Economic Reforms in Chile

Development and Inequality in the Market Economy

The purpose of this series is to encourage and foster analytical and policy-oriented work on market-based reform in developing and postsocialist countries. Special attention will be devoted in the series to exploring the effects of free market policies on social inequality and sustainable growth and development.

Editor:
Andrés Solimano

Editorial Board:
Alice Amsden
François Bourguignon
William Easterly
Patricio Meller
Vito Tanzi
Lance Taylor

Titles in the Series:

Andrés Solimano, Editor. *Road Maps to Prosperity: Essays on Growth and Development*

Andrés Solimano, Editor. *Social Inequality: Values, Growth, and the State*

Lance Taylor, Editor. *After Neoliberalism: What Next for Latin America?*

Andrés Solimano, Eduardo Aninat, and Nancy Birdsall, Editors. *Distributive Justice and Economic Development: The Case of Chile and Developing Countries*

Jaime Ros. *Development Theory and the Economics of Growth*

Felipe Larraín B., Editor. *Capital Flows, Capital Controls, and Currency Crises: Latin America in the 1990s*

Mitchell A. Orenstein. *Out of the Red: Building Capitalism and Democracy in Postcommunist Europe*

Ricardo Ffrench-Davis. *Economic Reforms in Chile: From Dictatorship to Democracy*

Economic Reforms in Chile
From Dictatorship to Democracy

Ricardo Ffrench-Davis

Ann Arbor

THE UNIVERSITY OF MICHIGAN PRESS

Copyright © by the University of Michigan 2002
All rights reserved
Published in the United States of America by
The University of Michigan Press
Manufactured in the United States of America
♾ Printed on acid-free paper

2005   2004   2003   2002   4   3   2   1

A CIP catalog record for this book is available from the British Library.

Library of Congress Cataloging-in-Publication Data

Ffrench-Davis, Ricardo.
    Economic reforms in Chile : from dictatorship to democracy /
Ricardo Ffrench-Davis.
        p.   cm. — (Development and inequality in the market economy)
    Includes bibliographical references and index.
    ISBN 0-472-11232-5 (Cloth : alk. paper)
    1. Chile — Economic policy.   2. Chile — Economic conditions —
1970–1973.   3. Chile — Economic conditions — 1973–1988.   4.
Chile — Economic conditions — 1988–   I. Title.   II. Series.
HC192 .F443 2002
339.983–dc21   2001003735

Preface

In this book, I attempt to put forward my views on several crucial developments in the Chilean economy since the 1970s. I have tried to organize it chronologically, in three subperiods: the first half of the Pinochet dictatorship, the second half of that regime, and the return to democratically elected presidents in the 1990s. In my view, under a restrictive definition they correspond to three different approaches to building a market economy, progressing from an extremely orthodox neoliberalism in 1973–82 to some significant deviations (pragmatism with a regressive bias) in 1982–89 and then to some meaningful trials intended to achieve growth with equity (pragmatism with a progressive bias).

Forty essays written since 1976 were initially selected as candidates for inclusion. Eight have been chosen. I wrote a new essay on income distribution and poverty for this book as well as a miscellaneous chapter on exports and growth and a brief conclusion that poses some issues and challenges for this new decade. I added several new sections, too, mostly on the 1990s. Here and there a line of thought has been expanded by incorporating sections or paragraphs from essays not included here. Naturally, duplications among chapters have been reduced as deemed convenient, and I have deleted what I judged to be details not relevant today.

I have made a serious effort to harmonize statistical series; for instance, the national accounts have experienced sizable jumps in successive official revisions, misleading many researchers and commentators on economic events. When relevant, data have been updated to year 2000. I have added several bibliographical references in cases in which significant work has appeared since the original publication.

The original tone and emphasis have been retained, as intellectual honesty demands. Happily, I continue to feel comfortable with them today. Although the knowledge informing them has improved and deepened (I hope), there is no discontinuity of approach, and I feel that the various pieces are consistent. But the reader is to be the judge. I have always attempted to deal with each issue and period in a way that combines pragmatism with a solid analytical base and to consistently take into account the objectives of growth with equity, while trying to keep my distance from fashion, myths, and extremes.

Most of the articles were written while I was working at the Center for Economic Research on Latin America (CIEPLAN) between 1976 and 1990, no doubt the most inspiring period of my professional life. The unnumbered note in each chapter includes references to comments contributed by research associates and valued assistants of the time. Four chapters were written while I was at the Economic Commission for Latin America and the Caribbean (ECLAC), one of which was coauthored in a highly fruitful association with Manuel Agosin and with valuable input from workshops held there. The first half of another chapter (the one opening the book) is based on a text written with Oscar Muñoz in one of our joint forays into economic history.

Eight years of activity at the Central Bank are reflected throughout the book. The support of former colleagues at the bank, their contribution in supplying statistics, and their collaboration in interpreting them are much appreciated.

I appreciate the authorization of Johns Hopkins University Press, Macmillan, the World Institute for Development Economics Research (Wider), and Oxford University Press, M. E. Sharpe, the *Cambridge Journal of Economics,* the Inter-American Development Bank, World Development, and Elsevier Science to make use of material published originally by them.

In selecting the essays, generous and invaluable help was provided by Sebastián Sáez (then in the Chilean Ministry of Foreign Affairs), from the initial stages all the way to the final polishing of the texts in Spanish. In the final stage, in which statistical series were updated and harmonized, figures checked, duplications eliminated, sections of other writings incorporated, and language improved, I enjoyed the excellent collaboration and efficiency of my research assistant Heriberto Tapia. I appreciate the fine work of Lenka Arriagada in preparing the typescript. It was Juan Carlos Sáez (general manager of Dolmen Ediciones, the publisher of this book in Spanish), years ago, whose prodding initiated this collection. Finally, I would like to express my thanks to CIEPLAN for its valuable support of this publication.

To all those mentioned, and to the many who contributed but have been unjustly omitted here, my deepest appreciation. All responsibility for the content of this collection and any errors it may contain is, of course, solely mine.

Contents

CHAPTER 1

Economic Development in Chile since the 1950s

Throughout its independent history, Chile had been one of the most politically stable and democratic countries in Latin America. Despite the destabilizing effects of external shocks, which were frequent, Chile succeeded in modernizing its institutions, fostering social mobility, and bringing about economic progress.

By 1970, Chile had one of the less uneven income distributions in the region. A sizable middle class had evolved, although it was concentrated in urban areas. During the 1960s, distribution generally improved, also extending into the rural sector. Nevertheless, social advances and political development increased expectations of improvement in the low- and middle-income sectors much faster than the actual rise in economic well-being.

The traumatic mismatch between political and economic development, repeatedly noted by leading observers of Chilean economic history (Encina 1911; Pinto 1973; Moulián 1982), became evident once more in the late 1960s. Early political development spurred expectations of change and modernization; economic and social strategies, however, lacked the coherence and effectiveness necessary for the achievement of productive development with the speed and direction required by political changes.

In this chapter, crucial features of the Chilean economy from the Great Depression of the 1930s onward are highlighted, quickly advancing to the period of focus of this book, that is, the Pinochet regime and the two following democratic governments of presidents Aylwin and Frei Ruiz-Tagle.

The survey of events prior to 1989 is based on an abridged version of "Economic and political instability in Chile, 1950–89," coauthored with Oscar Muñoz and published in *Toward a New Development Strategy for Latin America: Pathways from Hirschman's Thoughts,* Simón Teitel, ed. (Washington, D.C.: Inter-American Development Bank, 1992). Reprinted with permission from Inter-American Development Bank and ECLAC. The text has been extensively revised and updated to year 2000. I would like to thank Sergio Bitar, Manuel Marfán, Patricio Meller, Dagmar Raczynski, Joseph Ramos, John Sheahan, Simón Teitel, Joaquín Vial, and Ignacio Walker for their comments and Andrea Repetto for her assistance.

Economic Strategies in Retrospect

The outbreak of World War I found Chile enjoying prosperity, manifested in material progress and rapid diversification of consumption among the economic elites. This was partly due to the impetus provided by the export sector and its linkages, especially backward ones. An early political belief that the state should assume active responsibility for the promotion of economic progress also contributed to this success, although there were heated debates over this issue (see Muñoz 1986).

At the time of the Great Depression, the Chilean economy was one of the most developed of the region, in terms of both per capita income and productive and social transformation, which it was undergoing. It is a well-known fact that the Great Depression affected the Chilean economy severely. It has even been maintained that Chile was one of the hardest hit countries in the world. The decline in the terms of trade lasted for decades (until the 1960s). The collapse of the export sector was disastrous, with effects that have been thoroughly documented (see especially Marfán 1984). Following the worst years, however, the Chilean economy enjoyed a significant recovery, and until the early 1950s it sustained a rate of industrial growth that mitigated the constraints imposed by the slump in trade. In large measure, this was the result of economic policies that responded actively to the crisis with new industrialization strategies (Muñoz 1986).

The emergency created by the Great Depression compelled the state to undertake a number of palliative measures. The conservative second administration of President Alessandri Palma (1932–38) applied a series of fiscal measures and very selective controls over trade designed to offset the effects of the depression. State intervention, which had been tentatively undertaken during the previous decade, intensified. In 1938, the process received further impetus with the electoral victory of the Popular Front, which more decisively asserted the state's leading role in economic development and industrialization.

It became clear that, given the trade crisis, the substitution of manufacturing imports would require an enormous effort as well as the mobilization of domestic and external resources. The items required included financing and new industrial facilities — especially in infrastructure and basic sectors such as electric power, fuel, and intermediate and capital goods — plus entrepreneurial and technical skills, which were also scarce. As if these problems were not difficult enough, this stage coincided with World War II, which aggravated shortages by disrupting international trade and finance.

Not surprisingly, therefore, a clear political consensus emerged that the state should expand the scope of its responsibilities in support of production and business activity via the Corporación de Fomento de la Producción (CORFO), which was created in 1939. While the private sector had reservations about the degree of autonomy given to CORFO by statute to create public enterprises (see Muñoz and Arriagada 1977), in practice rather harmonious relations prevailed between the entrepreneurial state and the private sector. Industrial development got a boost and achieved considerable momentum in the 1940s. The massive unemployment of the preceding decade was reduced, and strides were made in institutional and technological organization. CORFO itself initiated programs of technological research and natural resource exploration.

During the 1950s, however, the development model began to encounter new problems. Many of the deficiencies of Chile's industrialization process made themselves felt; particularly the stagnation of agriculture. In addition, unbalanced emphasis on import substitution discouraged the development of new exports, severely restricting trade options and the management of the balance of payments. Such disequilibria intensified during populist periods. The instability of traditional export prices was transmitted to the domestic economy through recurrent balance of payments shocks. Growing inflationary pressures drove living standards down, bringing protests from labor unions and social activists.

Populist Expansion and Orthodox Stabilization, 1952–58

One of the signals warning of the intensity of the problems of the Chilean economy was the accelerating inflation of 1952–55, when the annual rate of increase in consumer prices jumped from 12 to 86 percent.[1] This led policymakers to the conclusion that new economic strategies had to be found. This inflationary episode began with a moderate surplus of installed capacity, associated with the restrictive policies applied in earlier years and some binding constraint in the external sector. The years 1952 and 1953 saw expansionary domestic policies, wage hikes, and an appreciating exchange rate, all accompanied by a positive terms of trade effect, which improved from 1951 to 1953. After two years of expanding aggregate demand, at a rate that nearly duplicated the creation of capacity, a higher rate of resource use was achieved, though in the context of disequilibria in the external and fiscal sectors. Exports diminished because of the increase in domestic demand and exchange rate appreciation. The impact was heightened by a sharp fall in the terms of trade in 1954.

The government of President Carlos Ibáñez, which had been elected by a large majority in September 1952 with the support of independents

---

1. The next three presidential periods, covering 1952–70, are described and analyzed in detail in Ffrench-Davis 1973.

Klein
Saks

and the Left, lost its popularity, encountered growing social unrest, and ended up adopting an orthodox stabilization program.

Both the money supply and government spending were sharply curtailed, and the complex system of regulations introduced during the years of the Depression and World War II was cut back. But recessionary effects soon led to the partial rollback of these initiatives on political grounds.

A Thwarted Attempt at Capitalist Modernization, 1958–64

President Jorge Alessandri tackled the reform of the economic system in a more comprehensive way, though with a simpler stabilization program. As a true exponent of business leadership and heir to a liberal-conservative tradition, he believed that the country needed substantive reforms in two areas: its institutional structure should allow the executive branch more freedom of action, especially in reforming the state, and its economic policy should make the private business sector the engine of development with the help of an active fiscal policy. This required a broader scope for the market and competition—especially from external sources. But, given the prevailing high inflation rate, Alessandri attached great importance to achieving stabilization in the short run. Only with price stability, in his view, could a climate stimulating long-term private investment be attained. Stabilization was to be achieved by eliminating the "inflationary financing" of the fiscal deficit and fixing the nominal exchange rate. Consequently, a stabilization program anchored to the exchange rate and supported by abundant foreign loans to the government was designed. These credits were to finance both the external imbalance expected in the transition period and the fiscal deficit (Ffrench-Davis 1973).

This program enjoyed temporary success. Inflation was indeed substantially reduced in 1960–61, but the balance of payments deficits were so great that the country's international reserves were soon depleted. As a result of this currency crisis, it became necessary to devalue in 1962. Import restrictions were resumed, and inflation shot back to its former level. While agriculture remained stagnant, the investment ratio and industrial growth rose, but the increase in exports was not sufficient to offset the great expansion in imports, which, despite an improvement in the terms of trade between 1959 and 1961, exceeded available external financing.

Seen in perspective, the experiment of the Alessandri government stands out as the first serious postwar effort to modernize the mixed economy and the nature of state intervention. An attempt was made to limit the state's direct entrepreneurial endeavors so that the private sector would increase its participation. The intent was not to reduce the state to a passive role but to follow a classic Keynesian model in which the state acts primarily through fiscal policy, stimulating private investment by means of public spending and seeking to create a climate of confidence, stability, and favorable expectations over the medium term. This approach was backed up with a moderate liberalization of import restrictions and various export incentives.

The policy's failure stemmed from a lack of understanding of short-term stabilization mechanisms and their medium-term repercussions. The stabilization scheme overlooked two predictable lags: as inflation declines from a level higher than the international rate, the real exchange rate appreciates; and as trade and foreign currency are liberalized, imports begin to outpace exports — a process spurred by the appreciating exchange rate. As was demonstrated at the time, and would be shown again later, a nominal peg of the exchange rate is usually a counterproductive instrument of stabilization.

Gradual Stabilization and Structural Reforms, 1964–70

The strategy of the Christian Democratic government of President Frei Montalva, elected in 1964, was based on a three-point platform: a gradual, multianchored, nonrecessionary stabilization program; an industrial modernization program that reactivated the role of the state as the generator of investment initiatives, introducing new, leading-edge sectors (such as telecommunications and the petrochemical industry) and developing nontraditional exports; and a program of structural and social change that included agrarian reform, the first steps in the nationalization of the nation's large copper mines, and the development of community and labor-based grassroots organizations designed to foster popular participation in an effective political democratization.

The stabilization program inherited a 50 percent annual inflation rate in October 1964. It was based on a package of economic policy instruments in addition to the monetary and exchange-rate instruments that had dominated policy programming in the past.

In 1964, productive capacity was underutilized and real wages were depressed, which made it possible to reconcile a boost in output, a wage increase, and a reduction of inflation, all within the ranges calculated by the government (Ffrench-Davis 1973). This was facilitated by significantly improved terms of trade in 1965–66. Nevertheless, an economic and social dynamic was unleashed that placed serious obstacles in the way of the program.

First, on the economic side, the increased fiscal outlays of 1965 were funded by a significant tax reform, which boosted revenue, reduced evasion, and improved tax equity. Spending continued to rise in 1966, however, exceeding projections and reaching unfinanceable levels, especially for public works and housing. In the second place, after strong growth of the gross domestic product (GDP) in 1965–66, underutilized productive capacity gradually became exhausted, while investment continued at moderate levels. In the third place, real wages also rose more than planned, with a sharp surge in the organized sectors. This resulted in cost pressures on consumer prices and had a negative impact on government spending and inflationary expectations. Strikes spread, and relations between the government and labor organizations deteriorated (except in agriculture).

Inflation, which had dampened in 1965–67, began to rekindle in the following years. Nominal wages of the organized sectors continued to climb to levels inconsistent with overall economic performance. Fiscal policy, after a minishock centered on public investment in 1967, remained repressed in subsequent years as a means of alleviating inflationary pressures.

The result was a gradual rise in the underutilization of productive capacity starting in 1967, and targets began to be missed. Nevertheless, no disequilibria as traumatic as those of 1955, 1962, or more recent decades were recorded. The regulation of the economic system was rather successfully maintained, adjusted to the excessive rise in wages, the variable that was most difficult to keep under control. It is interesting to note that during this process, instead of diminishing, the investment rate rose to over 20 percent in 1970.

Inflation reached 36 percent in 1970, which was somewhat less than the initial 50 percent. Productive capacity growth averaged around 4.3 percent per annum, and actual GDP grew throughout the period at an annual rate of approximately 4.0 percent (see table 1.1), spurred by heavy public and government-promoted private investment. Labor income improved noticeably, and social organizations such as labor unions and neighborhood councils expanded vigorously. The external sector achieved significant success in reducing the high propensity to crises with the pioneer introduction in 1965 of a crawling peg exchange rate policy (see chap. 4).[2]

2. Undoubtedly, the good performance of the copper market and its partial nationalization contributed to this balance. In 1968 and 1969, an improvement in the terms of trade was recorded, equivalent to 6 percent of GDP. In 1970, there was a terms of trade negative shock of 3 percent of GDP. A significant fraction of the net positive balance was captured by the Chilean government and saved as international reserves in the Central Bank in order to be able to face future deterioration of copper prices. This was a pioneering approach to the implementation of a copper stabilization fund.

TABLE 1.1. Comparison of Key Macroeconomic Variables, 1959–2000

Variable	During the Government of						
	Alessandri 1959–64	Frei Montalva 1965–70	Allende 1971–73	Pinochet 1974–89	Aylwin 1990–93	Frei Ruiz-Tagle 1994–99	Lagos 2000
GDP growth[a]	3.7	4.0	1.2	2.9	7.7	5.6	5.4
Growth of exports[b]	6.2	2.3	−4.2	10.6	9.6	9.4	7.5
Rate of inflation[c]	26.6	26.3	293.8	79.9	17.7	6.1	4.5
Unemployment rate	5.2	5.9	4.7	18.1[d]	7.3	7.4[d]	10.0[d]
Real wages (1970 = 100)	62.2	84.2	89.7	81.9	99.8	123.4	134.4
Investment (% of GDP)[e]							
In 1986 pesos	—	—	—	18.0	24.6	30.0	26.6
In 1977 pesos	20.7	19.3	15.9	15.6	19.9	24.1	22.3
Government surplus (% of GDP)	−4.7	−2.5	−11.5	0.3	1.7	1.2	0.1

Sources: Central Bank and the Budget Office (DIPRES); Jadresić 1986, 1990; Marcel and Meller 1986; Larraín 1991.

Note: Annual growth rates of GDP and exports; average of annual rates of inflation and unemployment.

[a]Until 1985 in 1977 pesos; for 1986–2000 in 1986 pesos.

[b]Exports of goods and services for 1959–85 in 1977 pesos and for 1986–2000 in 1986 pesos.

[c]From December to December.

[d]With emergency employment included; without these, it is 13.3 percent in 1974–89, 7.3 percent in 1994–99, and 9.2 percent in 2000.

[e]Gross fixed investment.

A great disequilibrium that increased over the years took place in the sociopolitical arena. It was also the 1960s in Chile! Political antagonisms prevented the formation of a broad coalition government. Social organizations could not be induced to join in the task of political and economic transformation that the government had set out to accomplish. In the final analysis, this revealed serious institutional and political failures, which contrasted with the expectations that had been aroused. The wisdom of hindsight suggests that without a broad and solid coalition this strategy's chances for success were slim. Turf battles and differences concerning the nature and degree of change prevented the formation of a large majority in favor of progressive reform.

Although the attempt ended in relative failure because it could not achieve political continuity and not all its aims were met, considering the magnitude of the challenge, the strategy arguably attained a fair degree of success. The Frei government performed a good diagnosis and instituted an adequate program of changes. The productive capacity growth rate could not be raised above the 4.3 percent just mentioned, but inflation was curbed and income distribution improved significantly. The share of wages in national income rose from 45 percent in 1964 to 52 percent in 1970 according to the national accounts. A significant reform of the tax system was accomplished and 51 percent domestic control over the large copper mines was achieved, leading to the capture of a sizable share of the economic rent from that natural resource. The rural sector — with the implementation of structural reforms, most notably the agrarian reform — and the industrial sector were modernized. Exports were diversified, with a steady increase in nonmining items, and there was a strengthening of Latin American regional integration, which was also instrumental in trade diversification. The state apparatus was also modernized by providing it with better qualified human resources and more responsive institutions. The sophistication of economic policy making was increased through better understanding of the role of prices and basic macroeconomic equilibria. A stable real exchange policy was put in place (see chap. 4) and maintained, and strides were made in rationalizing the import regime and export promotion (Ffrench-Davis 1973).

Additional Reforms and Macroeconomic Disequilibria, 1970–73

The Unidad Popular (UP) government sought farther reaching structural change, particularly with respect to property and without regard for macroeconomic equilibrium. It proceeded without a social and political working majority. In the view of the UP's economic policymakers, short-term policy had to pave the way for an electoral majority sufficiently large to implement deeper structural change. Accordingly, straight populism dominated macroeconomic policy.

When President Allende took office in late 1970, his government inherited a surplus of installed capacity (see fig. 1.1) and high international reserves. This allowed an expansionist policy with rapidly rising wages and social expenditures. Economic activity responded positively, with an 8 percent rise in GDP and no significant inflationary pressures or external gaps in 1971. However, the expansion was carried out with public revenue losses due to drops in real (public) utility rates, appreciating exchange rates, weakening public and private investment, and a rapidly expanding money supply. Meanwhile, structural changes, including completion of the nationalization of the large copper mines and the nationalization of the banking system and many other enterprises, were under way. In addition, many firms and farms were taken over arbitrarily by workers or political groups.

Aggregate demand rose disproportionately with respect to the creation of new productive capacity, while the equilibria of the external, fiscal, and monetary sectors worsened at an accelerating pace. This deterioration was intensified by the constant worsening of the terms of trade from 1970 to 1972.

Actual production declined during 1972–73 by 4.1 percent because of the sectoral imbalances and bottlenecks resulting from the external gap, innumerable strikes, distortions in official relative prices, a growing black market, and accelerating inflation (Bitar 1979). The investment ratio decreased, although there was still a minor increase in productive capacity (see fig. 1.1). In other words, the decreases in output recorded in 1972 and the months preceding the September 1973 coup reflected not a net loss of capacity but growing underutilization. The rise in output during the months following the coup proves this assertion.

Allende's economic policy ended up hurting the government politically when contraction, accompanied by growing inflation, set in. Idle productive capacity as well as the state's ability to regulate and administratively control price and trade imbalances and distortions were highly overestimated. The full force of the macroeconomic disequilibria made itself felt in the second year of the administration, and from there on the struggle for power absorbed most of the efforts and energies of both rulers and ruled. Economic disequilibria, low governance, and the growing inability to reach political agreements finally gave way to the institutional breakup and the prevalence of the coup supporters.

The Neoliberal Strategy, 1973–89

The initial concerns of Pinochet's dictatorial government lay with controlling the macroeconomic disequilibria and especially the high inflation rate.[3] Soon the focus shifted to the inefficiencies of the prevailing economic system in accordance with neoliberal beliefs, which became increasingly popular at the international level in the following years. As an extremist neoliberal group extended its power until it dominated public policy making, the range and depth of the economy's structural changes increased (see chap. 2).

The principal reforms were abolition of price controls; across the board import liberalization; financial market deregulation, both in terms of access by new institutions and of interest rates and credit policies, followed at the end of the decade by a broad deregulation of capital flows; reduction of the public sector and restrictions on the activities of public enterprises; the return of expropriated businesses and lands to their former owners; privatization of traditional public enterprises; suppression of most current labor union rights; and tax reform, which, along with eliminating some distortions (e.g., the cumulative effects of sales taxes corrected by implementing a value added tax), sharply reduced the share of direct and more progressive taxes.

The traditional role of the state, as entrepreneur and promoter of investment and industrialization, was to be curtailed as quickly as possible so that those functions might be fulfilled exclusively on the basis of decisions taken by private agents in liberalized open markets.

The implementation of this strategy was complicated by two developments that affected the Chilean economy during most of the 1970s: an extremely high inflation rate, which the monetarist stabilization policy had great difficulty bringing under control; and the first oil shock, which, coupled with a sharp decline in copper prices in 1975, created severe balance of payments problems.

Utilization rates recovered in the twelve months following the military coup of September 1973. The labor discipline imposed through the repression of unions, the liberalization of prices, exchange rate devaluation, increased public works investment, and high copper prices removed bottlenecks and favored greater use of installed capacity and potential GDP. Rising copper prices in 1973–74 more than offset increased spending on oil imports, with a net improvement in the terms of trade equivalent to almost 5 percent of GDP in 1974 compared to 1972.

These developments helped lower inflation to 370 percent in 1974. Nevertheless, the price of copper dropped sharply in the second half of 1974, while the oil shock persisted, with a net negative overall effect amounting to 6.4 percent of GDP in 1975 compared to 1972.[4] This

3. Prices in 1973 rose at an annual rate of 600 percent, and in the last four months of the UP government the annualized inflation rate reached 700 percent.

4. This is the difference between the terms of trade deterioration in 1975 and the improvement in 1973 and 1974. Copper prices began to rise in the third quarter of 1973.

shock, coupled with persistent inflation, prompted the government to introduce a sharp adjustment program, based on a reduction of aggregate demand, which was led by fiscal and monetary contraction, and a significant exchange rate devaluation.

Soon economic activity began to slow, with a sharp decline in imports and an increase in nontraditional exports. Once again, the intense and rapid response of the trade balance to large shocks of aggregate demand was demonstrated. The novel element for Chile was the strength of the increase in export volume (see tables 1.1 and 8.1). There were four causes of this increase: a very sharp real devaluation, export capacity installed in earlier years, removal of bottlenecks in the sector, and a sharp reduction in domestic demand (see Ffrench-Davis 1979b). Inflation, on the other hand, was slow to respond. Existing indexation and inertial expectations concentrated the impact of the restriction of aggregate demand mainly on the level of economic activity. For three years, the inflation rate hovered around 300 percent, diminishing only after mid-1976 when the government introduced other stabilization mechanisms besides money supply control (Foxley 1983; Ramos 1986). One of the mechanisms was rather peculiar, consisting of an implicit deindexation through the manipulation of the consumer price index, which was underestimated month after month from 1976 to 1978 (see Cortázar and Marshall 1980). Another mechanism consisted of a series of profusely publicized exchange rate revaluations (see chap. 4).

The sharp 17 percent drop in GDP in 1975 and the slow pace of subsequent recovery generated a high average underutilization of capacity between 1975 and 1979 (see fig. 1.1). The predominance of sharp demand-reducing policies over a weak set of switching policies explains the significant underutilization of productive capacity. This manifested itself in high unemployment, depressed wages, numerous bankruptcies, and low capital formation. Given the deep recession, subsequently Chile could sustain a vigorous recovery for several years, with significant actual GDP growth, while potential GDP rose slowly. The noticeable recovery generated an image of economic and financial success, which was advantageous in light of the plebiscite of 1980, which institutionalized the authoritarian regime. Something similar occurred in the 1980s, when the crisis of 1982–83 was followed by recovery and a period of economic expansion, reaching the productive frontier or capacity in 1989.

In 1979 a new stage of automatic macroeconomic policy was introduced when the government fully adopted the monetary approach to the balance of payments. It had achieved a fiscal surplus and a free import system, with a uniform tariff of 10 percent. In this framework, the nominal exchange rate was frozen. The aim was to anchor the Chilean economy to the current world inflation rate, which, although it was then

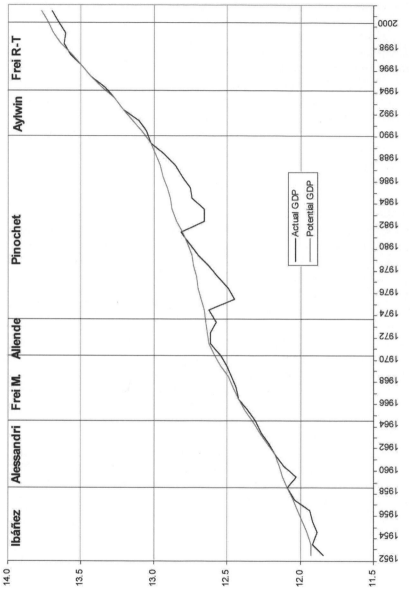

Fig. 1.1. Actual and potential GDP, 1952–2001 (natural log scale). Frei M. = Frei Montalva; Frei R-T = Frei Ruiz-Tagle. (Data from author's calculations on the basis of Central Bank data and Marcel and Meller 1986. A "consensus forecast" for effective GDP was used for 2001.)

at a two-digit level, was only one-third of Chile's 36 percent. This policy was supported by heavy foreign lending, which more than covered, until 1981, an expanding external deficit (see chap. 5).

The policy was successful in terms of curbing inflation, which at the beginning of 1982 stood at the international level. But once again the severity of other macroeconomic disequilibria was underestimated. Efforts were concentrated on bringing down inflation, while external equilibrium and investment in human and physical capital were overlooked. Since 1979, the real exchange rate had lost a third of its purchasing power, the external debt had doubled, the export boom had faltered in 1981–82, and the current account deficit had climbed to 21 percent of GDP in 1981.[5]

Underlying these disequilibria was a serious diagnostic error. The government assumed that since it had achieved a fiscal surplus and external borrowing was being decided by private agents a foreign exchange crisis would never occur. For the second time in a decade, the Chilean economy underwent a recession of considerable magnitude, the worst in Latin America in 1982–83, with GDP declining 14 percent.[6]

The productive sectors, including agriculture, manufacturing, and construction, faced massive bankruptcies. Political discontent spread, and demonstrations of opposition to a dictatorship that had been iron fisted proliferated, with many former supporters among the participants.

As the government's power weakened, it was compelled to revise its strategies in several respects. The climate of discontent and protest made possible the reconstitution of some social movements that had been dismantled, especially the labor unions and the political parties of the Center and Left. In the economic arena, several attempts at adjustment were made, including successive devaluations, the reintroduction of some protective tariffs, stringent regulation of the financial system, implicit nationalization of private debt, renegotiations of foreign debt with creditor banks, and massive financial aid to the private sector (see chap. 6).

The government yielded to business pressures to adopt a more pragmatic strategy. However, this greater pragmatism was biased in favor of upper-income sectors, including generous subsidies, while a tough position was maintained toward labor and grassroots organizations.

5. Figures were calculated on the basis of the exchange rate in 1976–78. With the appreciated exchange rate of 1981, the deficit was 14.5 percent of GDP. Keep in mind that GDP in current U.S. dollars was $15.4 billion in 1978, $32.6 billion in 1981, and $19.8 billion in 1983. Given the enormous volatility in these years, it is advisable to "normalize" the exchange rate in order to make intertemporal comparisons.

6. For 1974–85, I have generally used the series of national accounts published by Marcel and Meller (1986). According to Central Bank figures, the drop in 1982–83 was 15 percent.

The consequence was a further deterioration in income distribution (see chap. 9).

A strong, sustained recovery of economic activity and domestic production began in 1986. In 1986–87, the recovery proceeded in a sustainable macroeconomic framework. In the next two years, the situation changed: the expansion of demand and economic activity accelerated, culminating in the overheating of the economy in 1989, when GDP increased by 10 percent. The difference between that figure and the forecast of about 5 percent per year in 1988–89 was associated with an increase in aggregate demand resulting from expansion of the money supply, tax reduction, and import liberalization and some exchange rate appreciation, which made imports cheaper. A sharp improvement in the terms of trade (copper prices) in 1988–89 and the installed capacity still available made a sharp jump in economic activity feasible.

The 1980s ended with the Chilean economy enjoying a high rate of capacity utilization. The economy did, however, show some substantial disequilibria. During 1988–89, a number of macroeconomic variables showed inconsistent trends over the medium term. Aggregate demand had grown swiftly — by 22 percent — in two years, and GDP had risen by 18 percent. Exports grew vigorously in the two-year period, but imports rose even more. The gap between spending and production was compensated for by an improvement in the terms of trade equivalent to 5 percent of GDP in 1989 as compared to 1987. Output, in turn, grew swiftly due to idle capacity. Productive capacity was expanding by less than a total 8 percent in the biennium. The contrast with the 18 percent increase in effective GDP led to full utilization of installed capacity and overheating of the economy. This manifested itself in accelerating inflation and a deteriorating external sector. At the beginning of 1990, inflation reached 23 percent, twice the 1988 rate.[7]

The reforms had a significant effect on productive structure. Trade liberalization applied simultaneously with a tough monetary stabilization policy induced a depression that featured a 26 percent drop in industrial production in 1975. Despite numerous bankruptcies, the sector achieved a recovery based on a rise in productivity among the surviving companies and dynamic export expansion. While between 1969–70 and 1978 the industrial sector grew by only 0.2 percent per annum, exports rose by an average of 15 percent (Vergara 1980), with great heterogeneity in the sector. Some branches showed notable productivity and export dynamism, while others did not survive (see chap. 3).

The high rate of business bankruptcies cannot necessarily be attrib-

7. This is the inflation rate for the twelve months ending in January 1990. Between August 1989 and January 1990, the annualized rate of increase in the consumer price index (CPI) was 31 percent.

uted to inefficiency protected by the earlier development strategy. In fact, after 1973, the long recession, real annual interest rates at an average of 38 percent, and accelerated import liberalization, together with exchange rate revaluation, can be identified as the decisive factors leading to business mortality. Manufacturing lost a significant share of GDP. Exports, on the other hand, achieved great dynamism, particularly nontraditional goods. Between 1974 and 1980, the share of nontraditional exports (including industrial products) in total sales abroad rose from 8 to 20 percent. This was due to the notable growth of nontraditional exports at a rate of 18 percent per annum in that period (see chap. 8).

The rejuvenated business sector featured a surge of new groups exhibiting much innovative competitiveness. Furthermore, many classical conditions for development arose, among them the "correction" of some prices (especially exchange rate depreciation in the 1980s and the reduced cost of imported inputs), low real wages, market deregulation, guaranteed property rights, and the elimination of many union rights.

Nonetheless, it should be noted that "price corrections" were very contradictory until 1982. The neoliberal orthodoxy did not consider that financial liberalization could lead to high *outlier* interest rates or that trade liberalization could be accompanied by continuous exchange rate appreciation, as was the case between 1979 and 1982. Neither was it considered that the private sector would be promoted amid a sharp restriction of aggregate demand, as in 1975–76 and 1982–83. All this helps to explain why modernization was associated with economic growth of only 2.9 percent between 1974 and 1989 and why the average investment ratio was notoriously below the level of the 1960s.

As on many other occasions in Chilean history, economic policy was strongly influenced by transitory improvements in copper prices. During the last two years of the regime, copper enjoyed a notably high price. It is undeniable that 1988–89 would have been very different had there been a "normal" copper market in those years. However, it was obvious that external prices would eventually decline, as began to occur in late 1989. Thus, the Pinochet regime finally could boast an economy with impressive export figures, and a portion of the productive sector was modernized. But modernization had still eluded the large majority of firms, and evident macroeconomic disequilibria had to be corrected in 1990.

Income inequality was notably greater than two decades earlier (see chap. 9); for instance, in 1989, average and minimum wages were still below those in 1970. In political terms, the salient development was the effective organization of social movements and political parties, which were able to compel the democratization of the system, even under the rules unilaterally imposed by the dictatorial regime. Following the triumph of the opposition in the plebiscite of October 1988 and the presidential election of December 1989, a democratic president, Patricio Aylwin, took office in March 1990.

Democracy, Reforming the Reforms, and Development, 1990–2000

The 1990s were dominated by the administration of the Concertación de Partidos por la Democracia, which assumed power in 1990 with the successive elections of Patricio Aylwin (1990–93) and Eduardo Frei Ruiz-Tagle (1994–99). Both gave rise to a period of the greatest prosperity in Chilean economic history, with a sustained average growth rate of 7 percent between 1990 and 1998 that marked a clear break with the historical trend of expansion of GDP (see fig. 1.1), with high rates of capital formation and a generalized atmosphere of stability.[8]

The new administration of Patricio Aylwin concentrated its efforts on stabilizing the economy after the 1988–89 electoral boom of the Pinochet regime and achieving stronger, more stable, and more sustainable GDP growth. This required, among other things, an increasing investment ratio, the implementation of macroeconomic policies achieving sustainable equilibria and diminishing vulnerability to external shocks, and progress in the solution of the most urgent social demands by enabling larger segments of the population to benefit from the modernization of the economy. The aim was to reconcile macroeconomic and macrosocial equilibria and implement a style of economic policy that would become legitimate within the new democratic framework.

The government decided to avoid a radical change in existing economic policy, seeking "a change in continuity" and thus breaking with the rehashing tradition of several previous governments. In order to accomplish this goal, the government of Aylwin had to obtain the support of the trade unions and incorporate workers into the macrosocial decision-making process. This was intended to benefit the groups that had suffered most from the effects of the long period of adjustment of the 1980s.

The new administration had to cope with a potential conflict between macroeconomic stability and the demand that more resources be allocated to lower income groups. On the one hand, it changed the composition of public spending, increasing the share of social spending in the budget, and, on the other, it rapidly presented to the Parliament a tax reform package intended to increase fiscal income.

Likewise, in 1990 the government proposed a reform of the labor

8. Collections of studies with different perspectives can be found in Pizarro, Raczynski, and Vial 1996; Cortázar and Vial 1998; and Larraín and Vergara 2000.

code to Congress. Among other goals, this was aimed at balancing the bargaining powers of employers and workers and sought to endow current labor legislation with greater legitimacy. To get this law passed, an agreement was reached between the government, labor and employer organizations, and most political parties (Cortázar 1996). However, the reforms agreed upon (including the tax reform) were always less comprehensive than those originally proposed by the government. A determining factor was the group of senators that had been appointed under the Constitution designed by Pinochet, which more than compensated for the majority achieved by candidates of the new government in 1989 and 1993.

In 1990, a tripartite agreement was also reached between the government and the representatives of unionized workers and employers; this agreement provided for an increase of 28 percent in the real minimum wage between 1989 and 1993. In April 1991, it was agreed that after this recovery stage any future real increase in the minimum wage would be linked to labor productivity gains and that the criteria for nominal adjustments would be forward looking, not past, inflation.[9]

In the early 1990s, significant progress in income distribution and poverty reduction was achieved in this constructive climate. After 1993, progress in the achievement of equality seemed to come to a halt; nevertheless, poverty continued to decline. While 45 percent of the population lived in poverty in 1987, by 2000 this figure had been reduced to 21 percent (see chap. 9).

It should be pointed out that the greater social effort was attained with notable fiscal responsibility. As a result of the tax reform of 1990,[10] the expansion of economic activity and imports, a higher than expected copper price (captured by Chile thanks to the nationalization of large copper mines, now grouped under Corporación Nacional del Cobre de Chile [CODELCO]), and a decline in tax evasion, state income increased significantly, by 3 percent of GDP. This allowed the government to increase public spending, in particular social expenditure, and at the same time expand nonfinancial public sector savings from 2 percent in the 1980s to nearly 5 percent of GDP in the 1990s (table 1.2).[11] Higher savings not

---

9. Nevertheless, in 1998 a sizable additional triennial real adjustment was established by law. The minimum wage applied to about 12 percent of the labor force in the 1990s.

10. The opposition argued that the increase in the value-added tax included in the reform would tend to impose a recessive effect as low income families consumed a larger part of their income. Nevertheless, a consistent comparison also has to consider that most resources are transferred to these families through an increase in social spending. The net effect is evidently progressive.

11. Notice that these figures are net of depreciation of capital goods in public firms; this depreciation is included in private savings. Moreover, the fiscal sector generated

only financed public investment but generated an average fiscal surplus of 1.4 percent of GDP in the 1990s.

A new political agreement in 1993 enabled the approval of several previously transitory modifications on a more definite basis. Subsequent evidence rejected the prediction of critics of the reform that it would have a negative impact on investment. After a decline in 1991 — associated with the lagged effect of the 1990 adjustment — capital formation increased in 1992 and again in 1993, reaching record levels in the next five years (see table 1.1). This high productive investment was the principal explanation behind the outstanding annual GDP growth, which rose from below 3 percent in 1974–89 to 6.4 percent in 1990–99. As empirical studies show robustly, private investment, given its irreversibility, is positively correlated with macroeconomic equilibria whenever they appear to be sustainable and fulfill two key conditions. First, effective demand has to be consistent with the productive capacity being generated, and, second, macroeconomic key prices (the interest and exchange rates) must be *right* (see Agosin 1998; Coeymans 1999; Ffrench-Davis 2000, chap. 6; and Servén and Solimano 1993).

Given the macroeconomic disequilibria generated in 1988–89, a severe adjustment through the increase in interest rates was carried out in order to control the expansion of aggregate demand and a new outbreak of inflation. This adjustment was considerably complicated soon after by large capital inflows, which, like other economies in the region, Chile had been receiving since the early 1990s (Ffrench-Davis, Agosin, and Uthoff 1995). The gap between domestic and international interest rates had increased significantly, inducing a strong inflow of short-term "hot money" and an appreciation in the exchange rate in the second half of 1990 (with a drop from the depreciated ceiling to the appreciated floor of its 10 percent crawling band). The Central Bank was forced to buy large amounts of foreign currency to defend the band's floor.

The strong external supply of both short-term and portfolio capital threatened to considerably diminish the capacity of the authorities to conduct monetary policy independently of external events, since they intended to avoid excessive fluctuations in the real exchange rate and

---

financing to cover the deficit of the public social security system. Under the social security reform, the public sector continued paying retired workers and financed part of the new pensions while income was shifted to the private system. The figures do not consider the quasi-fiscal deficit of the Central Bank — which was initially caused by government intervention intended to prevent a massive bankruptcy of the domestic financial system in 1983; it was enlarged, subsequently, with heavy operational losses in sterilization to soften exchange rate appreciation in the 1990s (on this latter issue, see Ffrench-Davis, Agosin, and Uthoff 1995).

aggregate demand. The diminished effectiveness of monetary policy becomes particularly complicated when fiscal policy is too inflexible to regulate aggregate demand in the short term.

On the other hand, economic authorities faced the need to differentiate between permanent appreciation pressures, resulting from Chile's net improvement in productivity and from having surmounted the debt crisis, and transitory pressures. Having identified the former, an attempt was made to avoid the latter in order to maintain the competitiveness of tradables.

Faced with a massive capital inflow, the Chilean authorities sought to reconcile these two objectives — an interest rate suited for keeping domestic balances and an exchange rate consistent with external balances — by applying several policy measures. Among these were active exchange rate policy and monetary sterilization; selective liberalization of capital outflows; a reserve requirement (*encaje*) for foreign loans and liquid inflows; and the extension of a tax, which had previously applied only to domestic currency loans, to include foreign currency loans (see chap. 10).

These policies were successful in the sense of reducing short-term and volatile inflows. But foreign direct investment (FDI) — both risk capital exempted from the reserve requirement and associated credits subject to it — became increasingly large. FDI was stimulated by the attractive features of the Chilean economy: rich natural resources and the almost tax free transfer of the economic rent abroad (a loophole inherited from the dictatorship, which requires correction), high quality macroeconomic policies, and the positive perception of the democratization process. Therefore, a large surplus in the capital account, much higher than the deficit in the current account, was generated.

The set of policies, especially those affecting short-term capital inflows, contributed to keeping the deficit in the current account within sustainable levels (2.5 percent of GDP in 1990–95) and preventing an excessive increase in more volatile external liabilities. In so doing, Chilean economic authorities contributed significantly to macroeconomic stability, the export strategy, and overall growth. This became evident when Chile showed nearly complete immunity during the Mexican crisis of 1994–95 (see chap. 10; Ffrench-Davis 2000, chap. 10; Ffrench-Davis and Reisen 1998; and Stiglitz 1998).

In 1990–95, GDP growth surpassed 7 percent. If one compares the growth achieved in this period with that of other years of good performance in the past three decades (1966, 1971, 1981, and 1989), one can see that, in contrast to previous occasions, this time (1) GDP growth, both actual and potential, was sustained for several rather than one or two years; (2) growth occurred in a context of macroeconomic equilibrium, with high productive investment; (3) growth occurred without significant inflationary pressures or pressures on external accounts; and (4) an orderly fiscal balance was maintained. Both in 1966 and in the 1990s, considerable GDP growth was achieved without placing significant pressure on the rate of inflation, but in 1966 growth was based on an increase in public spending, while in the 1990s it was induced by exports and productive investment. In the other three episodes of a considerable rise in GDP (1971, 1981, and 1988–89), significant imbalances occurred. In 1971 and 1989, domestic productive capacity became exhausted, generating an inflationary surge, while in 1981 an external imbalance equivalent to 21 percent of GDP occurred.

After each of these years of unsustainable macroeconomics in the last four decades, an adjustment program with significant welfare costs had to be implemented. These significant changes in the macroeconomic environment reflect, on the external front, the instability of the terms of trade and financing. On the domestic front, they reflect the high sensitivity of external balances to aggregate demand, especially when the economy is operating close to its productive frontier.

The impact of the adjustment program in 1990 on other economic variables was less severe and quickly reversed. As mentioned earlier, investment ratios recovered in 1992 and reached record levels starting in 1993 (see table 1.1). The principal merit of policies in 1990–95 was that they resisted allowing increased domestic absorption of capital inflows and faster disinflation with an appreciating exchange rate and a large external deficit.

However, these policies lost their strength after 1995, and could not prevent real appreciation of the peso and imbalances in the external accounts in 1996–97. Thus, Chile entered the "vulnerability zone," where it was caught by the Asian crisis. What was the cause of the change? Various factors can be mentioned. First of all, the strength shown in face of the Mexican crisis in 1995 created a misleading sense of invulnerability. The immunity had been the result of a policy approach that prevented excessive exchange appreciation, a high current account deficit, and a significant stock of liquid external liabilities. Second, after 1995 a change in priorities could be observed, with the prevalence of anti-inflationary objectives. Third, the belief that financial crises would not occur in the future prevailed in international circles, and this implicitly or explicitly supported proposals for full financial opening; understandably, such overoptimism was absorbed domestically by private and some public authorities. Fourth, the outstanding record of Chile transformed it into a preferred destination for foreign investors in a context in which huge amounts of capital were being supplied to emerging economies. Chile, despite this larger capital surge, kept most of its regulations unchanged. The outcome was a net inflow equivalent to 10 percent of GDP in 1997.

Therefore, when the Asian crisis affected Chile in 1998, with a strong negative shock in terms of trade, the economy had accumulated a significant disequilibria: a real appreciation of 16 percent between 1995 and October 1997 and a current account deficit of 5.7 percent of GDP in 1996–97 (compared to 2.5 percent in 1990–95).

Again, adjustment, after macroeconomic disequilibria led by excessive capital inflows in 1996–97,[12] was costly. Beginning in mid-1998, aggregate demand fell sharply (with the drop reaching 10 percent in 1999, while GDP decreased by 1.1 percent). Since productive capacity kept rising, resting on the still high investment ratio up to 1998, a large gap emerged between actual and potential GDP in 1999 (see figs. 1.1 and 11.1), which was still significant in 2001.

It is useful to examine in some detail the existence of the gap. This is not obsolete physical capacity. It is economically productive capacity that was in use in 1997, to which we discount an estimate of nonsustainable output (see the discussion that follows); new capacity was being created at a speed of about 7 percent per year, which continued in 1998 and 1999, determined by the high investment ratios up to 1998 included. The recessive adjustment started by mid-1998, with effective GDP rising only 3.9 percent in 1998 and falling 1.1 percent in 1999. Altogether, this generated a gap of about 9 percent in 1999. That was the determinant of the sharp drop in the investment ratio in 1999 and 2000.

As I have shown repeatedly, a significant gap between effective GDP and the production frontier is followed, always, by a drop in productive investment. As in Mexico in 1995, Argentina in 1995 and 1999–2001, and Korea in 1998, in Chile the investment ratio diminished substantially (by 17 percent in 1999) and remained low during 2000; the output gap plus the drop in investment had a deepening impact on employment, too. Both reduced the speed at which the production frontier was moving in the 1990s: 7 percent per year.

Notwithstanding the gap in 1998–2000, actual GDP rose by 6 percent in the 1990s, more than twice as fast as in the 1970s and 1980s. The

---

12. Assertions that fiscal policy was mainly responsible for disequilibria are not supported empirically: 90 percent of excess demand in 1996–97 was located in the private sector and financed with net capital inflows. The fiscal expenditure was financed with new revenues, while public savings reached its highest level during the biennium (see table 1.2), as well as a significant surplus (2.1 percent of GDP). However, indeed, a countercyclical approach should have implied a moderation of fiscal expenditure or an additional increase in taxes during that biennium, but this would not have been enough to compensate for the great private sector imbalance. The source of disequilibria — that is, capital inflows — had to be tackled.

TABLE 1.2.   Gross Savings and Investment, 1985–2000 (percentage of GDP at current prices)

Years	Fixed Investment Ratio	Change in Stocks	Savings Ratio				
			External	National	NFPS	CBF	Other
1985–89	19.4	1.8	4.9	16.4	2.0	1.5	13.0
1990–95	22.9	1.7	2.5	22.1	4.4	0.7	17.0
1996–98	25.4	1.7	5.9	21.2	5.2	0.0	16.1
1999–2000	22.1	0.7	0.9	21.9	3.1	−0.4	19.2
1989	23.6	1.6	1.8	23.3	3.1	3.8	16.4
1990	23.1	2.0	1.9	23.2	2.5	2.3	18.4
1991	19.9	2.6	0.3	22.3	3.6	0.7	18.0
1992	22.4	1.4	2.3	21.5	5.0	0.3	16.2
1993	24.9	1.6	5.6	20.9	4.9	−0.2	16.2
1994	23.3	0.8	3.0	21.1	4.9	0.2	16.0
1995	23.9	1.9	2.0	23.8	5.4	1.1	17.3
1996	24.8	1.8	5.8	20.8	5.8	0.3	14.7
1997	25.5	1.7	5.7	21.6	5.6	0.1	16.0
1998	26.0	1.4	6.2	21.2	4.1	−0.5	17.6
1999	21.9	0.2	0.2	21.8	2.5	−0.7	20.0
2000	22.3	1.1	1.6	21.9	3.7	−0.2	18.3

Source: Calculations are based on data from the Central Bank and DIPRES.

Note: The figures for the nonfinancial public sector (NFPS) include the general government and cash profits of public firms, principally of CODELCO (the public copper producer), collected by the Treasury. CBF corresponds to the Copper Buffer Fund, which is deposited by CODELCO in a Treasury account at the Central Bank. Other includes net private savings plus the Central Bank balance, profits of public firms not transferred to the Treasury and capitalized by these firms, and depreciation reserves of all public and private firms.

leading force behind that outstanding performance was the vigorous investment ratio achieved in the 1990s. The average ratio (27.9 percent in 1990–99) was ten points larger than during the neoliberal experiment (18 percent in 1974–89; all in 1986 prices).

On the other hand, during the 1990s the national savings ratio averaged 22 percent (at current prices), the highest in recent decades, and one-third higher than the 16.4 percent achieved in 1985–89 (table 1.2). This provided financing for 87 percent of total investment. The high savings ratio was associated with the stimulating macroeconomic environment faced by firms, leading to greater use of installed capacity, high profit margins, and large reinvestment coefficients (Agosin 1998; Ffrench-Davis 2000, chap. 6).[13]

The savings capacity is strongly affected by the terms of trade.

13. As has been pointed out, the convergence between the productive frontier and effective demand is an essential element for efficient macroeconomic policies. The absence or disregard of this fundamental macroeconomic equilibrium has been characteristic of Latin American economies since the 1980s. See ECLAC 2000, chap. 8.

These continue to be extremely unstable in Chile. For instance, table 1.2 shows that in 1989 the high price of copper implied additional inflows equivalent to 3.8 percent of GDP into the copper buffer fund (CBF), which is a source of public and domestic savings. On the contrary, in 1999 the fund lost 0.7 percent of GDP. This represents a net difference of 4.5 percent, which ought to be used to adjust the gross figures of public and national savings in table 1.2 in order to improve the quality of data on effective savings effort in each year. However, that is only part of the story. The CBF covers just a fraction of the change in the proceeds of the large public firm CODELCO due to price fluctuations. Consequently, copper price changes have a residual effect on the net profits of CODELCO and all of these profits are transferred to the Treasury. Thus, fluctuations of that price have an impact on national savings beyond those on the CBF. But the savings of the private sector are also affected by the terms of trade, particularly when they affect exports of national firms.

In the 1990s, the volume of exports of goods and services grew at a rate of 9.5 percent per annum, while potential GDP expanded by 7 percent. Thus, exports and investment (which grew by 10 percent annually in this period) were the driving forces behind economic growth, increasing the external links of the Chilean economy and its potential for sustainable growth.[14] It is interesting to note that the rate of export growth was relatively similar in the last three decades. In this context, it is remarkable that GDP growth in the 1990s performed notably better because nonexports also grew dynamically, reflecting broader systemic competitiveness and the positive impact of sustainable macroeconomic equilibria (see chap. 8).

The Concertación administration compares favorably with all regimes since the 1950s in terms of GDP growth, inflation, real wages, and fiscal surplus (see tables 1.1 and 1.2). The performance of investment and savings and the generation of new productive capacity were also considerably improved. However, the unemployment rate, though lower than one-half the average rate under the Pinochet regime, did not recover to the level of the 1960s.[15] Moreover, by 2001 after a long recessive gap since 1998, unemployment was posing one of the greatest challenges

---

14. In 1999, exports of goods and services represented 42 percent of GDP (at 1986 prices), that is, 17 points more than in 1980. Expressed in 1999 current prices, the figure amounts to only 29 percent due to a decline in real prices of exports and exchange rate appreciation compared to 1986.

15. The lowest unemployment rate occurred during the Allende administration. Nevertheless, this rate was achieved with considerable public sector employment in nonproductive activities and enormous, hidden, macroeconomic imbalances made that low unemployment rate unsustainable.

for recovering growth with equity (see chap. 11). Another big challenge was to find the way back to sustainable macroeconomic equilibria and the recovery of productive investment after some confusing swings between the neoliberal and growth with equity approaches.

Long-Term Trends in Economic Growth

Macroeconomic policies intended to ensure high use of productive capacity are a key ingredient of a good public policy. In order to grow with equity — as we have shown throughout this book — the improvement of macroeconomic policies is unavoidable. For a better analysis of this issue, we need to examine the evolution of potential GDP or productive frontier (PF) or capacity, which has been estimated here for the last half century.

Potential GDP is the maximum aggregate supply of goods and services that can be achieved at any period, given the imperfections prevailing in the production process and factor quality. The determinant variable for achieving that maximum is an effective demand consistent with potential supply.

There is a significant asymmetry in the actual performance of the economy. Effective GDP can be placed much below the PF, while it cannot stay above that productive capacity in a sustained way. The PF can be surpassed only temporarily, as a result of exhaustion of inventories, growing inflationary pressures, or nonfinanciable external deficits or under transitory terms of trade positive shocks.

Counting with a credible estimate of potential GDP contributes to understanding economic history and to guiding future macroeconomic policies: monetary, fiscal, and exchange rate policies and prudential regulation of the capital account. How can the PF be estimated?

There are many sophisticated methodologies with which to estimate potential output, but they do not control for the effect of recessions. Therefore, these estimates account for the trend or historical average of GDP, including cycles, which implies a downward bias of potential GDP.[16] The use of these estimates affects the quality of both historical analyses and macroeconomic policy because it tends to reproduce past recessions in the future and hide the crucial variable: the sustainable economic frontier — of full utilization of capital and labor and efficiency in economic management — at which the battery of macroeconomic policies must be aimed.

---

16. Examples are the popular Hodrik-Prescott filter and estimations of production functions that do not correct for capital utilization or the sustainability of the growth path. One expression of the resulting biases is the erratic estimates of total factor productivity that are obtained.

The methodology used here focuses on estimating this frontier. First, I identified the peaks of use of capacity along the period studied. In this sense, there is wide consensus among economists: in the last three decades, the Chilean economic peaks were located in 1971, 1974, 1981, 1989, and 1997. I assume that in those years potential and actual GDP were similar.[17] Then, the net increase of output was calculated (GDP corrected by depreciation of capital) between two peaks and the net increase of the stock of capital (the sum of the net investment of each year lagged by one period). The ratio between both is usually called the incremental output — capital ratio or the coefficient of gross marginal productivity.[18] Subsequently, this ratio and annual investment were used to estimate potential GDP between peaks.[19]

In the early postwar decades, Chile lost ground among the countries of Latin America and the developing world. While the region's GDP grew by 5.5 percent per year in the first two postwar decades, Chile's average annual rate was 4.6 percent in the 1960s, and it fell below 1 percent in 1971–73 and to 2.9 percent in 1974–89. With population increasing by 2.3 percent annually in the first period and 1.6 percent in 1974–89, the per capita growth rates amounted to only 2.4 and 1.3 percent, respectively.

---

17. We search for the main biases in each of the annual *peaks* identified in getting a figure for potential GDP. We have corrected for the two main sources of bias. First, bias is introduced when the PF is underestimated by effective GDP; this happens when the peak is not achieved throughout the year (e.g., in 1974, with a recession starting in the third quarter). Second, bias can occur when the PF is overestimated, with an excess of imports without sustainable external financing; the excess allows a large value added in the marketing of imports (intensively in 1981, partly compensated by the underutilization in producing tradables, due to a much appreciated exchange rate; moderately in 1997).

18. I work with the reciprocal of the incremental capital-output ratio (ICOR). Here I am associating increases in output with net fixed capital formation. Apart from investment in human capital, there have been changes in the use of factors such as technology and natural resources (Marfán and Bosworth 1994). Employment grew by 1.9 percent in the 1960s, 1.7 percent in 1974–81 (with an increase of 3 percent in the labor force), and 3.9 percent in 1982–89. In addition, the use of natural resources intensified. Numerous empirical studies examine the quantity and quality of labor and capital. See Hofman 1999; Morandé and Vergara 1997; and Coeymans 1999. The latter author controls for cycles more than the others do.

19. Estimates by Marfán (1992) for 1960–88 yield annual rates of change in productive capacity similar to those obtained in this chapter. The similarity of the results, within the time frame common to both studies, is accounted for by the choice of the peaks method and agreement in the identification of peaks. Given the large cycles of the Chilean economy, empirical studies, which do not take the level of activity into account, can be significantly biased in their results for total factor productivity. For instance, Roldós (1997) gives a change in total factor productivity (TFP) per annum of −3.8 percent in 1981–85 and 0.9 percent for 1986–90, evidently distorted by the 1982 recession. Which estimate reflects better the trend in productivity changes? In this case, the average approximates to the real TFP.

Potential productive capacity expanded in fairly stable fashion in the 1960s, with relatively high capacity utilization, compared to the large gaps between actual and potential GDP of the 1970s and 1980s. In fact, capital formation and the growth of productive capacity were more unstable in these two decades (see fig. 1.1 and table 1.1). The low level of investment and slow expansion of the productive frontier seem to be associated with the low average capacity utilization and real macroeconomic disequilibria of these two decades. The gap between effective and potential GDP reflects the trend in aggregate demand, its relationship to effective demand (which is the one located in domestic resources), and the match between the structures of demand and supply of both products and factors.

The instability of economic activity had negative repercussions in two respects. First, underutilization of capacity tends to reduce the social and market profitability of capital; it diminishes the availability of investment funds and worsens the financial condition of enterprises. In addition to discouraging investment, it reduces effective productivity. On the other hand, this instability depresses productive employment and negatively affects the sustainable income level in the future.

Table 1.3 presents three indicators. Column 1 is the marginal coefficient *potential* output/capital, measured between peaks. Column 2 shows the gap between actual and potential output; that is, the rate of use of potential GDP. Column 3 presents the marginal coefficient *effective* output/capital.

The data suggest that potential productivity was similar in 1962–71 and 1982–89 and higher than 1975–81. How does one reconcile this with the belief that in the two more recent decades productivity was much greater thanks to the opening of the economy and the liberalization of

TABLE 1.3.   Effective and Potential Gross Productivity of Capital, 1952–98 (averages for each period)

	Effective GDP/Potential GDP (1)	Marginal Coefficient	
		Product/Capital (2)	Effective Product/Capital (3)
1952–61	0.96	0.26	0.25
1962–71	0.98	0.35	0.34
1972–74	0.96	0.12	0.12
1975–81	0.90	0.28	0.26
1982–89	0.88	0.36	0.32
1990–98	0.99	0.46	0.45
1952–98	0.95	0.33	0.31

Note: According to the data used for figure 1, column 2 is the ratio between the change in net domestic product and net investment between the peaks.

markets? The answer would be that the surviving enterprises in the 1970s and 1980s had higher productivity but that the mortality rate of enterprises was greater and that to measure economic performance all agents should be considered rather than just the winning segment.

Massive bankruptcies implied the destruction of capital (a lot of which would have been productive under normal demand and "right" prices). Losses resulting from sharp import liberalization and large exchange rate appreciation were very significant in the 1970s (see chap. 3). The situation improved in the 1980s, partly as a result of better macroprices (the exchange and interest rates), but it was restricted by the recessive effects of the binding foreign currency scarcity during the debt crisis.

In the 1960s, excessive protection and administrative obstacles fostered inefficiencies, but greater real macroeconomic stability helped improve efficiency and keep more enterprises afloat. It concentrated effort on creating enterprises rather than on transferring existing assets and provided more predictable patterns of demand and more stable relative prices (which stimulated productive investment, given its irreversibility). Development was also more integrated, which offered more productive opportunities for broader sectors of society. This environment, despite numerous inefficiencies, explains the better performance of productivity in the 1960s vis-à-vis the 1950s and the near match with potential productivity in the 1980s.

With respect to effective productivity, considering good and bad years in each subperiod, table 1.3 shows that the high underutilization of productive capacity in 1974–89 involved a sharp deviation between effective and potential productivity in the two corresponding subperiods. The years of great underutilization of capacity have been associated with deliberate or involuntary recessive adjustments following expansions, with fiscal, monetary, or balance of payments disequilibria. Underutilization also intensified when stabilizing policies rested on only one or two stabilization policy instruments instead of using multiple anchors (Ffrench-Davis 2000, chap. 6). Major gaps occurred in 1954–56, 1959, 1973, 1975–79, 1982–87, and most recently in 1999–2001.

Once all idle capacity was being used in 1989, the productive frontier increased vigorously at annual rates of around 7 percent in response to an increase in the investment rate by 10 points of GDP between 1982–89 and 1990–2000 (see table 10.4). Prevailing domestic stability throughout almost the whole decade, which was achieved by means of prudent countercyclical policies like the selective regulation of foreign short-term or volatile capital, determined the framework for a virtuous cycle of a higher utilization rate of existing capital, thus generating higher investment, and generally a more efficient use of productive resources, reflected in significant productivity growth of labor and capital.[20]

Growth of productive capacity is not a given immutable figure but the result of public action and the behavior of social, political, and economic agents. All of this occurred in the half century analyzed, in a context conditioned by the external environment and the ideas then in fashion.

The outstanding performance of the 1990s reached a turning point when the Asian crisis hit the Chilean economy. However, the inflection was also associated with two additional factors. On the one hand, there is a structural element: dynamism in exports, FDI, and domestic investment were strongly influenced by natural resource exploitation (as in copper and forestry) and the development of public services (as in energy and telecommunications) in megaprojects that will hardly be reproduced in the next decade (Moguillansky 1999). Consequently, a large number of smaller projects in sectors with systemic competitiveness will be necessary in this new framework. This will require a more intense effort to *complete* long-term capital markets; encourage diffusion, assimilation, and adaptation of technology; broaden labor training; and open external markets for Chilean nontraditional products (all with special emphasis on the development of small and medium enterprises [SMEs]).

The second factor is the macroeconomic environment. As we will see in chapter 10, policies applied in the second half of the decade lost coherence and the ability to control the vulnerability of the Chilean economy in the face of external shocks. Consequently, when the Asian crisis exploded, a climate of instability returned to Chile once again, opening a significant gap between effective and potential GDP since mid-1998. This gap, as will be demonstrated throughout the text, was the main cause of the sharp drop in the investment ratio in 1999–2000. There is a double challenge to resume high growth and improving equity.

---

20. Data adjusted for quality give a total factor productivity change of -0.4 percent for the 1970s, -1.4 percent for the 1980s, and 1.4 percent for 1991–95 (Roldós 1997).

CHAPTER 2

The Neoliberal Experiment: From Reforms to the Crisis of 1982

During the 1970s, the Southern Cone of Latin America witnessed the pioneering implementation of broad neoliberal economic reforms. The most orthodox and comprehensive neoliberal example is that of the model imposed in Chile between 1973 and 1982.[1]

There are four reasons for the particular relevance of the Chilean experiment. First, Chile was noted for its long democratic tradition and the broad pluralism characteristic of its institutions and citizens. After the coup in 1973, an authoritarian regime was established during which the neoliberal model was developed. Under the aegis of this regime, the executors of the economic model enjoyed exceptional autonomy in the design, implementation, and adjustment of their policies. Second, the Chilean experiment is an outstanding example of the contemporary application of monetarist orthodoxy because of its "purity," depth, and extensive coverage. Third, its prolonged survival, nearly one decade, provides a broad field for the assessment of its effects. Fourth, the case has been widely publicized as a "success," with the support of representatives of some international institutions, financiers, and "neoliberal" circles, which tend to give absolute priority to "economic freedom" over any other dimension of human activity. The experiment has frequently been cited by these media as a model for other developing countries. Hence, an understanding of its real features and the results it has provoked has a significance that goes beyond the particular case of Chile.

In this chapter, we shall study, first, the most characteristic features

This chapter is based on "The monetarist experiment in Chile: A critical survey," *World Development* 11, no. 11 (1983): 905–26. Copyright © 1983, with permission from Elsevier Science. The author gratefully acknowledges the comments of Eduardo García, Ricardo Lagos, Joseph Ramos, Jaime Ruiz-Tagle, Roberto Zahler, and the researchers at CIEPLAN, particularly José Pablo Arellano, René Cortázar, Alejandro Foxley, and Patricio Meller.

1. The model imposed in Chile has been variously described as orthodox or global monetarism. The authorities referred to it as a social market economy model. The last denomination leads to misinterpretation when it is confused with approaches such as that of the Federal Republic of Germany and those that give priority to social aspects. These are humanistic approaches as opposed to the "economicistic" approach of neoliberalism.

of the economic model. Then comes an analysis of the policies implemented in three strategic areas of the model, that is, the anti-inflationary program and the financial and trade reforms. There follows an exposition of the main results in relation to national production, income and wealth distribution, and the implications of the results obtained for future growth, especially with regard to the investment-saving process. The chapter closes with a brief recapitulation of the lessons provided by this orthodox neoliberal experiment.

My assessment shows the failures of neoliberalism in three strategic areas, which prevent it from working efficiently in developing economies. First, the heterogeneity of productive structures, sectoral and regional problems, and persistent market segmentation present demanding challenges to the efficacy of global economic policies. A growing but minor segment of increased productivity coexisted with numerous bankruptcies and a deterioration of income and employment quality in most areas of the economy. Second, the initial inequality among economic agents, which are indiscriminately thrown into competition among themselves, causes the overall liberalization and privatization, and the "neutrality" imposed on policies, to increase the concentration of economic power. Third, the presence of destabilizing and asymmetrical trends in the adjustment processes, in the macroeconomic framework created by neoliberalism, has made them notably procyclical and exceptionally costly from a social and economic point of view. The macroeconomic environment tended to encourage speculative forces at the expense of real capital formation and productive development.

Central Features of the Model

In Latin America, there have been many attempts to establish economic policies that allow the market a larger role than it had before.[2] This, however, can involve a wide variety of intensities of market action in the role of the state, the ownership of the means of production, and the participation of different social forces in decision making and the distribution of the benefits of development.

It is undeniable that in 1973 there were substantial macroeconomic imbalances that had to be corrected. Likewise the economy was over-intervened, with excessive "microeconomic" controls over private and public enterprises. Evidence of this appears in the self-criticism advanced during 1972–73 by various spokesmen of Popular Unity, the governing coalition under President Allende (Bitar 1979, chap. 5).

2. Chilean experiences in 1952–70 are analyzed in Ffrench-Davis 1973. A comprehensive analysis of economic reforms in Latin America can be found in Ffrench-Davis 2000.

The size of imbalances and the open inconsistency of public interventionism facilitated the introduction of the orthodox neoliberal approach after September 1973. Thus in Chile, in contrast to other authoritarian regimes in Latin America, an extreme version of global monetarism was imposed (see Foxley 1983, chap. 2). The model under discussion is an extreme case because of the amplitude of the role assigned to the market, the intensive privatization of the means of production, and the change imposed on the social organization of the country. Various channels of social participation and development, which had arisen in the continuing process of democratization in Chile during the preceding decades, were suppressed or controlled after 1973.

The implementation of the model gave rise to substantial changes in the economic role played by the public sector. It implied a general withdrawal, gradual or abrupt, from the broad field of action covered by the state. This embraced public ownership,[3] the active role of the state in development, and the orientation of indirect economic policies, which it was stated should become absolutely neutral.[4] The principle of the subsidiary state was applied within markedly narrow limits and on the premise that the private market could assume numerous functions, which in fact it could not perform satisfactorily.

The structural transformations in the economy were carried out without the government having resolved the serious conjunctural distortions and macroeconomic disequilibria confronting the Chilean economy. This procedure was due in part to the priority assigned to structural transformations; it was thought then that a delay in initiating them might mean the loss of the opportunity provided by the authoritarian political framework and the widespread anti-interventionist atmosphere prevailing in large social segments that had been traumatized by supply shortages and bureaucracy, among other things, in 1973. Additionally, the proponents of the model claimed that the existing problems had resulted from statist and interventionist policies applied both during the regime of President Allende and in the four preceding decades, transcending governments that covered the entire political spectrum.[5]

The main economic transformations took place in the fiscal, financial,

---

3. Notwithstanding the intensity of privatization, public ownership was still more significant in Chile than in several other Latin American countries in 1982. The norm, however, was the passivity imposed on public enterprises. The case of the state-owned copper enterprise, which is described later, is an example of this.

4. The more extreme aspects of the model were not fully apparent at the outset. The economic team was taking shape and consolidating its hegemony between 1973 and 1975 and at the same time imposing its neoliberal approach. The peak of orthodoxy was reached in the early 1980s.

5. See statements by public officials in DIPRES 1978 and Moulián and Vergara 1979.

and labor fields, international economic relations, and public ownership of means of production; while later a profound social security reform was also introduced. In all of these areas, economic action by the public sector was persistently reduced throughout this period (Vergara 1981).

Fiscal policy comprised a tax reform and a restructuring and reduction of the greater part of public expenditure. The tax reform included the elimination of taxes on wealth and capital gains and a reduction of the charge on profits. On the other hand, the adoption of a value-added tax was completed and the existing exemptions for basic consumer goods were in general suppressed. The target was to reduce the tax burden, concentrating it in taxes that, in the opinion of the economic team, were "neutral." The official speech claimed that any differentiation "distorted" resource allocation (DIPRES 1978).

Public expenditure recorded as a share of GDP was reduced by over a quarter from the levels it had reached by the late 1960s,[6] after having resulted in abnormally sizable expenditures and budget deficits in 1972–73. There was a dramatic decline in government investment, which diminished by more than half as a share of GDP between 1970 and 1979. Public expenditure also decreased in the productive sectors, in activities to support the private sector, in subsidies to public enterprises, and in infrastructure. Social expenditure, mainly on education, health, social security, and housing, increased its share in public expenditure. This was repeatedly proclaimed to be an indicator of the "social" character of the model. However, real per capita expenditure decreased, and it also declined as a share of GDP. As will be shown, the drop in public social expenditure per capita took place in the context of a marked increase in unemployment and deterioration in the real income of the middle- and low-income brackets. Therefore, the socioeconomic frame required, in contrast, a compensatory increase in expenditure.

In the financial field, a drastic reform was introduced in 1975. The banks that had been nationalized under the previous regime were returned to private ownership. Interest rates were left totally free, regulations respecting the terms and allocation of credit were eliminated, new financial entities were authorized with few restrictions, and easy access was given to foreign banks. Finally, there was a gradual relaxation of restrictions on capital flows.

With regard to international trade, practically all restrictions other

---

6. There are serious problems of comparability in the figures on public expenditure. Due to changes in definition and erroneous deflators, the official figures for social spending were overestimated. Homogenized figures for the period 1969–79 and an analysis of the main components appear in Marshall 1981. All the figures in the text come from that source. A comprehensive study of the distributive impact of public revenue and expenditure toward the end of the 1960s is contained in Foxley, Aninat and Arellano 1980.

than tariffs were removed, and these were rapidly reduced from the high level predominant in 1973 (a simple mean rate of 94 percent) to a uniform tariff of 10 percent for all goods since 1979. Likewise, trade liberalization resulted in the suppression of the price bands and public purchasing mechanisms designed to attenuate the transmission of external instability to the domestic economy. In line with the objective of the unilateral and across the board opening of the market to the world, Chile withdrew from the Andean Pact in 1976.

Privatization was not limited to transferring businesses expropriated during the regime of President Allende. It was also extended to enterprises created during successive governments after the establishment of the national Development Corporation (CORFO) in 1939. In 1970, CORFO controlled the ownership of forty-six enterprises, a number that rose to around three hundred in 1973.[7] In 1980 there were only twenty-four enterprises left in the hands of this institution, half of which were in the process of being sold. There were also some dozen public enterprises dependent on other governmental departments. Among these were the Copper Corporation (CODELCO) and the National Petroleum Enterprise (ENAP).

The sale of enterprises was largely conducted in periods of domestic recession and very high interest rates. Hence, very few groups were able to consider their purchases. This was one of the reasons for the acute concentration of ownership during those years.[8] In this process, there was little direct participation by transnational corporations, in contrast with the official expectations of a vigorous flow of foreign direct investment (FDI). However, a massive increase in loans from international commercial banks provided a substantial proportion of the financing required by the national economic groups acquiring the enterprises being privatized.

In the agricultural sector, the transfer of ownership had dramatic significance. The agrarian reform that had taken place during the governments of presidents Frei and Allende came to an abrupt end. After 1973, around 30 percent of the expropriated land was returned to its former owners and 20 percent was auctioned to nonrural dwellers. Barely one-third of the area was assigned to peasant farmers. Given the curtailment of one of the former functions of the state, that is, the provision of credit and technical support to peasants and cooperatives, these were some of the principal victims of the restructuring of public expenditure. It is estimated that as early as 1979 about half of the

---

7. This does not include about 220 enterprises subject to intervention in 1973. See Vergara 1981; Bitar (1979, chap. 10) examines the social property area program, its deviations, and resulting problems.

8. Additionally, it is estimated that the transfer was made at prices lower than *normal* market values. See Dahse 1979; Foxley 1983; and Marcel 1989.

peasants who had been assigned land had been forced to sell or rent out their farms.[9] At the same time, a massive expulsion of peasants from the farms on which they had been living before and during the agrarian reform took place.

The dismantling of state participation in economic life was also extended to other areas. In very concise and by no means exhaustive terms, the network making up the agricultural "infrastructure" (such as cold storage plants, supply centers for seeds and inputs, purchasing power, and technical assistance to medium and small farmers) and the mining network (mineral-processing plants) can be mentioned.

In 1980, another major step in the process of privatization was taken in relation to the social security system. The retirement pension scheme, hitherto financed through a pay as you go system, was replaced with a system based on individual capitalization in private social security financing societies (AFP) created by the new system.[10] Existing pensions and those of workers who would retire in less than five years continued to be the responsibility of the public sector; the rest of the workers could choose between remaining in the old system or transferring to an AFP. For merely making the transfer, the worker benefited from an automatic take-home pay increase of 11 percent. The choice between financing societies was to be made by the worker based on quality of service and an assessment of the expected return in each social security financing society during the length of time before his or her retirement. The expected return to the worker was determined by the various commissions he or she had to pay, which could be freely modified by each society, and the profits or interest obtained from the investments of each AFP.

One enterprise of great importance that resisted privatization was CODELCO. It underwent powerful onslaughts from the economic team but succeeded in warding them off. Even so, it suffered budgetary restrictions imposed by the Ministry of Finance despite the substantial profits it contributed to the Treasury. It was only permitted to make investments that allowed it to maintain the production level reached in 1977. Within the contradictions produced by the privatization dogma, the government encouraged, unsuccessfully hitherto, the development of other copper deposits to be operated by foreign companies. Paradoxically, these de-

---

9. Two financial factors that contributed to the pressure on peasants to sell or lease their allotted land were the high cost of credit in the domestic capital market and the lack of prior relations between the peasants and commercial banks. It seems to have been assumed that they would "compete" on equal terms with the other users. With reference to the agricultural and peasant situation, see Ortega 1987.

10. The characteristics of the pay as you go system, the new dispositions, and a comparative analysis with other options are discussed in Arellano 1985.

posits, although rich in a world context, were less so than those mined by CODELCO, which suffered systematic constraints on its expansion.[11]

One feature of the official antistate approach was the persistence of the privatization process, even during the serious 1982 crisis. The government constituted a commission to sell assets as part of an "economic recovery program."

Parallel with the changes in the economic field were structural reforms in social organization. According to the official rhetoric, these were part of the project to create a competitive society of "free men." This involved changes in the university system, in the organization and dependence of elementary schools, and in health services, professional, associations, and student and labor union organizations.[12] The last case was undoubtedly functional in imposing a policy that caused average real wages in 1981 to be even lower than in 1970 and 1971.

Neoliberalism in Three Strategic Areas

One of the distinctive features of neoliberalism is its globalism: its neglect of problems of a sectoral nature, of the heterogeneity of the productive structures and access to power of different sectors, of the significance of market segmentations, and of the difficulty of transmitting information to economic agents so that they can contribute to fulfilling the expectations of public policy. Ultimately, it underestimates the frequent presence of destabilizing adjustment processes and lags and overshooting. These elements represent inescapable obstacles that prevent "neutral" and indirect global economic policies alone from being effective in developing nations or those in the process of deep transformation like Chile was.

In this section, we consider three "neutral" policy reforms to which the government assigned a prominent role. This, in fact, they achieved but with an outcome different from what had been foreseen. First, the anti-inflationary policy and the extreme closed economy monetarism that was applied until 1976, and the subsequent extreme open economy monetarism imposed between 1979 and 1982, are considered. The financial reform introduced in 1975 is analyzed, and finally a brief discussion on trade and financial reforms is presented.

---

11. See Vignolo 1982. The main foreign investment, made by Exxon through the purchase of a deposit in exploitation, is discussed in Tironi and Barría 1978. Also see Bande and Ffrench-Davis 1989.

12. See Brunner 1981; Campero and Valenzuela 1981; Moulián and Vergara 1980; Vergara 1981; and various articles in *Revista Mensaje,* especially Ruiz-Tagle 1979; 1980; 1981; and Zañartu 1980.

The Anti-inflationary Policy

Until 1976, monetary policy constituted the instrument on which anti-inflationary action was based.[13] In the twelve months prior to September 1973, inflation had reached an annual rate of 400 percent, and from May to August of that year it was about 19 percent per month (an annualized rate of 700 percent).[14] The fiscal deficit was close to 14 percent of GDP, strongly influenced by price controls on the goods and services sold by public enterprises.

Price controls, which extended to broad areas of the private sector, involved heavily repressed inflationary pressures and an extensive black market (Bitar 1979). A few days after the coup, most of the controlled prices were freed within a context of high uncertainty. The foreseeable result was a dramatic upsurge in inflation, which soared to 88 percent in one month and reached 590 percent in the course of the first year of application of the model. Undoubtedly, there was an overshooting of market prices, which exceeded by far the inflationary pressures previously repressed. As the fiscal situation was being brought under control, the monetary policy became effectively restrictive in the course of 1974. The official line was that the new price fixers, the private entrepreneurs, had to take money supply behavior into account in order to define the price of their products. It was claimed that in their own best interest they would restrict price increases in order to maintain their market share. And this they would promptly do as soon as they observed a reduction in the expansion rate of the money supply.

The concrete fact is that the information on money supply became widely available with a delay of some months and with various divergent indicators, and that prices, given the high inflation, were often adjusted even more frequently than once a month. Under these circumstances, the main point of reference for each economic agent became the actual behavior of entrepreneurs as a whole, measured through changes in the official consumer price index (CPI), the only easily available and up-to-date indicator. This indicator was published early in each month with reference to the preceding period. The consequence was that annual inflation rates exceeding 300 percent persisted until far into the third year of application of the model, despite monetary restrictions and a fiscal budget already under control in 1975.

The monetary restrictions, rather than influencing prices, had a

13. Anti-inflationary policy is discussed in greater depth in Corbo 1985; Foxley 1983; and Ramos 1975, 1986.

14. All the inflation figures used here refer to the consumer price index as corrected in Cortázar and Marshall 1980. The official index significantly underestimated the effective rise in prices, mainly in 1973 and in 1976–78.

greater impact on the level of economic activity: during 1975 industrial production fell by 28 percent, GDP declined by 17 percent,[15] and open unemployment (including emergency programs) peaked at 20 percent.[16] The "price," which was in fact adjusted swiftly downward, was wages: around 1975 they had lost about 40 percent of their purchasing power owing to the legal readjustment based on an underestimated CPI and the drastic repression of unions.

The monetarist recipe for controlling inflation did not function in the way predicted by the supporters of the model. On the contrary, it multiplied the effects deriving from the international recession and involved a notably high cost both socially and in terms of economic activity (see Foxley 1983; Ramos 1986).

As late as mid-1976, the economic team recognized implicitly that monetary control was proving to be incapable of restraining inflation on its own. Then a second variable was incorporated into the anti-inflationary policy—the regulation of the exchange rate conditioned to that objective. Thus began a long process in which the exchange rate was used to slow inflation by reducing the cost of imported goods and attempting to influence inflationary expectations: analytically, it was a transition from closed to open monetarism. In June 1976 and March 1977, exchange rate revaluations were made (a reduction in the number of pesos per U.S. dollar), which were accompanied by a systematic mass media campaign.[17] The measure had a significant effect, since inflation rapidly fell to levels below 100 percent annually after the first revaluation and below 60 percent after the second. There was a belated realization that the inflation was not being generated by an excess of demand and monetary expansion; it is evident that misinterpretation of the workings of markets involved huge social and productive costs for Chile. The belated realization was, moreover, incomplete, since only one additional policy instrument was applied; that is, the exchange rate. This implied its excessive conditioning to the anti-inflationary policy, thereby sacrificing external equilibrium and the production of exportable goods and services.

---

15. In the course of 1975, a severe balance of payments problem arose. This was associated with a sharp fall in the terms of trade, which the government tackled by intensifying the restriction on the money supply, curtailing fiscal expenditure, and imposing a devaluation. The impact of the terms of trade deterioration was multiplied by three in the domestic economy. The direct impact of the deterioration in the terms of trade observed in 1975 is discounted in the figure for GDP decline. GDP measures real output; the terms of trade impact affects income.

16. The serious shortcomings of the official employment figures and a series corrected for the period 1970–85 are provided in Jadresić 1986.

17. After the publicized revaluations, daily minidevaluations were applied. The exchange rate policy is analyzed in detail in chapter 4.

The anti-inflationary policy culminated in 1979 in the freezing of the exchange rate, once again supported by the weight of publicity in the mass media. The new official version was that, with a fixed exchange rate in an economy with free imports, as the Chilean economy was then, domestic prices could not rise more rapidly than international inflation. At this late stage, therefore, they had adopted the "balance of payments monetary approach" then in fashion in several academic and orthodox financial circles. Thus, the implementors switched from a closed economy monetary approach, the official doctrine up to 1976, to an open economy model. In the former case, domestic inflation was considered to be the *exclusive* result of monetary expansion. In the latter case, domestic inflation was assumed to be due to international price changes plus exchange rate variations; with the exchange rate frozen, there should be rapid equalization of domestic and external inflation.

When the exchange rate was pegged (June 1979), domestic annual inflation was above 30 percent, while international inflation was near 12 percent. The convergence between the two rates occurred slowly; for a year and a half, domestic inflation was markedly higher than the international rate, so that the exchange rate lost purchasing power. Hence, the regime of free imports and an appreciated exchange rate caused a flood on the domestic market and an unsustainable disequilibrium in the current account during 1981; between 15 and 21 percent of GDP depending on the measurement criteria (see chap. 5). To face the external deficit, the official policy relied on an "automatic adjustment" in the style of the gold standard in force before the world crisis of 1929: it claimed that the real exchange rate would automatically adjust with the contraction of monetary liquidity associated with the current loss of international reserves in the Central Bank. This contraction should have provoked a drastic fall in domestic prices and nominal wages. However, a detail apparently overlooked was the fact that the exchange rate between 1979 and 1981 had accumulated a 30 percent appreciation (besides the lagged effect of import liberalization, as analyzed in chap. 3). The actual adjustment was in the right direction, but with a lag, and then only in a small proportion when negative inflation rates were achieved in some months of 1982. At the same time, however, there was a drastic fall in sales, production, and employment — the most severe recession experienced in 1981–82 in Latin America — and a progressive strangulation of business firms through increasing indebtedness at extremely high real interest rates.

Despite numerous tough restrictions on labor union activities and a real wage that remained below the average level of 1970, the authorities blamed salaries for their failure to achieve a fluent and rapid automatic adjustment.[18] In mid-1982, they tried to effect a general reduction of wages, but the economic team was unable to impose such a measure. Consequently, they turned to exchange rate devaluation.

The final outcome, in mid-1982, was an inflationary phenomenon repressed to levels lower than those of the industrialized nations[19] but with unsustainable disturbances in the productive and financial systems, which led to massive devaluations: between June and October of 1982, the exchange rate was devalued by more than 70 percent amid a general crisis.

Reform of the Financial System

At the end of 1973, the commercial banks were mainly in the hands of the state as a result of nationalization by the previous government.[20] During 1975, most banks were auctioned back to the private sector. The most important commercial bank, the Banco del Estado, founded in 1953, remained public, but its market share fell from about 50 percent at the beginning of the decade to 14 percent of all outstanding loans in 1981. Earlier in 1974, authorization had been given for the creation of private financing societies that could receive and lend resources at a freely determined interest rate. Meanwhile, banks remained subject to a legal maximum interest rate until April 1975. This and other measures that discriminated against banks while they remained public contributed to the boom of the new financing societies. Discrimination was also directed against the savings and loan cooperative system (SINAP), which was linked to the acquisition of housing. The notorious discrimination against this organization caused the funds received by SINAP to decrease from 28 percent of total financial loans in 1973 to 7 percent in 1977.

In addition to freeing the interest rate, in 1975 the government eliminated the norms relating to the quantitative control of credit in national currency and the selectivity of bank reserve regulations, which

---

18. The lower limit for the adjustment in wages was determined by the official CPI of the preceding period. Various authors blame this rule for the costly recessive adjustment. Nonetheless, there was no knowledge of cases of massive deflation that resulted from restriction of the money supply, which operates fluently, at the required intensity, and without causing severe problems for debtors or economic activity. The sticky prices model continued to be a reality around the world in addition to legal readjustment norms.

19. It is important to point out that the external inflation confronting the Chilean economy was negative, owing to the appreciation of the U.S. dollar in relation to the currencies of other industrialized countries: a weighted index of external prices, converted into dollars, from May 1981 showed deflation. Between that date and June 1982, external inflation reached an annual average of -2 percent.

20. Financial reform will be examined in detail in chapter 5.

were largely intended to channel funds into production rather than consumption. Moreover, restrictions relating to maturity terms were removed (except for a general restriction of thirty days minimum). Next a gradual uniformity was imposed on the different financing institutions for both the operations permitted and their conditions. Within this trend toward uniform treatment came the deregulation for foreign banks. In December 1974, the restrictions on their operation in Chile were eliminated. In 1982, there were nineteen foreign banks operating in the national market. But despite their accelerated growth they captured only 10 percent of banking loans.

The economic team expected that the liberalization of the domestic financial market, accompanied by the gradual opening of the capital account, would lead to an increase in national savings and the quality of investment, in response to the suppression of former subsidies and the removal of discrimination between credit users. The result was strikingly different and placed the financial reform and the handling of the external sector at the core of the economic crisis that surfaced in 1982.

The two most outstanding features of the functioning of the domestic capital market were the maturity terms and the interest rates that prevailed during the seven years between 1975 and 1982. The most common term for deposits and loans was thirty days, with a sharp drop in long-term funding. The average real interest rate (discounting inflation) was on the order of 38 percent annually during 1975–82, covering a range varying from 12 to 120 percent (see table 5.5). In other words, real interest rates in the domestic market, apart from a markedly high average level, varied enormously throughout the period.

Medium-term credits available at international rates were mostly those related to external loans. These were mainly available to enterprises connected with banks and to "economic groups" (principally, the so-called Piranhas), which grew like wildfire during the period under discussion (see Dahse 1979). The notable market segmentation to which this gave rise was partially recognized only shortly after the emergence of the crisis. In mid-1982, it became public knowledge that the principal bank of the largest economic group had 42 percent of its total loans (financed with domestic and external funds) in companies related to its directors or owners.

Repeatedly throughout the seven years of the financial reform, advocates of the model predicted decreases in real interest rates. Only during 1980 was there a significant drop in the real financial cost, which lasted for nine months. This was associated, on the one hand, with the freezing of the exchange rate during the whole year and with average domestic inflation still above 30 percent annually. Hence, the real cost of foreign loans was negative (-8 percent) for national debtors. On the other hand, the volume of external financing rose rapidly. Thus, external credit came to represent 40 percent of total bank financing (of domestic and foreign origin). Its high volume and negative real cost, despite the persistent segmentation of the domestic and external markets, brought down the cost of credit of domestic origin to 12 percent, twenty points higher than the rate applied to the large enterprises and banks, which had access to funds from international commercial banks.

Policymakers throughout the seven years anticipated that the market, once freed from public intervention, would achieve equalization of domestic and external interest rates, an integrated financial market, and increased investment and efficiency. The outcome was different: (1) there were persistent gaps between domestic and external rates of more than twenty points annually; (2) in the domestic market, the spread between active rates (loans) and passive rates (deposits) was around fifteen points; (3) the nominal and real rates were very unstable, as were the spreads mentioned; (4) consumer credit expanded, predominantly for imported consumer goods; and (5) the high cost of credit, its instability, and the short maturities (mainly thirty days) discouraged productive investment. What nonspeculative investment could pay real interest rates with annual averages of 38 percent?

In effect, the rate of capital formation (gross fixed domestic investment as a proportion of GDP) during the application of the orthodox model was lower than the historical figures, and the performance of saving was even more deficient. We shall return to this subject later.

Indiscriminate Trade Opening

The main feature of trade policy was the rapid reduction of protection to import substitution (protection was clearly excessive in 1973).[21] As discussed in chapter 3, the target of liberalization underwent major changes during the course of its implementation. In 1974, it was stated that in 1977 there would be no tariff higher than 60 percent. Then in 1975 it was announced that the tariff range would be between 10 and 35 percent and that it would be reached through successive adjustments in the first half of 1978. Nevertheless, the reductions were completed earlier, in August 1977. Finally, three months later a program of monthly adjustments was announced, which resulted in a uniform tariff of 10 percent for (almost) all imports after June 1979.

It was repeatedly stated that the real exchange rate would devalue as effective tariff protection decreased. Nevertheless, as noted earlier, shortly afterward the exchange rate began to be used to reduce

---

21. For more on trade opening in the period under study, see chapter 3.

inflationary expectations and compensate for the monetary effects of massive capital inflows. The result was that advanced phases of tariff liberalization were accompanied by intensive exchange rate revaluations, reinforcing the negative effects on domestic importables and contributing to a growing deficit on the current account. In practice, therefore, especially with the presence of voluminous capital surges, significant deviations occurred with respect to the supposed compensation between tariff reductions and the exchange rate.

Total imports, measured in constant purchasing power, considerably expanded in relation to domestic economic activity. This was mainly observable in consumer goods, particularly nonfood products, where the greater part of new imports were concentrated (see chap. 3). Nontraditional exports showed vigorous growth and diversification by both products and destination. Their share in GDP rose by around four points between 1970 and 1980. This brought total exports up to 20 percent of GDP in the latter year. Even so, there was an evident break in the expansive trend toward the end of the period. Additionally, the diversifying process showed a tendency to retract; in fact, those exports that continued to expand were mostly natural resource intensive (Ffrench-Davis 1979b, 1983b).

Just as import substitution has an "easy" stage, so there is an initial easy stage in the promotion of exports in emerging economies. The increase in nontraditional exports in the 1970s relates in general to this stage. In fact, it relied on rich natural resources and underutilized installed capacities. The underutilization characteristic of overprotected import substitution and exchange rate appreciation in 1971–73 was intensified by the great depression in domestic demand in 1975–76 and its subsequent slow recovery. This situation initially enabled exports to expand without major investments. The increase in exports was spurred by four additional factors. First, a crawling peg exchange rate policy of minidevaluations was applied, which, despite contradictory movements since 1976, in combination with the sharp drop in labor costs initially encouraged exports. Second, the presence of Chile in the Andean Pact until 1976 provided an enlarged market for more than one-third of the increase in new exports (Ffrench-Davis 1979b). Third, there was a reduction in the cost of imported inputs to those exporters who had not benefited from tariff exemptions previously. Finally, together with the above factors, the privileged position assigned to export promotion in the official rhetoric gave a significant impetus to the hitherto incipient export mentality of entrepreneurs.[22]

22. The official policy included active promotion through a public institution (PRO-CHILE). This involved a deviation with respect to orthodoxy, which claimed to base the promotion of exports exclusively on the liberalization of imports and the supposed compen-

The gap between imports and exports widened persistently after 1977. Several factors account for the external deficit and the poor performance of the production of tradables.

The most painful part of tariff liberalization was carried out abruptly and saw its negative impact reinforced by exchange rate revaluation (see chap. 4 and table 3.2). To make matters worse, this policy was applied in the context of very depressed domestic demand and notoriously high, open unemployment.[23] In consequence, the macroeconomic framework was not favorable for the identification of "comparative advantages" and corresponding investment opportunities. This contributed to the markedly low level of investment and the low rate of utilization of installed capacity and labor.

Underutilization of labor and capital, outlier macroprices (interest and exchange rates), and depressed domestic demand generated a framework quite different from the theoretical one on which the arguments in favor of free trade were based. The numerous changes made in the Chilean economy and the neutrality (passivity) of the public sector made it difficult, during the transition to a new equilibria, to identify "comparative advantages."[24] Not surprisingly, the resulting low level of domestic investment was concentrated mainly on resource intensive items and scarcely at all on activities intensive in value added over the natural component and in "acquirable comparative advantages."

There is no doubt that the phenomenon was aggravated by the freezing of the exchange rate in 1979 and its sizable real appreciation in the following years. Even those exports based on the most valuable natural resources, such as fruit, were discouraged. The unqualified adoption of the monetary approach to the "balance of payments" and the belief in an "automatic adjustment" were prejudicial even to one of the successes that economic policy could exhibit in its nine years of implementation.

As a consequence, the reallocative message provided by trade liberalization was clearer for the sectors that should have contracted than for those in a position to expand. The more rapid growth of imports than of exports was a decisive factor in the deterioration of the current account. The deficit was covered by increasing capital inflows.

The government expected a vigorous inflow of FDI in response to the "economic and political system" offered and to the favorable norms established for investors by the new statute for foreign investment (Decree

---

satory exchange rate devaluation. As the orthodox approach gained control in public action, PRO-CHILE rapidly lost importance.

23. Furthermore, there was high terms of trade instability, with a significant negative trend, particularly in the copper price.

24. *Neutrality* was an obstacle to the much needed efforts to *complete* markets. See ECLAC 1998, chaps. 7 and 8; and Ffrench-Davis 2000, chap. 1.

600). It was hoped that foreign investment would exploit the "comparative advantages" previously repressed, which the model was liberating, and that it would make a decisive contribution to rapid development. However, the response of FDI dashed the hopes of the economic team. There were promises of considerable amounts, but their realization was slow (see Lahera 1981 and Vignolo 1980).

In contrast, access to financial capital in private international markets represented the main source of financing for the growing current account deficit. Its main destination in Chile was the private sector. The fact that during a good part of the 1970s real interest rates in international capital markets were low or negative and access to private funds was expeditious led the economic team, and many policymakers and economists throughout the world, to believe that it was "good business" to borrow and that if the debtor was the private sector the funds would be invested efficiently (see chap. 5).

Once again the facts belied the expectations of the supporters of the model. A significant share of foreign credit was devoted to consumption. The massive net inflow of funds, in its turn, helped to promote excessive exchange appreciation and maintain it for several years. In fact, if foreign credit had been less accessible the government would have been forced to moderate the tariff liberalization and/or the exchange rate appreciation. Indeed, the loans available to Chile were larger than the country could absorb productively. After only a moderate increase in 1977–79, the level of debt accelerated in 1980 and grew spectacularly in 1981, rising by about 35 percent in the latter year. In contrast to other countries, which channeled external financing into investment, Chile, instead of having a "debt-led economic growth," incurred a "debt-led deficit on the current account," with a crowding out of savings and domestic output by imports and the discouragement of exports. Finally, external conditions worsened toward the end of the period: real interest rates rose abruptly, and access to funds became progressively more difficult in 1981–82 (see chap. 5).

The experiment in this area culminated in mid-1982 with a sudden exchange rate devaluation after several months of costly and inefficient "automatic adjustment" (Arellano and Cortázar 1982).

Production, Investment, and Income Distribution

In this section, I will make an appraisal of the results obtained in growth and equity. First, what happened with GDP and its main components? Second, to what extent was the performance of the economy generating new productive capacity and new sources of saving? And, third, how were the benefits and costs of the implementation of the model distributed? The background data show that (1) "growth" was largely fictitious, (2) the capital formation ratio was notably lower than in the 1960s, and (3) the limited benefits went to a minority while high costs burdened the majority alongside a sharp worsening of income and wealth distribution.

Global Production and Its Composition

National accounts, both official and corrected (Marcel and Meller 1986), show high "growth" between 1976 and 1981. However, in the first place the model was not initially put in motion in 1976 but (in partial form) in 1973. Second, in 1975 there was a sharp recession, which multiplied about threefold the depressive effects of external shocks. The overall result was a fall of 17 percent in GDP. Hence, to measure economic evolution from that low point is to record as "growth" that which in fact is simply a "*recovery*" of former levels. Whereas 1976–81 gives a per capita annual rate of increase of 4.7 percent, the period 1974–81 gives a rate of 1.4 percent. It is obvious that the greater the recession of 1975 the greater could have been the subsequent recovery. Thus, the greater the loss of production as a result of the recession (a true social and private cost) the higher will appear the "growth" if the period of recession is not taken into account and the measurement begins at the lowest point. This is an extremely gross error, but it is quite frequent.

Paradoxically, in several ways the domestic recession was useful for the promotion of the model. First, the model was able to show "growth" for several years, a circumstance that attracted extensive publicity in the national and foreign mass media; the degree of shortsightedness was impressive. This gave rise to the mistaken impression that Chile was growing vigorously and would continue to do so at rates on the order of 8 percent per year,[25] irrespective of what might happen in the rest of the world. Second, economists were able to show that employment was increasing (though only after the unemployment rate had risen from 6 to 22 percent and again ignoring the starting point). Third, on a more political level, after an intense recession — underestimated or ignored by the media under an authoritarian regime that allowed the orthodox neoliberal policy to continue — the subsequent gradual recovery brought a sensation of relief to both entrepreneurs and workers.

The weakness of the model is highlighted when the composition of GDP is disaggregated. Unfortunately, because there are no revised figures to follow this analysis, I use the official data here. This is shown in table 2.1. First, there was a rise in external indebtedness and its cost.

---

25. See, for example, the illustrative statements quoted in Foxley 1980, 5–6.

TABLE 2.1. Evolution of GDP and Its Composition, 1974–81 (annual rates of growth)

	Total		Per Capita	
	1974–80 (1)	1974–81 (2)	1974–80 (3)	1974–81 (4)
1. Gross domestic product	3.8	4.0	2.3	2.5
2. Gross national product	3.4	3.5	1.9	2.0
3. Value added				
(a) Marketing of imports	15.5	16.2	13.8	14.5
(b) Financial services	14.6	14.2	12.9	12.5
4. Gross national product excluding value added in (3)	1.9	1.8	0.4	0.3

Source: Calculations are based on official figures in Cuentas Nacionales de Chile, 1960–81, in pesos of 1977.

Note: Revised figures by Marcel and Meller (1986) give GDP growth of 2.6 percent for 1974–81; the main correction was in the industrial sector (here included in line 4). There are no disaggregated corrected figures in order to build a revised table.

Around a fifth of the per capita growth recorded between 1974 and 1981 was used to pay interest and profits abroad, which meant that the rate of expansion of the national product was lower than that of GDP. Second, the value added in the marketing of imported products and financial services contributed a high share to GDP "dynamism"; these two sectors, which were linked with the essence of the model, exhibited a dramatic cumulative expansion of 13 percent annually. The first sector expanded as a result of the rapid growth of imports of consumer and other goods. As was discussed earlier, most of these were financed not by greater exports but by an increase in private foreign debt. This source of dynamism was unsustainable in an economy that lacked vigorous real productive support. The second source of dynamism was associated with the financial reform and responded in large measure to the spread between the rates of interest on deposits and loans and to the transfer of foreign credits in Chile. Thus, these two sources of dynamism depended on outlier values of imports and financial spreads, both of which were prejudicial to productive activity and investment.

There can be no doubt that, owing to the distortion produced by both sectors in the Chilean economy, the overall performance contained a sizable share of artificiality. Hence, it is very significant that the rest of the value added per capita, which in 1974 amounted to 91 percent of gross national product, remained virtually stationary, as can be seen in column 4 of table 2.1.[26] Over and above this poor performance, GDP

26. As mentioned earlier, the value added in export production also grew at a significant pace. Therefore, a contraction in the rest of the economy—the nonexporting

fell by 14 percent in 1982–83, while Latin American GDP fell by only 3.2 percent in the same period.

The Nexus with the Future

The connection with the future relates to savings and investment.[27] The supporters of the model claimed that it would achieve a substantial increase in savings, investment, and efficiency. The foregoing analysis has shown that the results were negative with respect to production. However, this could be consistent with a vigorous process of slow maturing investment. Unfortunately, in each of the years between 1974 and 1980, the gross fixed investment ratio was lower than that of each year in the 1960s, and in the peak year, 1981, it was lower than in 1970 (Marcel and Meller 1986). In parallel, national savings financed a lower share of investment; in 1970, around 90 percent was covered by national savings, whereas in 1978–81 scarcely half came from this source. The sharp increase in inequalities of wealth and income observed in these years apparently expressed itself in a notorious differentiation in lifestyles rather than in higher levels of saving destined for productive investment; this is attested by the sharp fall in the rate of national savings.

Concentration of Income and Wealth

Here we shall take a brief look at the indicators of wages and pensions, employment, consumption, and wealth. Others are discussed in chapter 9.

Table 2.2 shows the evolution of some income indicators of wage earners and retired workers. All of these indicate a regressive performance. In 1974–81, average wages reached scarcely three-quarters of the level attained in 1970. After a sharp fall in 1973 and 1974, real wages began to recover somewhat in 1977 but without achieving, even in 1981, the level reached eleven years before,[28] labor income fell further given

---

sectors—occurred. Within this subset, the industry, which accounted for the major share of economic activity, suffered the negative pulls of the recession in 1975, trade liberalization, and then exchange rate appreciation. See chapter 3 and Marcel and Meller 1986.

27. There are many other connections to the future that are not considered here. These include the impact that the model may have had on the capacity for technological absorption and adaptation; the degree of creativity of the technical and university education systems; national cultural development; the channels of participation that could have served as a basis for development strategies, which represent the national consensus; and the dynamism and efficiency of the function of the state as the activator of development.

28. Note that 1970 was taken as a "normal" point of reference. Wages in 1971 were much higher and in 1972 somewhat lower than in 1970. See Cortázar 1983. The index available, calculated by INE, does not include firms with fewer than twenty workers or agricultural wage earners or workers in the Minimum Employment Program.

TABLE 2.2.   Indicators of Income and Unemployment, 1970–81

	Incomes (1970 = 100)			Average PEM Income (%) (4)	Unemployment (%)		
	Average Wage (1)	Average Pension (2)	Average Family Allowance (3)		Open (5)	PEM (6)	Total (7)
1970	100.0	100.0	100.0	—	5.9	—	5.9
1974	65.1	51.3	69.5	—	9.1	—	9.1
1976	64.8	52.3	61.8	80.5	16.6	5.2	21.9
1978	76.0	62.1	56.0	45.5	13.8	4.2	18.0
1980	89.0	74.3	54.4	37.6	11.7	5.2	16.9
1981	96.8	78.0	54.0	32.1	10.4	4.7	15.1
1974–81	76.1	61.9	59.3	48.8[a]	13.0	4.8[a]	16.8

Sources: Jadresić 1990 for column 1; Arellano 1985 for column 2; Cortázar 1983 for column 3, which is a weighted average of all family allowances.

Note: Column 4 indicates the net income of PEM (Minimum Employment Program) workers as a percentage of the minimum wage of 1970. All figures in current pesos have been deflated by the corrected CPI (Cortázar and Marshall 1980) up to 1978 and by the official index for the later years. Columns 5 and 7 are based on Jadresić 1986.

[a]Average for 1976–81.

the higher unemployment. Decisive factors explaining the drop in income were union repression, wage policies linked to the official index of inflation (which systematically underestimated it), the high level of unemployment, and the low level of productive investment. The pensions of retired workers and family allowances for wage earners' dependents (wives and children not working) also worsened considerably, as can be seen in columns 2 and 3.[29]

Despite some improvement between 1976 and 1981, open unemployment in the latter year was double the 1970 rate. As a palliative to growing unemployment, the government adopted in 1975 the emergency Minimum Employment Program (PEM), whose members worked mainly in municipalities and public institutions. In 1981, these workers represented around 5 percent of the labor force, and their income was equivalent to one-third of the minimum wage in force in 1970 (see table 2.2, col. 4). If the PEM workers are included, the unemployment rate is three times that of the year of reference (col. 7). As a result of the crisis of 1982, unemployment (including PEM) climbed to an annual average of 31 percent of the labor force in 1983.

The decline in real wages and employment was mirrored in the distribution of consumption expenditures. The data available refer to

---

29. In 1973, the family allowances for workers and employees were made equal. The equalization was made at the bottom, so all allowances diminished, though less in the case of blue-collar workers.

surveys conducted in 1969 and 1978.[30] With the households divided into quintiles, the poorest is found to have reduced its consumption by 31 percent between the two years of reference, and the second and third quintiles lost 20 and 12 percent, respectively. As total consumption remained stagnant, that drop equaled the percentage loss in the share of these groups. In contrast, the richest quintile was the only one that increased its share (see table 8.2).

There is one important indicator that showed significant improvement during this period. This is the infant mortality rate, which improved from 66 per thousand in 1973 to 33 per thousand in 1980,[31] despite the worsening of employment and income distribution. The main compensating factor for the negative impact of the economic environment for the majority of the population seems to be associated with the emphasis placed by the National Health Service on the maternal and child sector and on the nutrition programs directed toward breast-fed and undernourished infants (Raczynski and Oyarzo 1981; Monckeberg 1998).

In contrast to this specific area, as noted, total social expenditures of the public sector diminished between 1970 and 1981, falling in education, health, and housing by 17 percent per capita (Cabezas 1988; Ffrench-Davis and Raczynski 1990). Nevertheless, as total spending declined in even greater proportion, social expenditures came to represent a larger share of the public budget.

The distribution of assets and wealth also became highly concentrated. This phenomenon was associated with (1) decreasing wages and employment, (2) the privatization of public enterprises, and (3) the impact of the recession on entrepreneurs independent of the main economic groups in conjunction with the faulty functioning of the capital market.

There is no doubt that deteriorating employment and income among workers influenced the distribution of expenditures and wealth. Moreover, there was a striking improvement in the income of the highest paid workers, which increased the distributive gap. But the concentration was fostered by other components of the economic model as well. As mentioned, numerous enterprises in the public sector were rapidly privatized. This took place in an economy in recession and with high interest rates. Only a small segment of the private sector was able to take them over and at prices very favorable to the purchasers. Finally, the recession hit many private businessmen who lacked privileged

---

30. This information is based on household surveys conducted in Santiago by the National Bureau of Statistics. See chapter 9.

31. At the beginning of the 1960s, the infant mortality rate was 110 per 1,000, and in 1970 it improved to 82 per 1,000.

access to domestic or external credit. Hence, many of these entrepreneurs were forced to sell their businesses to the same economic groups that had acquired the former public enterprises. Differential access to foreign loans was another source of concentration. It signified, apart from the purchasing power it conceded, a capital gain corresponding to the large spread between the domestic and external interest rates (see table 5.5; and Zahler 1980, table 14).

The available data show the marked concentration of wealth, with two groups well ahead of the rest. At the end of 1978, the two main economic groups controlled enterprises representing around 50 percent of the wealth of the corporations registered in the stock exchanges of Santiago and Valparaiso, a figure notably higher than in 1970 (Herrera and Morales 1979, 148). Data on the 250 largest national and foreign private firms in Chile indicate that the two aforesaid groups controlled at least 37 percent of the capital of these firms in 1978 (Dahse 1979). The process of concentration continued in subsequent years; between 1978 and 1980, the capital of firms controlled by the two main groups doubled in real terms (Dahse 1982). Data provided by the Stock Exchange of Santiago in June 1982 on distribution of the shares of 177 open private companies indicated that the ten chief shareholders of each firm had direct control, on average, of 72 percent of equity capital.

Lessons from the Neoliberal Experiment

In the 1970s, neoliberalism came to the forefront in various countries and achieved a leading position in many academic centers in industrialized and developing countries. Nonetheless, its practical application in the postwar period had been generally limited and for brief periods. The case of Chile is particularly significant because of the depth, coverage, and continuity with which the orthodox neoliberal model was applied. The political regime that permitted its imposition likewise conceded great autonomy to its advocates, which invests this case, properly speaking, with the character of an "experiment."

The external situation prevailing during the years of application of the model had some negative shocks for the Chilean economy, which affected the success of the model. A case in point was the low price of copper, which persisted during most of the nine years considered. Even so, the external situation also contained features that facilitated the operation and duration of the model. One of the main features was that from 1977 on Chile had expeditious access to external financial loans, which, up to 1981, enabled it to more than offset the income loss caused by worsening of the terms of trade.

The increasing adherence to orthodoxy from 1974 onward met its first severe obstacle in 1981, and in 1982 it suffered several notable setbacks.[32] These were associated with the domestic crisis that erupted in 1981–82 with unusual virulence and spread to practically all sectors and groups in the domestic economy. During 1982, GDP and manufacturing output fell by 14 and 21 percent, respectively; construction was cut by one-half, and open unemployment was affecting one of every three workers in 1983. These and other indicators revealed a substantial worsening of the already poor levels attained in 1981, which have been analyzed in the course of this chapter. That left a long-lasting negative mark on equity in Chile.

The problems developing in the productive apparatus were closely linked to the functioning of the financial system and the indiscriminate trade opening. The model conceded a leading role to the financial reform. In fact, the financial system was transformed into the dominant decision-making center in the Chilean economy. In 1982, it became clear that indebtedness of firms and individuals was strangling economic activity and was growing rapidly owing to the prevailing high interest rates, while the revenue of enterprises was declining as a result of the domestic recession. The financial reform and the opening to capital flows constituted at first a determinant factor in the concentration of wealth and in the crowding out of productive investment (Agosin 1998). Then, toward the end of the period, it revealed the additional vulnerability that it had introduced into the national economy and the distortion of economic development created by the unbridled *financierism* to which it gave rise.

The results observed were actually the result of both intrinsic features of the model and errors in its implementation. For example, the freezing of the exchange rate at thirty-nine pesos per dollar is not an intrinsic element of the model, which was consistent with a more devalued fixed rate and/or a free rate.[33] However, given the model, the absence of an appreciated exchange rate would have prevented the reduction in inflation achieved in 1981, and this was the priority of the economic team when the exchange rate was frozen.

The intrinsic components of the model are observable in three

---

32. Examples of these are the establishment of a preferential exchange rate to enable private debtors to pay their foreign creditors, the reintroduction of controls on access to foreign currency, and the purchase by the Central Bank of nonperforming loans from the private banks. These had risen to more than 50 percent of the capital and reserves of the national private banks by mid-1982. See chapter 6.

33. Evidently, with a free exchange rate the level of appreciation would have been even higher, which would have led to a worse crisis. See Harberger 1985 for a similar argument.

areas, which form the pillars of orthodox neoliberalism. These are the assumption (1) that privatization and the suppression of state intervention rapidly result in integrated, flexible, and well-informed markets and spontaneously generate dynamic development; (2) that adjustment processes are stabilizing and characteristically speedy; and (3) that "competition," even among unequal competitors, leads to greater well-being for the majority. All three assumptions proved to be false in the Chilean experiment (see a comparison with reforms throughout Latin America in the 1990s in Ffrench-Davis 2000).

First, the indirect and "neutral" economic policies were introduced in a context of "competition" between unequals, which intensified the differences. Furthermore, the neutrality was broken in several decisive instances, so that institutions such as the cooperatives and a semipublic system of savings (SINAP) were discriminated against. The restraint on union activity accentuated the inequality between "suppliers" and "demanders." As has been shown, the concentration of income and wealth was dramatic. Second, the slowness of adjustment processes involves substantial costs because of the inefficient underutilization of resources and the disincentive it implies for capital formation (see Ffrench-Davis and Reisen 1998). The neoliberal approach fails to take into account the fact that to reach the long-term objective it is necessary to go through a succession of short-term effects that influence the final outcome and the quality of the transition (the so-called hysteresis in modern literature). Third, although a mistaken interventionism also severely accentuates the structural segmentation and heterogeneity of markets, the extreme alternative option, consisting of the cessation of state action and the indiscriminate privatization of the means of production as fast as possible, disregarding the conjuncture and balance of benefits and costs, does not lead to the rapid integration and flexibility of markets (these failures are characteristic of underdevelopment). Consequently, the resulting macroeconomic context is not propitious for the coexistence of the trilogy of growth, equity, and national autonomy, the three basic ingredients of a national development project. The solution to these failures demands an active state that is subject to strict norms of efficiency and accountability.

In summary, the neoliberal experiment produced a society with increased inequality on many fronts and a predominance of economicism over other human activities. A highly productive segment coexisted with impoverished large segments of the economy. It markedly deepened the unemployment problem, discouraged investment, and in general favored speculative and financieristic trends to the detriment of activities likely to increase overall productivity and capital formation. It intensified external vulnerability, as attested by the greater impact of the 1982 recession on the Chilean economy compared to the rest of Latin America.

CHAPTER 3

Import Liberalization: The Chilean Experience in 1973–82

The distinctive characteristic of trade policies implemented in 1973 was the sharp import liberalization, which was undertaken to a degree then unprecedented in modern economic history, either in Chile or in any other semi-industrialized country. By establishing a uniform tariff of 10 percent on nearly all imports, this liberalization suppressed all selective criteria for regulating them. Trade liberalization was accompanied by an opening to foreign investment, also unrestricted, and by a reduction in restrictions on foreign exchange dealings and capital flows (for a detailed analysis of the financial reform, see chap. 5).

The implementation of free trade raises four questions. First, did the policy allow more efficient use of available resources or did it produce significant new divergences between market and social "efficiency"? Second, what degree of dynamism characterized the process, compared to its historical behavior, and how did the intensity and timing of liberalization affect employment, investment, and consumption? Third, how much competition or economic concentration did the policy reform produce? Last, how effectively "neutral" were these "nondiscriminatory" economic policies? Policies, seemingly neutral, were applied to different segments of the economy that coexisted in a framework marked by inequalities and productive heterogeneity. This implies that these policies may produce asymmetrical effects among different productive and social groups.

It is evident that the effects of a deep process of reforms need a long time for completion. Nevertheless, given a positive time preference rate, it should be kept in mind that a peso today will be worth more than twice as much as ten years later. On the other hand, many other policy changes were implemented together with trade reform, making it difficult to distinguish between the effects of each of them. Finally, there were different

---

This chapter is based on "Import liberalization: The Chilean experience, 1973–82," in *Military Rule in Chile: Dictatorship and Oppositions,* Samuel J. Valenzuela and Arturo Valenzuela, eds. (Baltimore: Johns Hopkins University Press, 1986). Reprinted with permission from Johns Hopkins University Press. The author would like to thank Augusto Aninat, Vittorio Corbo, René Cortázar, Jaime Estévez, Alejandro Foxley, Dominique Hachette, and Pilar Vergara for their comments and Jorge Scherman for his assistance.

effects on tradables, giving a positive impulse to the production of export-ables and a negative one to importables. Mainly, we are referring to the transfer of innovations through exposure to foreign competition (Lüders 1980; Tybout, de Melo, and Corbo 1991).[1]

At the beginning, I would like to remove from consideration the sim-plistic dilemma that the only alternative to the reform implemented, with all its details, would have been to maintain the chaotic situation of 1973. Why, for instance, was the pragmatic version of the trade reform applied between 1968 and 1970 not continued? Its main features were gradual im-plementation, complementarity of export promotion, reduction of the variance and average of effective protection (i.e., of variance and average of the import tariff), and an active crawling peg exchange rate policy con-sistent with the reform (see Ffrench-Davis 1973, chaps. 3 and 4).

The next section shows the path followed by the reduction of import restrictions, focusing on tariff liberalization and the evolution of the real exchange rate in order to determine to what degree this macroeconomic price played the compensatory role assigned by official policy. I then analyze the behavior of the principal categories of imports (in particular, consumption goods) and examine some distributive effects. Next the general impact of import liberalization on manufacturing and employ-ment is investigated, and the effects of liberalization are illustrated by examining the impact of disaggregated information on the performance by industrial branches. Finally, I present the main conclusions.

The Import Liberalization Process

Chile's trade liberalization scheme is the oldest and longest continuously applied program in Latin America. In late 1973, before the introduction of reforms, Chilean foreign trade was subject to a great deal of govern-ment control:[2] a simple tariff average of 94 percent, countless nontariff restrictions, and multiple exchange rates.

A remarkable reduction in the extremely high barriers that pro-tected import substitutes constituted the core of the new trade policy. The rapid liberalization process, which began in 1973 and ended in June 1979, induced a drastic change in market comparative advantages by modifying both the profile of effective protection and its average.

1. In this chapter, I will focus on import policies. Export policies, their effects, and the interrelationships between both dimensions are examined in Ffrench-Davis 1979b; and Ffrench-Davis, Leiva, and Madrid 1992. The export model in the 1980s and 1990s is analyzed in chapter 8.

2. Notice that this was the situation in 1973. However, in the second half of the 1960s there was a reform in progress that included the gradual rationalization of the import regime and the improvement of mechanisms of export promotion (Ffrench-Davis 1973).

During the period of liberalization, the target of the process underwent significant changes. What initially appeared to be a moderate reform, with maximum tariff rates of 60 percent, in the end became a drastic revamping of the tariff structure with a final uniform tariff of 10 percent.

The first steps in the process consisted of suppressing the main nontariff barriers and dropping to 220 percent all tariffs that were above that level. Most import prohibitions and deposits were eliminated. These import deposits, with a rate of 10,000 percent, which were charged on more than half of the imports, constituted one of the most common mechanisms used to regulate imports in 1973. The deposits were waived on the condition that importers fixed their volumes within the quotas recommended by the government. Since this mechanism was applied along with an undervalued exchange rate to several thousand products, it generated countless supply bottlenecks and speculative windfall gains for importers. The "normalization" of the foreign exchange market (see chap. 4), which took place in October 1973, and a significant increase in the price of copper during the second half of that year facilitated the rapid removal of quantitative restrictions and initial tariff reductions.

In early 1974, the government announced a tariff liberalization scheme that would take place gradually over a three-year period and indicated that it would proceed pari passu with real exchange rate depreciation. The finance minister asserted that it would generate export-led growth and that workers would benefit, "as it would create more jobs in expanding sectors than the number of jobs that could disappear in some highly inefficient sectors."[3] The announcement gave no indication of the levels tariffs were projected to reach.

The first such indication came in May 1974, when the government declared that "in 1977, no tariff will be higher than 60 percent. This clearly defines the tariff policy that will be followed in the future, so that domestic industries can make whatever adjustments are necessary and prepare themselves so that they will be in good shape to meet foreign competition."[4]

Despite these announcements, the tariff policy still was not really defined, as strategic differences emerged between proponents of a fully orthodox policy and other important government officials possessed of a more pragmatic bent. Toward the end of 1974, it was informally hinted that the maximum tariff rate in the future would only be 30 percent. Internal government documents mentioned a range of 25 to 35 percent, within which the majority of tariff rates would fall (De la Cuadra and

---

3. Statement of January 7, 1974, reprinted in DIPRES 1978, 61.

4. Comments of the finance minister, October 1974, reprinted in ibid., 107. The minister reconfirmed this goal on April 24, 1975 (172).

Hachette 1992; Hachette 2000). Later, in 1975, the government announced that the range of tariff rates would be placed between 10 and 35 percent and that it would be reached during the first half of 1978, by gradual reductions.

Although step-by-step the apparently more pragmatic official policy gave way to the free trade approach, the policy as it was presented by 1975 contained two important heterodox elements. On one hand, it contemplated nonuniform tariff rates (from 10 to 35 percent) according to the degree of elaboration of different categories of products. On the other hand, it also contemplated maintaining the tariff preferences agreed upon under the Andean Pact, which meant that tariff reductions for several products stopped at the minimum common external tariff in place in 1972–76, according to the Cartagena Agreement (Aninat 1978).

The gradual tariff reductions were made approximately once every six months, as can be seen in table 3.1. Nevertheless, the final reductions, scheduled for the first half of 1978, were completed in August 1977, when 99.6 percent of all tariffs reached the 10 to 35 percent range, with a 20 percent simple average.

It seemed from repeated official statements that the reduction of protection for import-substituting firms had been completed in August

TABLE 3.1.   Tariff Liberalization, 1973–79 (rates on *cif* value)

Date	Maximum Tariff		Modal Tariff		Simple Average Tariff (%) (5)	No. of Items (6)
	Rate (%) (1)	% of All Items (2)	Rate (%) (3)	% of All Items (4)		
12/31/73	220	8.0	90	12.4	94.0	5,125
3/1/74	200	8.2	80	12.4	90.0	5,125
3/27/74	160	17.1	70	13.0	80.0	5,125
6/5/74	140	14.4	60	13.0	67.0	5,125
1/16/75	120	8.2	55	13.0	52.0	5,125
8/13/75	90	1.6	40	20.3	44.0	4,958
2/9/76	80	0.5	35	24.0	38.0	4,952
6/7/76	65	0.5	30	21.2	33.0	4,956
12/23/76	65	0.5	20	26.2	27.0	4,959
1/8/77	55	0.5	20	24.7	24.0	4,981
5/2/77	45	0.6	20	25.8	22.4	4,984
8/29/77	35	1.6	20	26.3	19.8	4,985
3/12/77	25	22.9	15	37.0	15.7	4,993
6/78	20	21.6	10	51.6	13.9	4,301
6/79	10	99.5	10	99.5	10.1	4,301

Source: Central Bank of Chile.

Note: Dates refer to the official decrees on general changes of custom tariff rates between December 1973 and December 1977. On the latter date, the government issued a decree of monthly adjustments that lasted until June 1979.

1977. Three months later, however, the finance minister announced another policy change: a target tariff of a uniform 10 percent to be reached in mid-1979. The additional tariff liberalization was carried out in monthly steps between December 1977 and June 1979. By the later date, a uniform tariff of 10 percent was being charged on nearly all imports into Chile. Nontariff restrictions, which were generally inefficient and generated capital gains, had been mostly eliminated; and several hundreds of tariff exemptions in favor of firms, regions, or individuals had been suppressed (De la Cuadra and Hachette 1992). But mechanisms softening the transmission of external instability were also eliminated. Imports of nonproduced capital goods, which had been generally exempt from tariffs, now became subject to them, although they were paid in installments.

Evidently, relative prices changed as compared with those of imports of capital goods and in favor of imports of consumer goods.

The 10 percent flat rate was unusually low for developing countries in the 1970s, and even in developed countries a uniform rate was exceptional. Some comparative information illustrates this. In a semi-industrialized country such as South Korea, even after a decade of following its successful overall economic policies, tariffs still ranged between zero and 150 percent, with many locally produced items enjoying nominal rates of protection between 30 and 60 percent.[5] Korea as well as Taiwan and other Asian countries had carried out a profound trade reform led by export promotion rather than import liberalization (see Ffrench-Davis 2000, chap. 3).

Developed countries, despite their position at the forefront of world industry, usually maintained selective (nonuniform) rates of protection for different products, with levels notably higher than 10 percent for significant groups of items. Effective tariff protection in the United States, Japan, and the European Economic Community was relatively high for product categories such as textiles and clothing, processed food, and light manufactures. For instance, textiles and clothing enjoyed effective tariff protection of about 40 percent in these countries. In Japan, the effective tariff protection on processed food was 68 percent.[6] Imports

5. See Balassa 1977, 148–51; and Frank, Kim, and Westphal 1975. For other developing countries analyzed in a comprehensive project by the National Bureau of Economic Research (NBER), see Bhagwati 1978. An earlier study by Little, Scitovsky, and Scott (1970) includes a fine theoretical analysis that supports the use of selective (moderate) tariffs. See also Ffrench-Davis 1979a, chaps. 7–9.

6. Mendive 1978. The dispersion of effective rates of protection by items or "products" was very high; for example, cigarettes had a rate of 405 percent in Japan, refined oil a rate of 466 percent in the United States, and butter a rate of 1,300 percent in the European Economic Community. The background information refers to the pre-Tokyo round of the GATT negotiations.

into these countries were restricted by many nontariff mechanisms (Baldwin 1981) that were significantly affecting a growing number of industrial exports from developing countries. Estimates for 1973 covering France, the United States, Japan, and Sweden indicate that for twenty-six chapters of the tariff schedule the average ad valorem rates of protection of nontariff regulations (such as health regulations, import quotas, "voluntary" export restrictions, and import licenses) were as high as 40 to 90 percent (Roningen and Yeats 1976).

After 1973, public officials stated repeatedly that the real exchange rate would depreciate as effective protection dropped (DIPRES 1978, 275, 291). The government declarations implied an extremely naive view of causal relationships in the economy, one that is valid only for a competitive model without capital flows. In practice, however, the large capital inflows implied significant deviations from this supposed univocal causal relationship.

In fact, during periods in which the most sizable tariff reductions were made, the real exchange rate appreciated in tandem. Table 3.2 shows the evolution of the real exchange rate (col. 1), nominal rates of protection for items subject to the maximum and average tariffs (cols. 3 and 4), and the total cost per dollar of imports (col. 5) on selected dates. Dates were selected according to the evolution of the cost of imports and

TABLE 3.2.   Cost of Imports, 1973–82

Phase	Date	Real Exchange Rate[a] (1)	Change in (1) in Each Phase (2)	Nominal Tariffs (%) Maximum (3)	Nominal Tariffs (%) Average (4)	Average Total Exchange Rate[b] (5)	Change of (5) in Each Phase (6)
	10/73	59.20		220	94	114.85	
1			67.2				31.0%
	4/75	98.98		120	52	150.45	
2			−39.4				−51.4%
	7/77	59.96		45	22	73.15	
3			14.2				2.9%
	6/79	68.46		10	10	75.31	
4			−31.3				−31.3%
	6/82[c]	47.02		10	10	51.72	

Sources: Central Bank of Chile, *Boletín Mensual,* various issues; Ffrench-Davis 1984; table 3.1.

[a]Nominal exchange rate deflated by the corrected CPI (see Cortázar and Marshall 1980) and multiplied by the index of external prices in 1986 prices.

[b]Obtained by multiplying column 1 by $[1 + (4)/100]$.

[c]Monthly average until the day before devaluation.

the relation between the two components that are considered here: the exchange rate and nominal tariffs.[7]

Using this information, we can distinguish four phases in the liberalization process (see fig. 3.1).

The tariff reductions in phase 1, which lasted from the end of 1973 until April 1975, were made when exchange rates were very depreciated, particularly following late 1974. Moreover, a significant portion of the notably high tariffs were then redundant, which meant that the initial reductions did not have substantial effects, as they represented mostly "water" in nominal protection.[8] Because of this, there were no significant increases in "nontraditional" imports during this phase.

During phase 1, the average cost of a dollar's worth of imports increased by 31 percent. Hence, the reform process was principally one of "rationalization" in which the large dispersion of effective protection rates was diminished without causing a substantial impact on manufacturing of import substitutes. However, the latter industries suffered the negative effects of the strong recession then in progress. Import liberalization and exchange rate depreciation did have a positive effect on exportables; given that exports previously enjoyed customs exemptions for imported components, it was the exchange rate policy that had stronger effects on increasing exports (Ffrench-Davis 1979b).

The situation faced by importable goods changed substantially during phase 2, which lasted from April 1975 until mid-1977. During this period, reductions in nominal protection were more effective than in phase 1, dropping from an average of 52 to 22 percent, and the maximum nominal protection decreased from 120 to 45 percent. The exchange rate appreciated by 39 percent, strongly reinforcing the effects of reduced tariffs. Thus, for two years, as the tariff liberalization was carried out, the real exchange rate was revalued in parallel. Consequently, the thirty-point reduction in the average nominal tariff meant a 51 percent fall in the average cost of each dollar's worth of imports (table 3.2, col. 6). There was little chance for the market to gradually adjust to the

---

7. The selected dates are somewhat arbitrary, since the real exchange rate levels are sensitive to the price indexes used to calculate them. The average tariff also can be calculated in very different ways. I present here the simple average used by different government and independent sources. It is well known that the simple average is very sensitive to the extent of disaggregation.

8. Obviously, the nominal tariff for several items, in particular for consumer goods, dropped notably more than the decrease in the average tariff. The corresponding reduction in effective protection was even sharper. Therefore, for many of these categories the real exchange rate depreciation did not compensate for the effects of tariff liberalization. Data on effective and nominal tariffs before tariff liberalization appear in Behrman 1976, 137–44; and in De la Cuadra 1974.

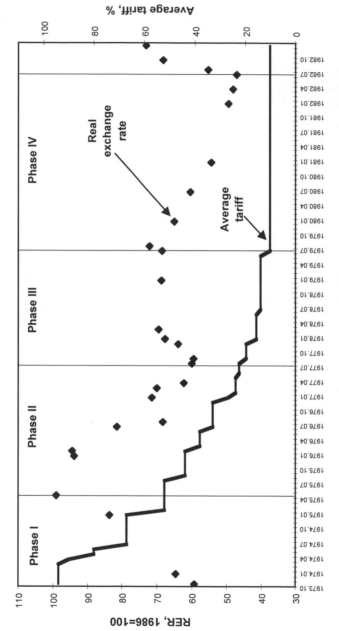

Fig. 3.1. Average tariff and real exchange rates, 1973–82. (Data from Ffrench-Davis 1984 and tables 3.1 and 3.2 in this volume.)

strong impact of this rapid liberalization, unexpected because it contradicted repeated official statements that the exchange rate would "indissolubly" compensate for the dismantling of tariffs.[9] The net result of tariff reforms in phase 2 was a rapid increase in nontraditional imports, particularly nonfood consumer goods.

In phase 3, which lasted until mid-1979, when the nominal price of the dollar was frozen, the exchange rate was periodically adjusted to compensate for tariff reductions, as can be seen in column 2 of table 3.2. Consequently, at the end of phase 3 the average cost of the import dollar was about the same as at its beginning. Naturally, products that were relatively more protected at the start of phase 3 lost their privileged position as customs duties converged toward a uniform 10 percent. These changes occurred in an economy growing more sensitive to the evolution of the international economy, including a constantly rising import coefficient. The average tariff had dropped from 94 to 10 percent during these three phases (and nontariff restrictions had disappeared); while the real exchange rate at the end of the process was only 16 percent above the price at the outset of the reform. Exports also benefited from the broadening of the range of imported inputs, then either liberalized or subject to a uniform tariff. Substitutors, on the other hand, had to compete with imports that on average were 34 percent cheaper than in late 1973.

Finally, in phase 4 the real exchange rate was revalued steadily. This appreciation was a consequence of the fixed nominal rate and a domestic rate of inflation higher than the international rate during the three years in which the exchange rate remained frozen. In the end, foreign currency finished 21 percent cheaper than at the beginning of the reform, while average tariffs were eighty-four points lower. In June 1982, this phase ended with an abrupt devaluation.

In summary, import policy took shape with successive official announcements, with each one of them presented as the final one. Thus, the policy evolved from a moderate opening to trade, explicitly declared to be consistent with the process of Andean integration, to a sharp, across the board trade liberalization. As for the supposed compensatory role of the exchange rate, the facts show that in general the policy did not fulfill this function as it should have according to the assumptions of the economic model. Therefore, an outcome that differed so much from that expected by the economic team is not surprising.

---

9. In this phase, Chile left the Andean Pact. As a result, producers of importables faced less Andean competition while exporters lost their significant advantages in that market.

Import Composition

The drastic changes in the structure and level of protection had a significant impact on the composition of imports. As could be foreseen, consumer goods, which had previously been the most restricted category,
were the most favored by across the board tariff liberalization. Within
this category, imports of nonfood consumer goods were the items that
showed the greatest growth.

Many variables other than trade policies affected the behavior of
imports. Among the most significant variables were the sharp contraction in aggregate demand in 1975–76 and the recovery in 1977–81, the
low investment ratio during nearly the entire liberalization period, and
the rise in oil prices.

Between 1970 and 1981, total imports increased by 127 percent in
real terms, as shown in table 3.3.[10] If purchases of oil and lubricants are
subtracted, the increase is 104 percent. We must keep three factors in
mind. First, the increased oil price (along with a drop in domestic production) was for Chile a permanent feature that required the country to
generate additional resources to meet the greater expenses, either by
reducing other imports or by expanding exports. Second, until 1981
imports of equipment and machinery, as a share of GDP, were significantly below 1970 levels and insufficient to recover historical growth
rates. Third, GDP per capita barely increased 10 percent in 1970–81,
while imports other than equipment and machinery per capita grew by
115 percent between 1970 and 1981 (table 3.3).

This outcome was predictable given the drastic import liberalization.
In fact, increased imports were not a response to an income effect, as per
capita output was practically stagnant, but were predominantly due to the
liberalization program and exogenous changes in the supply and demand
of importables (e.g., oil prices and changes in income distribution).

Different import categories behaved heterogeneously. The influence of liberalization can be observed mainly in nonfood consumer
goods, where the greatest number of "new" nontraditional imports are
concentrated. Purchases of nonfood consumer goods increased by 534
percent between 1970 and 1981 (and by 518 percent in 1973–81).

The share of machinery and equipment in total imports dropped
from 21 to 11 percent, and their participation in GDP fell by one-tenth
between 1970 and 1981, with an even more noticeably lower share in the
intermediate years. This drop reflects the lack of productive investment
in the period (see chaps. 1 and 2).

---

10. Since 1973 presents significant distortions, in table 3.3 I shall use the figures for
1970, which was considered a relatively "normal" year.

TABLE 3.3.   Main Imports of Consumer Goods and Total Imports, 1970, 1980, 1981 (U.S.$ millions in 1977)

	1970	1980	1981	Percentage Change, 1970–81
Confectionery items	0.2	8.2	10.5	5,150
Leather and fur manufactures	1.3	9.0	17.5	1,246
Alcoholic beverages and cigarettes	1.1	22.8	27.5	2,400
Carpets, clothing, knitwear, textiles, and fabrics	24.8	171.9	271.6	995
Photographic and cinematographic products	8.0	17.4	25.2	215
Footwear, hats, and umbrellas	2.1	24.0	43.3	1,962
Musical and optical instruments	4.4	18.1	28.7	552
Toys and recreational goods	3.5	32.0	42.4	1,111
Processed foods from cocoa, meat, shellfish, vegetables, and market produce	5.3	34.6	41.3	679
Perfumery and cosmetics	0.1	13.7	19.6	9,500
Television sets	0.7	49.0	66.2	9,357
Radios	4.7	46.0	45.8	874
Cars and motorcycles	19.5	144.4	263.9	1,249
I. Total main nontraditional consumer imports	75.7	591.1	902.6	1,093
II. Wheat, maize, and sugar	43.6	309.9	262.1	757
III. Fuels and lubricants	118.0	666.9	689.5	484
IV. Other consumer and intermediate goods	1,155.5	1,561.2	1,714.3	48
V. Transport equipment	157.4	317.5	395.8	152
VI. Other capital goods	408.6	376.6	480.6	18
Total imports	1,959	3,823	4,445	127

Sources: National Customs Authority for 1970 and import registers of the Central Bank of Chile for categories II, III, V, and VI in 1980 and 1981.

All imports were directly affected by liberalization. Thus, due to a reversal of the import substitution of final products, a reduction of demand for intermediate goods took place. At the same time, reduction of national integration requirements for industrial activity caused an additional increase in the share of imported components in consumer goods in which substitution survived. This occurred in the auto industry, for instance. Consequently, the structural changes in the pattern of production means that the net expenditure in foreign currency involved in these "new" imports was less than their gross value. Likewise, the gross industrial production figures tended to overestimate the level of domestic activity due to the falling integration of domestic inputs.[11]

Conscious of the limitations of the figures, table 3.3 shows the groups of consumer items (food and nonfood) that increased most between 1970 and 1981. The thirteen groups disaggregated in this table

11. This is the main source of overestimation of GDP in the national accounts calculated with a fixed matrix. See Marcel and Meller 1986 and Scherman 1981.

cover 50 percent of all consumer goods imports in 1981. During the eleven-year period they grew by 1,093 percent (i.e., twice the increase in fuels) while all other imports expanded by 62 percent. As can be seen, most of these nontraditional imports were items that had traditionally been considered "dispensable" or "luxury" goods. In several cases, a variety of these new imported items were not locally produced, even though they did replace similar domestically produced items. There was, then, a significant diversification in the composition of consumption.

The consumption of goods whose imports grew most significantly was concentrated among high-income groups. Naturally, this phenomenon was related to the worsening of income distribution, although this effect was magnified by the fact that consumption by income bracket is more concentrated for importables than for total consumption.

Undoubtedly, the low-income sectors were able to buy new varieties of consumer products, but these purchases were bound by their limited and declining earnings. According to family budget surveys conducted in Santiago by the National Bureau of Statistics, families in the upper quintile increased their share of total consumption from 44.5 to 51.0 percent between 1969 and 1978, while families in the lowest quintile decreased their share from 7.6 to 5.2 percent (see chap. 9). The 1978 survey also reflects the concentration of the consumption of nontraditional imports that year (see table 3.4).

In eleven of the thirteen groups of importables included in table 3.4, the richer quintile consumed a higher percentage than its share in total expenditure (51 percent in 1978). The two groups in which this richer bracket purchased proportionally less than its average include "inferior goods" (negative income elasticity) for the higher income levels. For example, as income rose purchases of black-and-white television sets were replaced with purchases of color televisions, and transistor radios were passed over in favor of stereo sets and tabletop radios.

Overall Effects of Trade Liberalization on Industry

Evaluating the effects of import liberalization is a complex task. First, the effects were significantly different in each phase. Second, many other important changes took place simultaneously. On the one hand, there was a drop in aggregate demand, wages, and investment and a rise in unemployment; these factors strongly influenced the nature of the adjustment process. On the other hand, export expansion, which began before the impact of liberalization was substantial, contributed to the recovery of economic activity and offered opportunities for investment in the production of exportables.

In the first part of this section, we will examine the global changes in the industrial sector. In the second part, we will try to progress to a disaggregate analysis.

Macroeconomic Effects

We will examine the overall changes in the manufacturing sector on the basis of production, value added, and employment indices. The corresponding data appear in table 3.5.

Manufacturing production was drastically affected by the economic recession of 1975. That year, industrial output dropped by 26 percent, while GDP fell by 17 percent. As could be predicted, this meant that the subsequent recovery was more intensive in the manufacturing sector than in the others, producing high rates of "growth" from 1977 to 1979. Still, this was only a partial recovery. More than eight years after the neoliberal economic policy was first implemented, industrial value added per capita was 18.5 percent below its 1973 value, as can be seen in table 3.5.

This performance resulted in a notorious drop in the share of manufacturing in GDP from 26 percent in 1970 to 20 percent in 1981. Finally,

TABLE 3.4. Distribution by Income Brackets of Consumption of Imported Goods: Main Nontraditional Imports in 1978 (percentages of total consumption)

Item	Highest 20% of Households	Middle 60% of Households	Lowest 20% of Households
Color television sets	100.0	0.0	0.0
Automobiles	98.6	1.4	0.0
Imported whisky	94.0	6.0	0.0
Imported cigarettes	92.0	8.0	0.0
Cassettes	72.8	26.8	0.4
Tennis racquets	71.8	28.2	0.0
Electric blenders, mixers, and food processors	71.8	28.2	0.0
Motorcycles	65.3	34.7	0.0
Watches	59.7	34.7	5.6
Toys	56.1	41.4	2.5
Stereo equipment, record players, and tape recorders	51.3	48.5	0.2
Transistor radios	32.9	57.8	9.3
Black-and-white television sets	18.8	71.2	10.0
Share of each bracket in total consumption	51.0	43.8	5.2

Source: Instituto Nacional de Estadísticas, *III Encuesta de Presupuestos Familiares,* 3 (May 1979).
Note: Only includes those products that could be identified in the survey as "nontraditional" imports. Unless otherwise specified, includes consumption of domestic and imported goods.

this deterioration was also revealed in industrial employment: from 1976 on, it has remained at levels markedly lower than those of 1970. This was caused in part by the diminished importance of labor-intensive industrial activities such as textiles and garments. There was also a drop in employment in areas where output increased; but remember that the value added per unit of gross production decreased, which naturally resulted in a reduction in labor demand.

Consequently, the figures reveal the lack of realism in statements that claimed that the industrial sector had been behaving dynamically. On the contrary, overall production and employment in the manufacturing sector was deficient from 1973 through 1981. After the spectacular drop of 1975, the sector recovered strongly between 1977 and 1979, losing its velocity in 1980 and falling off in 1981. Evidently, the invasion of imported consumer goods in 1980–81 played a crucial role in this. Finally, without even having recovered its 1973 or 1974 levels, the sector suffered another spectacular drop of 21 percent in 1982.

It is revealing to compare the evolution of output in the manufacturing sector to its trend in the 1960s. A short digression to examine the period in between, 1970–73, will be useful. "Normal" production was estimated for the 1970–73 period using the historical growth rate for industrial value added during the 1960s (5.9 percent per year).[12] Output was 5 percent less in 1974 than in 1971. The negative outcome can be explained by two facts: investment was low in 1971–73 and the sector's organization was severely disrupted, with some of the deterioration being irreversible. Nevertheless, assertions by supporters of the military coup that the industry was "destroyed" in 1973 are belied by the resumption of production immediately after the September 1973 coup: there was no generalized destruction, although there definitely was a halt to growth. The loss of accumulated production in 1971–73, estimated with our explicit assumptions, would be between 11 and 14 percent of the value added for 1973. This was one of the costs of the disorder, lost discipline, and macroeconomic disequilibria predominant in these three years.

Let us return to 1974. The methodology that takes the actual level of industrial production as representative of its "normalized" level in 1974 does not overestimate, but rather underestimates, the actual productive capacity: the sharp contraction of aggregate demand had already begun in the second half of 1974 and was negatively affecting the annual

12. Since in 1970 actual output was lower than "normal," partly owing to the effects of that year's presidential election on domestic production and sales, the normal growth rate is also applied to the actual production of 1969 in order to provide a hypothetical estimate for 1970. It appears that this method does not overestimate potential output, as the actual figure for 1971 was 3 percent larger than the "normalized" figure for that year.

level of output.[13] The effect can be partially seen by observing that between October 1973 and September 1974, that is, during the first twelve-month period of the new government, industrial output was 3.4 percent higher than during the 1974 calendar year.

To estimate figures for 1974–80, we applied the 1960s growth rate to the actual value of production in 1974. Finally, in order to take the international recessionary environment into account, the growth rate of manufacturing in less developed countries (LDCs) (0.9 percent) was used for 1981–82.

From mid-1974 until 1981, the sector operated below its productive capacity and significantly below its historical trend: The gaps between actual and trend production were caused by a series of events. Output losses in 1975 were due primarily to the contraction of aggregate demand.[14] During the 1977–81 period, however, production responded principally to the changes in demand patterns induced by the across the board import liberalization with exchange rate appreciation, the concentration of income, and the drop in domestic investment as a result of a recessive and unstable macroeconomic environment and high outlier interest rates (Mizala 1992; Agosin 1998). Negative pulls for desubstitution were significantly stronger than the positive pulls for specialization and export dynamism. In 1975–81, effective production was on average about one-quarter below the "normal" level.[15] This forgone production, between 1975 and 1981, measured by the method just described, was remarkably large.[16] At its worst, 1982 saw an additional drop of 21 percent.

---

13. There was a large drop in real wages; the surveys conducted in January, April, and July by INE show that the average decrease was 16 percent compared to the same months in 1973. The decrease strongly influenced sectors that produced goods intensively demanded by middle- and low-income consumers. An outstanding example was that of the textile and clothing sectors.

14. The contraction of aggregate demand was associated in part with a significant worsening of the terms of trade beginning in the second half of 1974 (see chap. 5). The negative terms of trade shock was 6 percent of GDP in 1975 compared to 1972. It must not be forgotten that this worsening followed a strong 5 percent improvement in 1973–74. In fact, during the first year in which the new economic policy was applied, the copper price was extremely high. Nevertheless, the transitory high revenues were not saved.

15. Estimates based on the output index of the Manufacturing Association (SOFOFA), disaggregated by group (three digits of the ISIC rev. 2) show that productive capacity would be 37 percent greater than actual output in August 1978 using the "maximum historical" method with moving bimesters. It should be noted that the index of actual output for the period October 1973 to September 1974 was 10 percent higher than in 1978.

16. Adoption of a free trade policy should reduce, presumably for several years, the pace of expansion of the manufacturing sector. This reduction should be compensated for by growth in other economic activities. This did not occur, and per capita GDP growth in 1974–81 was one half that recorded in the 1960s.

Table 3.5 shows the contrast between the evolution of the manufacturing sector in Chile compared to the sets of developed and developing countries. Moreover, it shows an absolute decrease in sectoral employment (col. 5).

It is undeniable that import liberalization did not "destroy" national industry, just as it is undeniable that it was not destroyed in 1973. The liberalization did, however, contribute strongly to the overall poor performance of the industrial sector and of the entire Chilean economy between 1973 and 1981. The productive capacity of the sector was seriously damaged, and many firms were needlessly destroyed; survivors, naturally, tended to be stronger. Was the period too short to judge and a necessary investment in the future? Altogether, despite the evident need to reduce the average level and dispersion of effective import protection in 1973, the net balance appears to be overwhelmingly negative. The information presented in the next subsection provides additional support for this hypothesis.

Effects on the Structure of Manufactured Production

The structure of industrial output changed significantly during the 1970s. To identify the impact of import liberalization more precisely, we will examine the behavior of the different production branches.

The close relationship between the domestic industrial sector and foreign trade can be seen first in the global evolution of exports and

TABLE 3.5. Manufacturing Output: Chile and the World Economy, 1974–82 (1973 = 100)

| Year | Total Value-Added | | | Value Added per Capita of Chile (4) | Industrial Employment (5) |
	Industrialized Countries (1)	Developing Countries (2)	Chile (3)		
1974	100.1	106.3	99.1	97.5	97.5
1975	91.8	108.1	73.0	70.6	88.8
1976	100.1	116.7	74.9	71.4	86.1
1977	103.7	125.3	79.9	75.1	87.1
1978	107.9	133.6	85.0	78.8	88.8
1979	113.3	139.7	91.0	83.1	88.2
1980	112.3	146.8	93.3	83.9	88.8
1981	112.8	147.0	92.1	81.5	87.3
1982	108.5	149.6	72.8	63.4	71.0

Sources: For Chile, calculations based on Central Bank data; Jadresić 1986; and Marcel and Meller 1986. For developing and industrialized countries, United Nations' *Monthly Bulletin of Statistics,* May 1983.

imports of manufactured goods. Exports grew significantly from 1974 until they totaled 10 percent of the gross value of the sector's output in 1981, while imports rose to 35 percent. The respective figures for 1969–70 were 3 and 17 percent. It is well known that in the real world the behavior of exports is not univocally tied in a unique way to import policy; in fact, export promotion can be fully consistent with a policy of selective import substitution, as the East Asian countries have demonstrated beyond any doubt.[17] Because of this, the effects of import and export policies on domestic production can be analyzed separately.

Information broken down into twenty-nine groups (International Standard Industrial Classification [ISIC], rev. 2, three digits) compares the 1969–70 average to 1978, that is, a year before the freezing of the exchange rate in 1979. The composition of consumption, output, and trade changed substantially during the decade (see Vergara 1980). First, trade was dynamic in the sense that exports increased in sixteen groups while imports rose in eighteen; both imports and exports grew in ten of these groups, implying that, at three-digit information, there was intra-industrial specialization. There were drops in output and consumption in seventeen groups each, while in fourteen of these branches both output and consumption decreased. This suggests that domestic demand decisively influenced output in this period.

At the level of disaggregation at which we are working, many of the groups include goods whose production processes and marketing channels are quite diverse. Notwithstanding this heterogeneity, the data allow us to advance some conclusions (Foxley 1983, chap. 3; Vergara 1980).

First, only two groups show output growth that is associated with exports (wood and paper); in two other groups, exports play a significant role (food and industrial chemicals), even though their role is not as dominant as in the preceding groups.[18] When the data are broken down still further, it can be shown that a large share of export expansion was concentrated in only five groups: pulp and paper, wood, molybdenum oxide, fish meal, and semimanufactured copper. After a sizable diversification in the period 1974–76, the share of these products fell in 1976 to 58 percent of industrial exports, but in 1978 it rose to 64 percent and in 1981 to 66 percent.

For imports, diversification was greater, as was shown earlier. This diversification is also reflected in the large number of groups for which imports became significant. Three groups were strongly affected by

---

17. An account of different country experiences appears in Bhagwati 1978, chap. 8; see also Sachs 1987.

18. The main exported food products are fish meal, fish oil, and frozen seafood. The most important exported chemical substance is molybdenum oxide.

imports: electrical machinery, transport equipment, and professional equipment. In the first two groups, the rise in domestic demand ameliorated the negative impact of imports on output, while in the third group a receding domestic demand exacerbated the negative impact. In six groups, opening to trade together with a significant reduction in domestic demand led to a decline in output (textiles, clothing, leather, oil derivatives, pottery and china, and nonelectrical machinery). In four other groups (footwear, printing and publishing, nonmetallic minerals, and iron and steel), the determinant variable in declining output prior to 1978 seems to have been the decrease in domestic demand. One group (other chemical products) showed remarkable increases in consumption and production with low levels of trade. Finally, miscellaneous "various industries," predictably, showed significant growth in production, consumption, imports and exports. Data on the other groups are more difficult to interpret, as the results depend largely on which years are compared and the methodology used to estimate the change of each variable.

As shown, the behavior of domestic demand had a determinant effect on the level of output. To a certain degree, this effect makes it difficult to evaluate the impact of import liberalization, while depressed domestic demand contributed to increased exports of items in excess supply in the local market. Naturally, to the extent that domestic demand recovered subsequently, the relative weight of different variables changed; thus, after 1978 the effects of import liberalization gained importance vis-à-vis aggregate demand as an explanatory factor of the poor performance of manufacturing. It was clear that by 1978 the effects of import liberalization had not yet been fully felt. At that stage, the trends shown by the data indicated that export growth was losing speed, while imports, particularly of consumer goods, were rising fast. This trend was at work in 1978 and 1979, before the nominal exchange rate was fixed. Subsequently, the sharp real appreciation of the peso that followed reinforced the lagged effects of import liberalization. Consequently, the trade reform had detrimental effects on manufactured output, which went beyond the implementation period. The negative impact of nontraditional imports increased compared to changes in domestic demand and the positive effects of exports. Aggregate demand became more intensive in imported components, the quantum of non-resource-based exports ceased growing in 1980, and imports (especially of consumer durables, as shown in table 3.3) rose in 1980–81 notably faster than in the previous two years.

The sector adjusted to foreign competition in three ways. Some went into bankruptcy or closed down plants. In other cases, firms began to specialize within the industry in two ways: merging with other firms and suspending lines of production within a firm. Finally, some firms also began to import goods that they marketed in place of those they had previously produced.

Marketing imported products enabled firms affected by import liberalization to capitalize on the relative advantage they had because of their sales outlets and knowledge of demand. This adjustment mechanism had several interesting effects. First, in this case production and importing were not independent functions but were managed by the same decision unit; thus, for a while foreign competition would be operating in a more limited fashion than is assumed by orthodox theory. Second, a larger percentage of businesses leaned toward commercial and financial activities rather than producing goods. The extent of this bias is shown by changes in the composition of GDP recorded in the national accounts (see table 2.1). The resulting growing current account deficit, which was created by the asymmetrical response of producers in sectors hurt by new trade policies and in sectors favored by them, was financed by an increase in foreign debt. Third, although some producers defended themselves by switching to marketing imports, this change negatively influenced employment; in fact, as is obvious, productive employment decreased per unit of sales and even per unit of output.[19]

Elements for an Evaluation

In these concluding remarks, we will look first, briefly, at the global effects of trade policy on the balance of payments. Next some points will be raised about the effects that those policies could have on the efficiency, dynamism, and competitiveness of the Chilean economy. The macroeconomic implications are covered in detail in chapters 5 and 6.

Balance of Payments and the Current Account

Practically all components of foreign trade expanded during the period under study, especially the categories of nontraditional imports and exports. The export quantum registered a most dynamic behavior. After an abrupt jump and diversification in 1974–76, exports continued to

---

19. This is a *microeconomic* increase in productivity. However, it has negative social and economic consequences (1) when it implies a greater reduction in employment than in production, instead of a greater increase in production than in employment; and (2) when it takes place within a framework of widespread unemployment and worsened income distribution, as was the case.

increase until 1980. The key factors for this development were an initially depreciated exchange rate, better availability of imported inputs, a recessive domestic economy, and the development of an "export mentality." Undoubtedly, exports became the dynamic productive sector of the Chilean economy. They even provided some dynamism to the highly depressed agricultural sector. But the net effect was limited since, after the "disciplinary adjustment" of the agricultural sector in 1974, growth reached merely 2 percent between 1974 and 1981. The dynamic agricultural exports, consisting mainly of fruit and forestry products, shared the sector with traditional agriculture, which decreased spectacularly (especially in grains, sugar beets, and oil seeds).

The expansion of manufactured and total imports was much larger than that of exports, causing a growing trade deficit that increased markedly between 1976 and 1981 (see table 3.6). Because of "abnormal" levels of significant trade components, the content of trade flows must be examined more closely. Two components that deviate most from "normal" values were imports of equipment and machinery, whose share of total imports lost ten percentage points, and the copper price,[20] which recorded a level one-fifth lower than the normal price.[21] Nevertheless, foreign exchange proceeds from copper exports increased as a result of two factors. On the one hand, investments made between 1967 and 1970 made it possible for copper production to increase by 50 percent immediately after "discipline" was imposed. On the other hand, the 1971 nationalization of the large mines allowed the government to capture a greater share of the economic rent derived from the rich Chilean copper deposits. These two positive effects were "permanent," while the low price was assumed to be "transitory."

The current account deficit in 1981, which was 1.2 times all exports, was covered with extraordinarily large capital inflows. These inflows, which were primarily caught by the private sector, not only financed the current account deficit but allowed the accumulation of international reserves (table 3.6). In the meantime, external debt grew significantly, leading to the debt crisis that exploded in 1982 (see chaps. 5 and 6).

In the face of the evolution of the sector, the authorities held on to two valid assertions, though with a faulty interpretation of their significance. It was stated that if the exchange rate were to be liberalized by the Central Bank the rate would strongly appreciate. This evidently would

20. A third component that shows a notable change is the price of molybdenum, a copper byproduct whose real price increased sixfold during the 1970s. The higher value of this export was equivalent to 46 percent of the increased expenditure on oil imports in the same period.

21. See a methodological discussion of the "normal" copper price in Ffrench-Davis 1973, chap. 4; and Ffrench-Davis and Tironi 1974.

TABLE 3.6.   Balance of Payments, 1973–82 (U.S.$ millions 1977)

	1973	1974	1975	1976	1977	1978	1979	1980	1981	1982
I. Current account	−442	−256	−535	160	−551	−960	−925	−1,361	−3,213	−1,600
1. Trade balance	32	434	76	693	34	−376	−276	−527	−1,817	43
Exports (f.o.b)	1,968	2,612	1,734	2,282	2,185	2,171	2,984	3,250	2,605	2,573
Copper	1,577	1,971	947	1,330	1,161	1,076	1,469	1,467	1,180	1,170
Non-copper	391	641	787	952	1,024	1,096	1,515	1,782	1,425	1,403
Imports (f.o.b)	1,936	2,179	1,657	1,588	2,151	2,547	3,260	3,777	4,422	2,529
2. Nonfinancial services	−328	−478	−313	−212	−295	−214	−186	−269	−476	−385
3. Financial services	−165	−225	−310	−352	−365	−432	525	−642	−994	−1,334
4. Unrequited transfers	20	13	11	30	75	62	62	78	74	76
II. Net capital inflows[a]	507	94	305	143	669	1,589	1,740	2,220	3,259	791
III. Balance of payments	65	−163	−230	303	118	628	815	859	45	−809

Source: Calculations based on data from Central Bank of Chile, *Balanza de Pagos*.
Note: The figures were deflated by an index of external prices (see Ffrench-Davis 1984).
[a]Includes errors and omissions.

have happened, confirming that foreign exchange flexibility under a capital surge tends to exacerbate imbalances (see chap. 10 and Harberger 1985). A lesser evil had been the fixing of the exchange rate at $39, but the most efficient policy would have been to moderate capital inflows and give way to a real devaluation in order to enhance a positive restructuring of production. The other weak point was the assumption that the excess of imports would slow down spontaneously. Slowing did tend to occur but with a lag. On the other hand, as the exchange rate continued to appreciate until 1982 it stimulated a fast-rising expenditure on imports, which crowded out domestic output and savings. These effects left indelible footprints on the Chilean economy over a prolonged time span. As underlined in other chapters, the deficit on the current account of 21 percent of GDP in 1981 revealed an impressive and absolutely nonsustainable disequilibria.

Efficiency, Dynamism and Competition

The theoretical foundation of reforms asserted that the market, free of government interference, would allocate resources according to a sort of unmistakably identifiable "comparative advantage." Actually, market comparative advantages depend on the level and stability of the exchange rate, the degree of activity in domestic and world markets, international price fluctuations, and many other factors (such as the availability of long-term funding, infrastructure, and trained labor). Market and social comparative advantages tend to diverge because of the disequilibria and distortions characteristic of developing economies.[22] The differences between the two can be striking in a country facing a radical change in economic policy, with high unemployment, and with a public sector that abruptly abandons its guiding role in stimulating productive activity and maintaining the consistency of reforms. The resulting disequilibria and distortions can be significantly more costly than the inefficiencies of an active public sector, as the recent Chilean experience suggests.

The Macroeconomic Framework and Efficiency
The efficiency of any economic policy depends on the context in which it is applied. The generally recessive domestic economic situation of this period was relatively conducive to export promotion, but on the other hand it constituted one factor that increased the transition costs of import liberalization.

---

22. See Ffrench-Davis 2000, chaps. 1 and 2, on the implications of *incomplete* markets and multiple equilibria for investment allocation.

The expansion and diversification of exports provided an outlet for excess production that otherwise would not have had a market. In fact, the sharp contraction of domestic demand (in particular, during the period from mid-1974 to 1976) left a significant share of industry with underutilized installed capacity. The depreciated exchange rate, access to the Andean market, and the efforts of PROCHILE (the government export promotion agency) supplied a market abroad for many firms with excess capacity. Later, productive capacities were expanded, and nontraditional and traditional natural resources were exploited, enhanced by investment during the 1960s in the forestry, fruit, and fishing industries, the still depreciated exchange rate, and the accelerated liberalization of imported inputs. Dynamism was reversed in the early 1980s, when growing exchange rate appreciation induced a generalized drop of exports. In general, the expansion of nontraditional exports promoted efficiency in the allocation of resources, principally through an increase in the rate of utilization of capital and labor and the use of natural comparative advantages.

For imports, the situation was the opposite. In fact, if a trade liberalization process goes too far, is too rapid, or is undertaken at the wrong juncture, it will provoke premature and unnecessary plant shutdowns, the underutilization of capital and labor, and a decrease in investment. Therefore, to evaluate the effects on the Chilean economy we must distinguish between the different stages of the liberalization process and take into account the macroeconomic context in which it was implemented.

In phase 1, clearly redundant levels of protection were eliminated. But the first tariff reductions served to limit national producers' capacity to set monopolistic prices. In phases 2 and 3, the additional tariff reductions, which lowered the maximum nominal protection from 120 to 10 percent, had a much greater effect. The most painful part of import liberalization was carried out rapidly, and its negative effects were reinforced by exchange rate revaluations. This policy was implemented during a time in which (1) wages were deteriorating, (2) domestic demand was very depressed, (3) investment was low, and (4) open unemployment was remarkably high. These four factors must be closely examined to evaluate the effects of lifting tariffs.

First, wage repression acted as an artificial protection mechanism that, although it was obviously regressive, compensated for reduced tariffs on imports. In fact, in 1976 the ratio of wages to the exchange rate was less than half that of 1970, and in 1979 it had recovered to only 64 percent (see table 4.3).

Second, given the depth of the recession, recovery rates for demand and production were bound to be high. Since tariff liberalization took place during recovery, a superficial examination of the data has led many to the wrong conclusion that the liberalization process encouraged the increase in output. As was demonstrated earlier, however, exactly the opposite occurred. The implementation of free trade contributed to maintaining the recovery of domestic production at a level lower than that of the recovery of aggregate demand; output and aggregate demand became increasingly import intensive. The recession itself negatively affected the efficiency of the process. The underutilization of productive capacity and the extremely high interest rates (averaging 38 percent between 1975 and 1982; see chap. 5) tended to raise the average cost of production to domestic producers, making it more difficult for them to face foreign competition.

Third, the widespread underutilization of installed capacity discouraged domestic investment (see Servén and Solimano 1993 and Ffrench-Davis and Reisen 1998). The low level of investment was also associated with the high real interest rates, which distorted relative prices and the "comparative advantages" observed in the market. This depressed investment ratio was clearly insufficient to facilitate a symmetrical or positive adjustment between the sectors that contracted and those that expanded in response to the curtailment of effective protection of importables. A high unemployment rate and abnormally low investment implied a low probability of achieving an effective reallocation of resources. These factors also suggest that the opportunity cost of resources freed by the sectors negatively affected by reform was lower than their market price.

Consequently, a drastic dismantling of tariff protection, instead of a gradual and more comprehensive reform, including all ingredients for productive development (see Ffrench-Davis 2000, chaps. 1 and 2), should not have been undertaken in a macroeconomic environment such as the one predominant in the Chilean economy. Some proponents of this policy argued that if the policy had not been implemented so rapidly it would have been impossible to carry it out at all. The answer to this argument is threefold. First, it would have been better not to undertake tariff reductions as drastic as those performed since 1975 (covering phases 2 and 3) rather than attempting to impose them in the midst of a depression. It is evident that "corner" solutions were not the optimal choice. Second, foreign exchange appreciation should not have been allowed during tariff liberalization. This misstep also flagrantly contradicted the government's repeated assertions. Third, unemployment, low investment, and depressed demand generated a real environment that differed substantially from the theoretical framework on which the arguments in favor of free trade were based. As a consequence, the corresponding desubstitution of imports, predictably, was higher than naturally necessary and therefore was inefficient in many cases.

Neither excessive protection nor extreme liberalization was the appropriate solution. It should be kept in mind that it was also claimed that with free trade and a privatized economy Chile would be better equipped to face an external crisis. Nonetheless, in 1982 Chile suffered the worst crisis in all of Latin America. Economic dogmatism had left the Chilean economy more and not less vulnerable.

Dynamism and Efficiency
The conclusions of the preceding paragraph are reinforced when dynamic aspects are incorporated into the analysis. The discussion will be confined to three interrelated points concerning the degree of symmetry of the adjustments, the investment rate, and the "dynamic comparative advantages." The speed of adjustment in the sectors that were hurt and those that were favored by the change in trade policy was asymmetrical. Presumably, the message to reallocate resources was clearer for sectors that were hurt by liberalization. This phenomenon was reinforced by the widespread depression of aggregate demand and by high real interest rates, which made it difficult for affected firms to continue to stay in business, whether or not they were efficient under "normal" or socially optimum conditions. All of these factors made it hard for potential investors to identify those productive areas with a comparative advantage.

A remarkably low level of gross domestic investment contributed to the asymmetrical character of the adjustment. It is obvious that reallocation is easier in an economy with a high rate of capacity utilization and sustainable growth. The stagnation exhibited by the national economy during the period made it necessary for many of the hurt sectors to reduce absolute output in order for the relative adjustment to take place. Limited sectoral and regional mobility of resources and the reduced rate of investment were obstacles to the effective reallocation of freed resources: it was predominantly the expansion achieved in the export sector that compensated, partially, for the resulting lack of dynamism in the economy. As I have stated elsewhere (Ffrench-Davis 1979b), a growing proportion of the scarce domestic investment was channeled to the export sector. This investment was mainly concentrated in activities intensive in natural resources. It was less significant in products intensive in value added to a natural resource base and in "acquirable" comparative advantage. In fact, available background information supports the hypothesis that it was easier to identify comparative advantages that possessed a defined base of natural resources or were already acquired. The many changes taking place in the Chilean economy, depressed domestic demand, unstable and outlier interest and exchange rates, and strategic incomplete markets made it difficult to identify the whereabouts of potential and acquirable comparative advantages. The diffuseness of comparative advantages was presumably one factor explaining the low rate of investment.

Competition and Efficiency

One result the government's economists expected from import liberalization was increased "competitiveness" in the domestic market. This would be achieved by means of the effective or virtual presence of foreign importables, which would put an upper limit on the domestic price. It is undeniable that this did happen to a significant degree. What also happened, however, was that there were important deviations from the types of relationships that were supposed to characterize a "competitive" economy.

First, a significant proportion of nontraditional imports belonged to categories in which product differentiation played a decisive role. Consequently, competition among suppliers of these products was based on product differentiation to a larger degree than on pricing. The segmentation of the capital market (one example is the persistent gap between domestic and foreign interest rates) also introduced an element of competition based on the terms of suppliers' credit. These factors provoked effects quite distinct from those that "competition" should have generated according to orthodox theory. Second, marketing channels were not completely open to every competitor; for instance, in a number of cases the producer of import substitutes became an importer of "competitive" goods. Third, the abrupt-cum-appreciation opening to trade promoted greater concentration in the ownership of domestic productive activities. This phenomenon was reinforced by the depression in aggregate demand and by the manner in which the capital market operated. These factors gave a significant advantage to economic groups that were linked to financial activities and had access to foreign credit.

Finally, two types of problems arose in cases in which the domestic price was in line with the external price. One problem was that foreign suppliers dumped into Chile leftovers from the previous season abroad; this happened, for instance, with powdered milk and textiles. The other problem was linked to the sizable fluctuations in international prices, as occurred, for example, in the cases of wheat and sugar. The elimination of redundant protection and the absence of antidumping mechanisms and other stabilizing nontariff barriers expedited the transmission of instability from international markets to the domestic economy. The sensitivity of domestic output to occasional dumping and the fluctuations of international prices induced a reallocation of resources that tended to be inefficient for the national economy. Subsequently, in 1984 there was a substantial policy reversal that reintroduced price bands for agriculture and an antidumping mechanism (see chap. 6).

A crucial argument for free trade policy refers to the benefits that competition allegedly brings to consumers, with the availability of a wider variety of goods, lower prices, and greater efficiency. Within the framework of orthodox consumer theory, the opening to foreign trade is seen as positive because it allows demanders to equalize their marginal utility with the marginal cost of importing (which is assumed to be the same as the international price for a "small country"). The diversification of consumption is seen as welfare increasing, as it would increase the freedom of choice of the consumer.

Ceteris paribus this is perfectly true. However, it is appropriate to add two comments, one concerning the indirect effects on consumers in their role as producers and the other concerning the impact on overall efficiency and the level of economic activity.

First, the "desubstitution" of imports served, during the adjustment process, to directly generate unemployment and delay the recovery of aggregate economic activity. This latter factor indirectly discouraged investment, which in turn had a negative impact on the creation of new job opportunities. Therefore, low-income consumers (who suffered the highest levels of unemployment), in their roles as producers (workers), bore much higher costs than the contingent benefits derived from the diversification of the basket now available in the market to those with purchasing power.

Second, the diversification of consumption enabled a small, high-income sector to rapidly assume the consumption patterns of the well off in the richest economies. The notorious increase in inequality that took place during these years manifested itself more in a noticeable differentiation of lifestyles than in higher savings rates and productive investment. The collapse in national savings supports this hypothesis (it dropped to 8.2 percent of GDP in 1981 and to 2.1 percent in 1982, in current prices of each year). Finally, from the point of view of economic activity, freeing imports in a rather sudden move contributed, as said, to a fragmentation of demand for those types of goods for which product differentiation is significant. Naturally, abrupt liberalization made it difficult for domestic producers to take advantage of economies of scale and contributed to the rise of average production costs.

The Chilean experience definitely taught heterodox lessons. The national economy in 1973 had excessive margins of protection for numerous import categories; therefore, a significant trade liberalization was required. However, trade liberalization was excessive and ill-timed; it was not coordinated with exchange rate policy and disregarded the need to *complete* factor markets. A gradual procedure should have been adopted and a deliberate search for a dynamic complementation between import substitution and export promotion should have been undertaken in the

East Asian style (see Sachs 1987; and Ffrench-Davis 2000, chap. 3). Positive export expansion would have been essentially consistent with a more pragmatic tariff policy than the one adopted. It could have involved a greater conversion of import substitutes into exportables and a more diversified export basket that would have been more intensive in value added.

What was lacking, as in other fields of economic policy, was the adaptation of theoretical concepts to the specific nature of the Chilean economy. On the other hand, it appears that the overall economy and the industrial sector had some capacity to adjust to changes in relative prices, even under the unfavorable conditions that the domestic market suffered. At the same time, it is clear that part of the capacity to respond, particularly in the export sector, was based on the industrial development previously achieved through import substitution and the development of "nontraditional" natural resources (including forestry, fresh fruit, and fisheries). Finally, the conventional hypothesis that an unrestricted opening to trade would promote the expansion of labor-intensive tradables and result in a contraction of capital-intensive activities was at least partially contradicted by the characteristics of changes that occurred in the productive structure. This performance was directly linked to the framework in which trade was liberalized, to the excessive intensity and lack of selectivity of the reform, to the passive role that was imposed on the public sector, and to the absence of a comprehensive national development strategy.

CHAPTER 4

Exchange Rate Policies: The Experience with the Crawling Peg

Chile was a pioneer in implementing exchange rate (ER) policies that belong to the family of crawling peg approaches. This happened between April 1965 and July 1970, making Chile the first country to implement a policy of this nature systematically.[1] Subsequently, from October 1973 to June 1979 a second experiment in this kind of exchange rate system was carried out. Finally, in the 1980s, after the 1982 crisis, a crawling peg was reinstated that evolved into a crawling band and survived until September 1999. Here we concentrate on the first two experiences; the latter is covered in chaps. 6 and 10.

The two policies involved frequent upward adjustments of the exchange rate, lasted more than five years, and were established during periods of acute balance of payments difficulties and sizable inflation rates. However, they differ with respect to the political environment in which they were implemented and with respect to the role assigned to the exchange rate, the stability of the policy, the size of the individual nominal adjustments, and the criteria used to determine modifications of the real rate.

We begin with a brief discussion of some specific aspects that are relevant for an evaluation of exchange rate policies in the two particular experiences covered by this chapter. Next a description of the main features of the specific policies applied is given, along with an examination of the similarities and differences among and within each period. Finally, a short discussion of the more important conclusions and pending questions is attempted.

This chapter is based on "Exchange rate policies in Chile: The experience with the crawling peg," in *The Crawling Peg: Past Performance and Future Prospects,* J. Williamson, ed. (London: Macmillan, 1981). Reprinted with permission.

1. After Chile, Colombia and Brazil implemented a crawling peg system in 1967 and 1968, respectively. These and other country experiences are analyzed in Williamson 1981.

Some Introductory Aspects

We have emphasized that it is hard to evaluate any public policy experience objectively. Policies have effects in very diverse domains and indirect and long-run consequences that usually are difficult to trace.

Both the domestic and external environments have an important influence on the selection, effects, and interpretation of the results of exchange rate policy. In table 4.1, macrodata related to the Chilean economy are provided.

The initial domestic economic situation of both experiences was characterized by balance of payments difficulties, low reserves, substantial debt service, widespread nontariff restrictions, and high and variable inflation. All of these disequilibria were much larger at the outset of the second experience than in the first one. The public sector was an important operator in the foreign sector, a role that was enhanced after the nationalization of the main copper-mining enterprises in 1971, with copper generating over 60 percent of export proceeds.

Finally, the domestic capital market witnessed a deep transformation during those years. In the first period, it was more regulated and there was some noninterest credit rationing, although the banks' real lending interest rate was positive, close to a policy target of 6 to 10 percent per year (see table 4.3, col. 4). In the second period, the domestic capital market was largely liberalized, the controls on interest rates having been completely removed; the real interest rate fluctuated widely, averaging 38 percent per year in 1975–82. A large segment of the domestic financial market operated on a thirty-day basis (see chap. 5).

The external framework exhibited a highly unstable copper price, with an average high price during the first episode. With respect to the second one, the raw materials price boom of 1973–74 was very favorable to Chile because of the importance of copper in exports. However, in 1975–78 the terms of trade worsened when copper prices became depressed—about one-fourth below "normal" levels—until mid-1979, when they moved closer to their trend line. Furthermore, Chile is a net importer of oil, which increased from 6 percent of imports in 1973 to 13 percent in 1980. Finally, Chile made use of the increased availability of funds in international capital markets. In both experiences, it received a capital flow larger than that needed to finance the deficit on the current account (table 4.1, lines 8 and 9), leading to an accumulation of reserves (and to an expansion of base money) larger than that presumably desired by the authorities.[2]

---

2. The lack of a deeper financial market did not allow massive monetary sterilization.

TABLE 4.1. Macroeconomic Indicators, 1964–82

	1964	1965	1969	1970	1972	1973	1974	1978	1980	1982
1. GDP index (1970 = 100)										
a) Total	78.9	83.0	96.5	100.0	107.9	103.6	109.2	109.4	124.7	112.6
b) Per capita	89.4	91.9	98.3	100.0	104.0	98.2	101.9	96.1	106.3	93.0
2. Industrial value-added index (1970 = 100)										
a) Total	78.8	83.8	98.7	100.0	116.9	109.3	108.3	92.9	101.9	79.5
b) Per capita	89.2	92.8	100.6	100.0	112.7	103.6	101.0	81.6	86.9	65.7
3. Investment rate (% of GDP)	21.4	19.9	19.6	20.4	14.8	14.7	16.5	14.7	17.6	15.0
4. Unemployment rate										
a) Open	7.0	6.4	6.0	5.9	4.0	4.8	9.1	13.8	11.7	19.6
b) With PEM	7.0	6.4	6.0	5.9	4.0	4.8	9.1	18.0	16.9	26.1
5. Inflation rate (Dec.–Dec.)	40.4	27.3	33.1	36.1	260.0	606.1	369.2	37.2	31.2	20.7
6. Real copper price (1977 U.S. cents)	73.1	85.0	139.1	120.1	85.2	120.1	113.3	54.6	68.5	46.6
7. Fiscal surplus (% of GDP)	−4.0	−4.3	−0.8	−3.5	−14.1	−10.5	−6.6	2.2	5.5	−2.3
8. Current account balance (1977 U.S.$ millions)	−312.8	−131.1	−185.4	−166.7	−689.2	−442.0	−256.2	−960.4	−1,361.0	−1,599.7
9. Balance of payments[a] (1977 U.S.$ millions)	−55.6	−108.2	269.8	233.3	−411.5	64.6	−162.7	628.5	859.2	−808.7

Sources: Lines 1 and 2 based on Marcel and Meller 1986. Line 3 based on Central Bank of Chile data. Line 4 based on Jadresić 1986. Line 5 shows the CPI rate of annual change. The 1964–69 period is from Ffrench-Davis 1973. The 1970–78 period is from Cortázar and Marshall 1980 and official INE figures. Lines 6, 8, and 9 are from Ffrench-Davis and Tironi 1974 and Central Bank of Chile data, deflated by the external price index from Ffrench-Davis 1984. Line 7 is from Larrain 1991.

[a]Up to 1972, international reserves include private sector reserves; from then on, they correspond only to Central Bank reserves.

The definition of the *crawling peg* adopted here is that used by Williamson (1981). It is a policy with a nominal rate fixed by the government with or without a formal band; the peg is adjusted in small steps in order to follow some sort of "equilibrium" path. *Small* can be defined in relation to the influence on relative prices and opportunities for speculative gains. The latter can be based on objective criteria, corresponding to the costs involved in exchanging domestic for foreign currencies (and of investing and divesting in alternative income-earning assets). It is obvious that the larger the net rate of domestic inflation the more frequent each ER adjustment must be in order for them to remain "small," that is, of a size estimated to avoid speculative activity and capital gains at the expense of the Central Bank.

Both the policy package within which the exchange rate is placed and the associated specific objectives attached by policymakers are of crucial importance. In both experiences, the explicit desire was to have a "realistic" policy that sought to impose an "equilibrium" rate and bring greater stability to price relations. However, the interpretation of *equilibrium* was not uniform. In the first experience, it was related to some (not completely specified) level of the balance on the current account, which was estimated with a trend or normal price of the main export and with a certain level of indebtedness, lower than in the previous regime. In the second period, the authorities appeared to be trying to return the ER to the purchasing power parity of 1970, but subsequently they were strongly influenced by the change in gross reserves, and the ER became more of a monetary policy tool than a stable resource allocator. Finally, the ER was used as the main instrument regulating inflationary expectations and as anchor for tradable prices, rather than as the tool equilibrating the balance of payments or seeking a given current account target. The changing role of the ER — the changes in policy priorities and (subjective or objective) restrictions on the availability of policy tools — meant large variations in the real exchange rate (RER).[3]

Once the indexes suitable for measuring the RER are available, there remains the more difficult challenge of determining the optimal trend and the optimal degree of stability of the RER.

---

3. By RER, I mean the nominal exchange rate divided by an index of domestic prices and multiplied by one of the external prices (see table 4.3). With respect to external inflation, it is common to use the wholesale price index of the United States. But, since the geography of Chilean trade was diversifying and price relations and exchange rates among the country's main trading partners had changed notoriously, it was much more relevant to utilize a weighted index that reflects these phenomena (see Ffrench-Davis 1973, app. 1; and Ffrench-Davis 1984).

The Evolution of Exchange Rate Policies

Exchange rate policies applied in Chile after the 1929 world crisis and until the mid-1960s share much with the policies enforced throughout South America during that period. For long periods, Chile had a fixed nominal ER; since the domestic economy was characterized by a rate of inflation persistently higher than that prevailing abroad, real rates declined through time and generated recurrent balance of payments crises. The response of authorities was to make use of various restrictive practices without ER adjustments, although sooner or later the use of ER policies would become inevitable. Sometimes such measures involved the devaluation of a unified rate. On other occasions, multiple rates were created, with higher rates for "nonpriority" groups of commodities and continuous changes in the coverage of each group. At some points in time, apart from widely diverse tariff rates and quantitative restrictions, several hundreds of multiple rates coexisted, with ranges as large as one to fifteen between the lower and the higher rates.[4] From time to time, flexible or free rates were established, covering all of the market or some segments of it, which actually either fluctuated freely (and vigorously) or were subject to intervention by the Central Bank. In a few cases, the government performed a series of small devaluations, though for short periods and without a clearly defined policy.

The predominant policy feature was the intent to maintain a nominal peg, but in fact it became an adjustable peg in response to balance of payments crises, with large jumps in the nominal rate and instability in the real rate.

A "Programmed" Exchange Rate Policy: 1965–70

In late 1961, Chile suffered a sizable balance of payments crisis after three years of a pegged nominal rate and an extensive liberalization of trade and capital flows. The fixed rate had been given a crucial role as an anti-inflationary expectations builder, and in fact it worked as such during the period when it remained pegged, between 1959 and 1962. However, when it was drastically modified, after being frozen for four years, expectations changed its sign and ER depreciated strongly (72 percent between October 1962 and January 1963). The devaluation was forced by three factors: exports had increased much less than expected and imports much more than expected; and capital inflows—which had

---

4. The policies applied in 1952–70 are analyzed in Ffrench-Davis 1973, chap. 4.

closed both the current account and the fiscal gaps — had experienced a decline beginning in 1961. The ER had been helping to repress domestic price increases, and devaluation opened the way to a large upsurge of inflation (from 9 percent in 1961 to more than 40 percent per year in 1963 and 1964).

Two other features of the initial situation influenced policy choices in 1965. On one hand, large speculative capital movements had taken place, together with huge capital gains for economic agents who had "anticipated" the 1962 crisis. On the other hand, in 1961 a dual ER market had been created, with a "broker's" market for foreign exchange related to tourism, several services, and capital movements; both access to the market and the price in the broker's market were free. The rate suffered large ups and downs until it came under the control of the Central Bank, remaining pegged up to the end of 1964. My conclusion was that both the nominal peg and free rates — the two corner solutions that were then the options in fashion in the literature — had a negative impact on both macroeconomic stability and resource allocation (Ffrench-Davis 1964).

In November 1964, a new six-year presidential term began. The economic authorities had designed a gradual program to reduce the 50 percent annual rate of inflation recorded by October, which it was assumed would persist at decreasing but still significant rates for several years. Furthermore, the new government wanted to pursue in a more rational fashion the substitution of imports, to expand and diversify exports, and to avoid speculative movements and balance of payments shocks to the domestic economy, including those on inflationary expectations, which had been so recurrent in the previous decade (Ffrench-Davis 1964; Ffrench-Davis 1973, 98; Molina 1972, 110). Nonetheless, there was no consensus with respect to which trade policies ought to be implemented to achieve those objectives. It took several months of internal discussion before the authorities agreed on the new exchange rate policy, which was implemented in April 1965.

A crawling peg was adopted. The official rate was to be announced periodically by the Central Bank, with "small" upward adjustments. The purpose was to have a reasonably stable real exchange rate without large jumps in order to provide better allocative signals and avoid speculative capital gains and shocks to the domestic economy.[5] The trend of the RER was to depend on "the medium and long-run prospects of the Chilean foreign sector."

5. It was thought that the ER influenced prices in proportion to its direct incidence on the costs of production and that larger inflationary effects were tied only to abrupt large devaluations through their impact on expectations. It should be noted that exportables had a low share of domestic expenditure and thus a small incidence on overall domestic prices.

The new policy design retained three exchange rates: a main rate for the bulk of trade (called the forward bank rate); one for the large copper-mining enterprises, which were then foreign owned (the spot bank rate); and one for tourism, financial capital flows, and various services (the broker's rate).

The so-called forward bank rate worked in such a way that in each foreign exchange operation the flow of domestic funds (payments by importers and payments to exporters) took place about two months before the flow of the foreign currency at the ER prevailing during the occurrence of the former; this, apart from eliminating the exchange risk during that period, implied that an interest-free loan was granted by importers to exporters. The value of the "forward" component amounted to roughly 2 percent plus the "credit availability" effect in somewhat restricted and segmented financial markets such as those prevailing in Chile (Ffrench-Davis 1973, chap. 5).

The spot bank rate had traditionally been lower than the forward rate in order to tax indirectly the economic rent accruing to foreign copper producers. The spot rate was increased gradually, thus reducing the gap between the two rates. This step was part of an agreement, between the Chilean government and the foreign firms Anaconda and Kennecott, to increase investment in the production of copper, with taxation based on net income (rather than the exchange rate), but it was also intended to foster a rise in the ratio of domestic to imported inputs in copper output.[6]

The broker's rate was kept permanently above the forward bank rate in an effort to make the total implicit price for the average demander of foreign currency roughly the same whether it was used to import goods or undertake tourism abroad. The target gap between the two rates was 20 percent, a figure intended to reflect the estimated average net tax on imports.[7]

The nominal rates were devalued once or twice a month; the average rise was 1.5 percent, covering a range from 2.9 to 0.4 percent (see table 4.2). The real forward bank rate was increased by 35 percent during the sixty-three months that the policy lasted (table 4.3, col. 1).

The main variable guiding the nominal ER adjustments was the

---

6. The response of the domestic/foreign inputs ratio to relative prices and direct regulations is examined in Ffrench-Davis and Tironi 1974, 227–32. It is found to be a significant effect of the exchange rate and other public policies on the level of integration of the copper industry with the domestic economy.

7. This estimate, based on actual customs tax proceeds, as is well known, tends to underestimate the average nominal protection of import substitutes. The gap was increased in moments of foreign currency shortage in order to deter tourism abroad and foster capital inflows.

TABLE 4.2. Nominal Adjustments of the Exchange Rate, 1965–76

Date	Number of Adjustments (1)	Average Number of Days between Adjustments (2)	Rates of Adjustment (%)		
			Maximum (3)	Average (4)	Minimum (5)
1965 (May–Dec.)	8	30.0	2.9	1.52	0.4
1966	12	30.4	2.3	1.75	1.2
1967	16	22.8	2.4	1.78	0.7
1968	24	15.3	1.9	1.17	0.8
1969	19	19.2	1.7	1.40	0.8
1970 (Jan.–July)	12	17.6	1.9	1.71	1.4
1973 (Oct.–Dec.)	3	30.7	19.3	9.00	1.8
1974	24	15.2	15.9	7.16	3.3
1975	26	14.0	18.2	6.06	1.8
1976 (Jan.–June)[a]	18	10.1	−10.1	3.35	0.9

Source: Central Bank of Chile, *Boletín Mensual,* various issues.
Note: Refers to the so-called forward bank rate.
[a]After June 1976, adjustments were made daily.

expected rate of domestic inflation. It was the purpose of the authorities to achieve a real devaluation: first, because there was a desire to reduce the upward trend of the previous decade in foreign indebtedness; and, second, because the average level of protection for import substitutes was to be reduced gradually, thus requiring a compensatory adjustment in the ER.[8]

Three factors strongly influenced the real trend shown by the ER in 1965–70: the rate of external inflation, a balance of payments problem in 1967, and the behavior of the price of copper and capital flows.

The existence of external inflation — for that period about 2.4 percent per year on average — contributed to a real devaluation. A conjuncture that allowed an additional real depreciation was a balance of payments deficit in 1967. As part of its economic policy, the government had improved and extended a system of periodic projections of reserve movements, import intentions, and the current account. These projections showed an imbalance that needed timely action. The set of trade measures adopted by mid-1967 (Ffrench-Davis 1973, 104) included a reduction in fiscal expenditure and a faster devaluation (with more frequent adjustments); as a consequence, between July 1967 and February 1968 the RER was devalued by 12 percent (with a larger broker's rate devaluation). The real devaluation contributed to solving the balance of pay-

8. Most prohibitions and import deposits were eliminated, and a rationalization of tariffs, implying a moderate liberalization and reduction of the variance of effective protection, was begun (Ffrench-Davis 1973, 96–116).

ments imbalance while avoiding a serious shock to the domestic economy; apparently, the crawling peg approach had removed the ER from its former role as the main expectations builder.

During the remainder of the period, because of a higher price for the main export of Chile (copper, which represented about two-thirds of total exports) and an increase in the share of its economic rent accruing to the government, the balance of payments showed sizable surpluses from 1968 onward. This also induced an increase in short-term capital inflows into a "successful" emerging economy. The inflows were fostered by the larger reserves, an expanded debt-servicing capacity, and relatively tight domestic credit. Obviously, strong pressures were exerted within and on the government in order to freeze the ER. In this environment, it became more difficult to continue increasing the RER, but the economic authorities managed to retain the improvement achieved in 1967–68 and to enlarge it by continuing to crawl nearly pari passu with the rate of inflation; thus external inflation provided a positive differential.[9]

Given the balance of payments surplus and the nature of the pressures against the policy being enforced, it is probable that actual expectations were predicting a declining RER; those expectations, in combination with the natural gap between the external and domestic interest rates, were some of the incentives that encouraged the huge inflows of capital in 1968–70.

Probably the main obstacles faced by ER policy in the period 1965–70 related to coordination with other economic policies. On the one hand, the ER policy intended to limit the transmission of copper price instability to the domestic economy: thus, "normal" balance of payments estimates assumed a copper price lower than the actual high price. Apart from guiding policy according to the "normal" price, it was necessary to ensure that the recipients of copper export proceeds also had their incomes stabilized. This was largely done by the government with respect to the large copper producers. In the case of fiscal proceeds this was done (through annual agreements between the Central Bank and the Treasury on the use of the tax revenue from large copper producers) by using an account in dollars in the Central Bank where the "excess" of revenues were deposited. This was the "informal" birth of the Copper Buffer Fund.

On the other hand, capital flows tended to be destabilizing. The government had at its disposal only weak tools with which to check or compensate for them. It was able to establish a minimum repatriation

---

9. It must be stressed that in the 1960s there was very limited understanding of the implications of external inflation for the RER.

period for new inflows and to reduce domestic credit to partially compensate for the increased high-powered money originating from the accumulation of reserves. In a rather segmented capital market, the drastic change in the composition of money creation produced some financial bottlenecks. This phenomenon was repeated more intensively and had a more severe impact during the second experience.

In summary, given available policy tools, in 1965–70 it was desired to have more stability in the RER than in reserves, (1) because of its direct allocative effect, particularly with regard to exports; (2) because of the fear of ratchet price effects if the ER started following transitory changes in the terms of trade or capital flows; and (3) because of the belief that the actual price of copper was above its "normal" level and would fall drastically some time in the future, as it did by mid-1970.

The Crawling Peg in 1973–79

In October 1973, a crawling peg was again adopted. In this period, three different phases can be distinguished. The first phase ends in June 1976, the second extends to February 1978, and the third continues until June 1979 when the crawling peg was replaced with a nominal peg.

The First Phase, with Binding External Constraints

During most of 1973, there was a critical balance of payments situation and inflation was at an annual rate of close to 400 percent.[10] The government had established a system of multiple exchange rates in December 1971, and by August 1973 this involved six rates, with the lower one being only 3 percent of the highest. Although the government adhered to the nominal peg, it had been forced by the economic situation to make large devaluations; furthermore, by March 1973 it had reintroduced the crawling peg in the main area of the broker's market. However, most of the ERs lagged notoriously behind the climbing rate of inflation.

Some weeks after the coup of September 1973, the government announced a new economic policy directed toward reducing public intervention in the economy. Despite the fact that most price controls were abruptly lifted, the exchange rate continued to be controlled. The multiple rates were reduced to three, as had been the case until the end of 1971. The main rate, that of the forward bank market, was devalued by approximately 300 percent. The intention was to obtain a real rate approximately equal to that of 1970 (apparently, the role of the external

---

10. The official rate of increase of the index of consumer prices in the twelve-month period ending in August 1973 was 304 percent; an estimate of the incidence of black market prices increased the rate to 402 percent (Yáñez 1979).

inflation was ignored). Even though the main broker's rate was revalued at 53 percent, it still remained above the forward bank rate, while that for copper returns was kept at a low level (40 percent of the forward bank rate). The crawling peg was adopted for all three rates, with converging movements.[11] By August 1975, the government achieved the target of a fully unified official exchange rate, divergent only from the black market rate.[12]

The rates were adjusted between one and four times a month, with a frequency similar to that prevailing during the first experience. But, because of the high domestic inflation rate, the average nominal devaluation was much larger in the second period (see table 4.2); there were "crawls" as large as 18 percent, and within a two-week period in March 1975 the cumulative effect of two jumps was a 40 percent change. Thus, adjustments were not "frequent" enough to constitute a systematic process of minidevaluations.

The real forward bank rate experienced a significant net increase between 1974 and January 1976 (see table 4.3, col. 1). The improvement was directly determined by the behavior of the copper price. During the first ten months following the coup, the effective price of copper in Chile was the highest recorded in recent decades, but in the second half of 1974 it fell abruptly while imports continued mounting. The cycle led first to real revaluations and then to an accelerated process of devaluation that involved a 38 percent change in the RER between average 1974 and January 1976.

The fears of a balance of payments crisis had been superseded during this period by a severe recession. Despite the seriousness of the problem, import liberalization had continued: the average nominal tariff had been reduced (between mid-1974 and January 1976) from 67 to 44 percent. Real devaluations compensated approximately for the average fall in nominal restrictions on imports during this subphase, and both factors combined to enhance the competitiveness of exports. A 98 percent rise in nontraditional exports in 1974–77 covered one-third of the loss of copper export proceeds; exports were fostered by greater competitiveness (including preferential tariffs in the Andean Pact) and by the capacity left unused by a drastic restriction of aggregate demand (see chap. 3). This latter phenomenon, linked to an anti-inflationary policy

---

11. The nominal broker's rate was revalued until May 1974, bringing it closer to the bank rate. Also a tax rate of 53 percent was reduced to 13 percent in August 1974 and eliminated in February 1975.

12. Apart from import tariffs, the value added tax (VAT) with a rate of 20 percent, based on taxation according to the destination of products, meant that importers of goods paid more per dollar purchased and exporters (who were exempted from the VAT) received more per dollar sold.

shock, generated a large drop in imports, which contributed to the bulk of the external sector adjustment. Thus, more balanced trade was achieved, but GDP declined by 17 percent in 1975 (Marcel and Meller 1986) and open unemployment rose to 21.9 percent (including emergency employment programs; excluding them, the figure was 16.6 percent).

Subsequently, a growing balance of payments surplus (owing to the external credit boom experienced by Chile since 1976) and a rising

TABLE 4.3. Exchange Rate, Wages, and Interest Rates, 1965–82

	Real Exchange Rate Index (1970 = 100) (1)	Real Wage Indexes (1970 = 100)		Real Interest Rate (4)
		Deflated by Exchange Rate (2)	Deflated by CPI (3)	
1965	80.1	84.1	67.3	−0.5
April	77.8			
1966	84.2	89.6	75.4	8.8
1967	91.0	94.2	85.7	10.8
1968	95.6	89.5	85.6	6.5
1969	99.0	92.8	91.8	5.6
1970	100.0	100.0	100.0	6.9
July	104.7			
1973	83.9	56.0	82.0	n.d.
October	113.4			
1974	130.5	45.0	64.8	n.d.
1975	179.0	31.9	62.0	121.0[a]
1976	144.6	49.8	65.0	51.2
January	180.7			
June	155.9			
July	130.8			
1977	120.3	60.6	71.0	39.4
July	114.8			
1978	133.5	58.1	75.0	35.1
February	133.1			
1979	133.4	64.3	81.8	16.9
June	131.1			
1980	116.6	80.1	88.9	12.2
1981	99.2	102.6	96.8	38.8
1982	115.1	88.2	97.1	35.2
June	90.0			

Sources: For 1965–70, Ffrench-Davis 1973; for 1970–82, based on figures from the Central Bank of Chile; Cortázar and Marshall 1980; and Ffrench-Davis 1984.

Note: In column 1, nominal exchange rates were deflated by CPI and inflated by the Chilean external price index (EPI). Monthly figures are given when important changes in exchange rate policy occurred. Columns 2 and 3 have as a numerator the general wage index by INE and as denominator changes in CPI and in nominal exchange rates multiplied by the EPI, respectively. Column 4 shows the annual nominal interest rate, deflated by CPI.

[a]Second semester, after the interest rate liberalization.

monthly rate of inflation invited a change in the trend of the RER. In the remainder of the phase, the real rate fell rapidly, with gradual adjustments below net inflation, losing 14 percent in the last five months. In this same period, import liberalization became effectively more drastic because tariff reductions already had a clearly lower redundant component (the average tariff was reduced from 44 to 33 percent). Now they came together with an RER appreciation rather than the reverse, as the authorities had repeatedly announced.

The Abrupt Revaluations Phase

The second phase began with an abrupt revaluation of 10 percent in June 1976, which represented a notorious change in the policy and caught public attention not so much because of its intrinsic economic effects but because of the conditions and arguments that surrounded it.

The main characteristics of the second phase, which covered the period up to February 1978, were the daily frequency of minidevaluations, according to schedules announced monthly, and a series of four abrupt changes (two revaluations and two devaluations).

The June 1976 revaluation was announced with great fanfare. After an introductory speech by General Pinochet, the minister of finance read a series of policy announcements. The main one was the already mentioned 10 percent revaluation. Beginning in July, the rate would be adjusted daily; during July, the ER would be devalued by 5 percent (compared to the 12 percent inflation in June), and adjustments in each of the following months would be equal to the inflation rate of the immediately preceding month.[13]

The minister argued that (1) in 1975 the ER had increased faster than domestic prices, producing an "unrealistic" ER that was not sustainable in the long run; (2) the new parity would be adjusted systematically because its new level was realistic; (3) the new system would allow the exporter to work with certainty; (4) the revaluation would reduce industrial costs and inflation from July onward, thus, he asserted, increasing real wages; (5) imports and economic activity would be fostered by revaluation; and (6) money expansion originating in net reserve purchases by the Central Bank would be reduced.[14]

The decision to revalue can be traced to a combination of factors. First, economic policy was under heavy attack from government

---

13. There was no mention of external inflation, nor was that issue systematically developed in the literature concerning real exchange rate measurement. See the contrasting estimates of RER in the 1960s in Ffrench-Davis 1973 and Behrman 1976.

14. Speech of the minister of finance, June 29, 1976, in DIPRES 1978, 261–62. About 80 percent of the changes in high-powered money had been originating in the net purchase of reserves.

supporters. The monthly rate of inflation had been rising, complicated by a slow recovery from the downswing in economic activity achieved by the policy approach taken in 1975, and open unemployment was at a very high level. It appeared that a spectacular event was needed to ensure the survival of the drastic orthodox policies being imposed. Second, the purely monetarist approach to stabilization (à la Friedman) had been weakened by the negative experience with the dynamics of inflation in previous months (Foxley 1983). Thus, the emphasis was placed on the anti-inflationary effect that a widely announced revaluation could exert via expectations.[15] Third, an overall balance of payments surplus allowed the authorities to "burn" foreign currency, which would also contribute to a reduction in the printing of money.

The fact is that all the weight of the government-controlled mass media was put into promoting the newly announced policy. The revaluation actually did change expectations, reducing the monthly rate of inflation to 6 percent in August and September, but it stagnated at that level for two quarters. The minister of finance announced in March 1977 a new revaluation of 10 percent, with the set of minidevaluations fixed at 4 and 3 percent for March and April, respectively. This was to be followed, again, by adjustments according to the rate of inflation in the preceding month. Most of the arguments provided by the government were the same as those given for the first revaluation, though with more emphasis on the assertion that exports (except for "marginal" ones) would hardly be affected because the ER "was 20 percent above October 1973 and only slightly below the average of the second semester of 1976."[16] The rate of inflation was indeed reduced to 3 or 4 percent a month, but it again stagnated at the new level.

Despite the first revaluation, the overall balance of payments showed a positive performance. In 1976, there was a surplus in the trade account and also, which was extremely unusual, in the current account. This fact facilitated the March 1977 revaluation. But the surpluses, despite a low price for copper, were the result of the drastically depressed level of

---

15. The orthodox closed economy monetarist approach to inflation that had prevailed until mid-1976 was questioned by the appearance of an open economy monetarist approach, to which most official economists seemed to have been converted rapidly. The predominance of the latter approach appeared to be definitive when the nominal ER was pegged three years later. It is curious that economists who in the previous period had stated that if the money supply was held constant the ER would have no effect on the level of prices later argued that the ER determines the price level. Trade liberalization does not justify such an extreme change of approach. Thus, we witness, once again, the importance of fashion in economics at the expense of pragmatism.

16. Speech of the minister of finance, March , 1977, in DIPRES 1978, 308–9. The official figure clearly overestimated the RER. See table 4.3; and McKinnon 1977, table 5. Recall that the official CPI rate systematically underestimated actual inflation.

aggregate demand, reflected in low imports. This situation was notably reversed in 1977 and 1978 in response to some recovery of aggregate demand, tariff reductions, and an appreciating RER. The consequence was the appearance of a sizable deficit in the current account, which was more than compensated for by financial inflows.

In the second half of 1977, two abrupt, though relatively small, devaluations took place: 6 percent in August and 4 percent in December. The former was compensated for by a fall in tariffs that corresponded to an anticipation of the "final" step of the trade liberalization process, by which customs duties would be limited to the range 10 to 35 percent. Thus, supposedly the import tariff liberalization process had ended in August 1977 (DIPRES 1978, 337).

Nonetheless, in December the minister of finance announced that tariff discrimination was to be suppressed, gradually establishing between December 1977 and June 1979 a uniform tariff of 10 percent (DIPRES 1978, 358–59). In order to compensate for the average effect of the tariff reduction made in December, there was a devaluation of 4.3 percent. Again, with the purpose of influencing price expectations, daily rates of minidevaluations were announced for the two following months, totaling 2.2 percent for December (the official inflation rate of the previous month) and 3 percent for January. It was asserted that subsequently the ER would be increased slightly faster than the previous month's domestic inflation in order to compensate for the concomitant import liberalization. This was not done, however, because the policy was changed shortly afterward, in February 1978, bringing an end to the second phase.

The ER was assigned a quite different role in this second phase. The higher frequency of adjustments could be associated with the purpose of making real rates more stable. However, the changed role of the ER made the real rate more unstable. In fact, the appreciating trend of the RER, which began in January 1976, continued until mid-1977. Then it resumed a depreciating trend, reinforced by the two forward jumps. During the last part of the phase, the RER improved by 16 percent after having lost 26 percent during the first year of the phase, with a net appreciation of 15 percent (see table 4.3).[17] In the meanwhile, nominal average tariffs had been reduced from 33 to 16 percent (see table 3.1).

The exchange rate was used actively as an expectation builder. Previously, according to widespread government arguments, expectations could not be regulated efficiently except through monetary policy. In this phase, on two occasions the ER was assigned the role of a

---

17. In this period, external inflation of 17 percent was a crucial variable in explaining the RER trend. The high external price index was the result of growing inflation in developed countries and a U.S. dollar devaluation.

substitute for monetary policy in that field, and it fulfilled this assign-
ment rather well. Of course, its efficiency was related to the specific
economic framework that had prevailed since 1974: expectations of
price fixers (entrepreneurs) built strongly on the behavior of prices in
the preceding month in the absence of a clearer anchor.

On the other hand, the RER movements were strongly influenced
by short-run fluctuations in the balance of payments. Reserves responded to changes in imports tied to the downswing and recovery of
GDP, to large capital flows, and to exchange rate adjustments that
destabilized the resource allocation. Given the instability of reserves,
the role assigned to the ER made the real rate notoriously unstable
during the phase. The transmission of instability to the RER implied
the usual misleading signaling to producers of tradables. This was reinforced by the fact that the Chilean economy was now clearly more
open to trade; thus, price relations and the allocation of resources
were more influenced by changes in the ER than they were in the
1960s. The economy was also more open to capital inflows, which were
now operated predominantly via the private sector. The significant
ups and downs of the RER, coupled with high domestic interest rates,
brought sizable capital gains to borrowers of foreign loans (Zahler
1980).[18]

The phase ended in February 1978 when the monthly schedule was
replaced with a daily schedule for the remaining eleven months of the
year. The formula used in the previous eighteen months, based on endogenous nominal ER dependent on previous inflation, was replaced
with an exogenous schedule, determined by the annual inflation target.

The Final Phase: Toward the Return to a Fixed Rate and the Crisis

In February 1978, the minister of finance announced a schedule of daily
changes of the ER that contemplated decreasing adjustments, starting
with 2.5 percent (roughly the official rate of inflation in the previous
three months) and ending with 0.75 percent for December. He asserted
that "given the excellent balance of payments situation, the opening to
foreign trade and the announcement of the exchange rate for 1978,
competitive imports would rapidly enter if prices of domestic products
were increased excessively" and that "the government is providing the
foundations, so 1979 will mark the start of a period of unprecedented
price stability."[19] On this occasion, the content of the official announce-

---

18. In chapter 5, estimates of differentials between domestic and external interest
rates, and of the funds involved in these operations during 1975–82, are provided.
19. Speech of the minister of finance, February 3, 1978, in DIPRES 1978, 369–71.

ment, and of conferences and interviews of several government representatives, gave the impression that, more than the regulation of expectations, the crucial factor was the belief that the economy was already so open that the *law of one price* would apply.[20]

Domestic inflation, measured by the official CPI, fell from 64 percent in 1977 to 30 percent in 1978 (from 84 to 37 percent, according to the corrected CPI). This apparent success led to the adoption of the same approach for the following year. In December 1978, a schedule of daily adjustments was announced for 1979. The compound annual rate of devaluation to be implemented was 14.7 percent, similar to the rate of inflation that had been announced informally as the rate expected for that year. There was no consideration of either external inflation (which was over 14 percent per annum in 1978–79) or the declining gap between effective and potential GDP. If it was to be true that the law of one price applied, exchange rate policy would clearly lead to inflation above 15 percent. It is possible that the economic authorities were still in transition from an expectations theory to a law of one price approach.

The fact is that during the first half of 1979, instead of decreasing, inflation began to rise. In the twelve-month period ending in June, inflation was 35 percent. All indicators signaled that inflation, rather than being reduced by half, as announced by the government, would be higher than in 1978.

This last phase ended abruptly in June 1979 with the freezing of the ER at a level 5.7 percent above the level prevailing then; the new level anticipated the rate schedule for the end of the year.

By mid-1979, after almost six years of several policy variants and oscillations of the RER, the rate was at a level close to that established at the outset. However, during the process import restrictions had been drastically reduced: most nontariff obstacles disappeared, and tariffs were reduced from an (unweighted) average of 94 percent to a flat 10 percent. Additionally, the ER was fixed in a context of the 35 percent inflationary trend.

When the ER was frozen in June 1979, it was asserted that it would be maintained until February 1980, "bringing more stability to the external sector, without danger for a reasonable equilibrium in the balance of payments." A brake would be put on price increases, and inflationary expectations would be reduced. It was strongly emphasized that credit

20. This law implies that domestic and external prices of tradables corrected by tariffs and ER are equal. As a result, it is argued that in a small country domestic prices have no ability to change except through tariffs or ER changes. According to the extreme view, prices of nontradables similarly have no autonomy because they are determined by their interrelation with tradables through goods and factors markets.

availability and public expenditures would be significantly restricted, and thus traders would not be able to transfer all of the RER increase to prices.[21]

The ER was held at $39 per dollar up to mid-1982. In that three-year period, there was real appreciation by one-third. Annual domestic inflation decreased from 35 percent to less than 10 percent, but during the transition a disequilibrium between external and domestic prices by the magnitude mentioned arose. As a result, in order to return to the previous level of RER, in appearance estimated as one of equilibrium by authorities (McKinnon 1981, 34), a domestic inflation thirty points lower than the external one was required. During the last months of 1981 and the first half of 1982, a slight domestic deflation was registered.[22] But, in parallel, unemployment increased sharply and a rapid fall in the production of manufactures occurred.[23]

The fact is that, after some months of automatic adjustment, the outcome was disastrous. An initiative to accelerate the adjustment process, through a legal reduction of nominal wages, could not be imposed by the economic team. An abrupt devaluation was applied in June 1982 by a new minister.

The initial devaluation was 18 percent, and a table of minidevaluations was announced. Then a totally flexible exchange rate regime, with free access (with immediate huge outflows by the market), was implemented. Subsequently, a system of bands and minidevaluations, based on past inflation and regulated access to the foreign exchange market, was developed (see chap. 6).

The commitment to reduce inflation has the highest priority for the government; given that reserves continued to grow because of capital inflows, it would be feasible to keep the nominal exchange rate fixed in 1980, notwithstanding its real appreciation.[24]

Supporters of a permanent freezing include, of course, importers

21. Speech of the minister of finance, June 29, 1979. Additionally, the spread between the selling and buying rates applied by the Central Bank was increased to plus or minus 2 percent.

22. On the one hand, the wholesale price index fell by 8 percent between May 1981 and May 1982. Also the CPI declined 1 percent between February and May 1982. On the other hand, international markets exhibited negative inflation as well: the external price index fell by 4 percent in the first half of 1982 as a result of a U.S. dollar revaluation.

23. Open unemployment (excluding public emergency programs) grew from 11 to 23 percent between September 1981 and June 1982. Value added of manufacturing fell by 21 percent in 1982.

24. The original study was finished in November 1979. Here I have deleted several paragraphs on the conjuncture from the version published in Williamson 1981. However, two paragraphs, slightly abridged, that contain my views about what I expected would happen in the next few years have been retained.

of consumer goods, and those influenced by the monetary approach to the balance of payments. The response of non-tradables prices in periods of accumulation of reserves and of their output during decumulation periods, and the slow speed with which the law of one price applies to tradables, are crucial. Apart from the standard criticism of the optimistic assumptions in these two areas, the critical view brings into the discussion the belief that (i) the present ER is too appreciated (the deficit on current account amounted to 7 percent of GDP in 1978 and import liberalization has not yet exerted all its effects); (ii) monetary management will be based on deeper restriction of public expenditure, with a low public investment and quality of basic social services; (iii) the large overall unemployment is concentrated more heavily in industries producing importables, and non-tradables that usually have been highly dependent on public expenditure; and (iv) the probable changes that the economy will continue to suffer, either from external or domestic origin, are difficult to predict. A crawling peg policy provides flexibility to adjust to deviations from predictions, while the fixed nominal ER makes abandoning the parity traumatic. Consequently, pegging the nominal rate imposes a harder adjustment process on the real economy, though in the next months it will probably contribute to more stability of the price level.

The appreciation that the real ER will probably suffer will tend to have a negative effect on employment, economic activity and investment. In fact, on the one hand, the desubstitution of importables will be encouraged. On the other hand, investment, which is already low, will tend to be deterred by the uncertainty with respect to the level of the ER and its corresponding impact on market comparative advantages; this could be particularly relevant with respect to investment in exportables. Despite its probable negative effects, the present policy might be retained for a rather long period. First, the external payments situation looks favorable in the near future because the price of copper will probably increase, as usual overshooting the normal level. Second, gross reserves are large, and can support an increased deficit on current account. Third, foreign capital in sizable amounts should still continue to flow despite the fall in domestic interest rates and the real ER appreciation; given the nominal ER, the dollar equivalent of domestic annual interest rates is still over 40 percent; real appreciation adds a growing risk, but experience shows that a large deterioration can accumulate before international lenders react, as long as the other "attractive" features of the model remain in force. (Ffrench-Davis 1981, 168–69)

All of this, what we were predicting in 1979, happened in the following two years and ended in the collapse of 1982.

Final Remarks

My concluding remarks can be divided into two groups. The first are related to some of the answers that the Chilean experience suggests and the second to some of the questions that remain open.

Some Lessons

This discussion will touch on four points, which refer to (1) the feasibility of changes in the RER, (2) expectations, (3) stability, and (4) the correction of policy errors.

The two experiences show that not only the nominal rate but also the RER can be modified substantially by means of policy decisions. The law of one price, even in an economy as open to trade as the Chilean one, has limited validity. In particular, lags can be very long and imply imbalances for several years, generating wrong signals, misallocation of resources, and a low rate of productive capacity utilization. In fact, there is a wide range of outcomes characterized by multiple equilibria and RER for a long time far from its medium-term sustainable level.

In the cases analyzed here, the main variables interacting with the ER have been the terms of trade, the level of economic activity, and external financing. Notwithstanding, the relation of the ER with other macroeconomic variables can also suffer drastic and persistent changes: in 1973–79, wages were depressed by a policy decision at the outset, and the wages/ER ratio remained at levels one-third to two-thirds that of the ratio prevailing in 1970 (table 4.3, col. 2); on the other hand, domestic interest rates fluctuated widely and departed drastically from parity relations with international markets (col. 4).

The effect of the ER on inflationary expectations is closely tied to the specific policy design adopted. Different variants of the crawling peg have divergent effects. A policy of the sort implemented in the first period, and to some degree between October 1973 and June 1976, reduces the impact on expectations of changes in the ER. On the contrary, the widely announced annual schedule of the ER established in 1978 operates in the reverse direction; as such, it can be used "actively" to regulate expectations, but simultaneously it behaves "passively" if the objective is to alter the RER. The larger the influence on expectations, the less will be the degrees of freedom to modify the RER; the extreme case is that of the nominal peg. Of course, the net effect depends on how well other variables that influence expectations and production costs are performing.

The behavior of the ER seems to have a significant influence on nontraditional exports. In both experiences exports expanded and diversified (Ffrench-Davis 1979b, tables 4 and 6). This phenomenon is the result of multiple variables, but the depreciating trend and the larger stability of the crawling peg, compared to the jumping peg or the purely free float, seem to have played a positive role.[25] The greater stability of the real rate also tends to deter speculative movements, which were frequent with the fixed peg. However, if the RER policy responds to short-run changes in reserves, the policy can become destabilizing and replicate the overshooting of a free exchange rate, as happened partially during the second experience. Consequently, changes of the RER that try to avoid large fluctuations, away from the trend suggested by the real economy, seem to provide improved allocative signals and increase the demand for domestic assets.

Finally, a crawling peg policy, managed with flexibility by the economic authorities, appears to make it easier to correct disequilibria resulting from errors in predictions in the trend of relevant variables, when these can be corrected via adjustments in the nominal ER. One obvious case relates to the adjustment in response to import liberalization. The managed flexibility increases the feasibility of avoiding balance of payments crises and cumulative disequilibria.

Some Open Questions

When the world and the domestic economy are in equilibrium, there is no need for changes in macroeconomic price relations. But the world economy is changing and is not in equilibrium: neither natural resources nor capital markets seem to be in long-run equilibrium. These conditions recommend a managed flexibility in ER policy — of the sort that a crawling band can provide — in order to face the corresponding structural adjustment in the real economy.

It is important to identify the circumstances under which permanent ER adjustments must be made, for instance, in response to autonomous changes in the terms of trade, the composition of domestic output, or the foreign capital supply. Furthermore, it is crucial to determine what to do with respect to transitory changes. The general line seems to be to stop their transmission to the ER. But there are two aspects that call for some flexibility of the RER. One is that ER policy is seldom sufficient

---

25. Econometric data referring to 1974–75 support this hypothesis (Behrman 1976, table 7.2). See also ECLAC 1998, chap. 4.

by itself to avoid the transmission of instability; there is also a need for other policies, such as fiscal, credit-monetary, and foreign debt policies, each one implying some cost. What is the optimal mix of policies? The other refers to the implications of uncertainty or limited knowledge. It is impossible to distinguish the exact frontier between normal and transitory components of the balance of payments; in fact, there is a range where the frontier is ambiguous. Thus, in order to minimize policy failures, it is convenient to accept some instability in the short run; this can contribute to avoiding the forced adjustments that are necessary in the long run when errors accumulate. Where is the optimum cutting point and what are the components of trade that must be "normalized" as an input for policy purposes?

One recurrent feature has been the enlarged size of private capital flows and the associated abrupt changes in reserves and base money observed in different historical episodes in Chile. Their effects are far from neutral: (1) funds accrue mostly to some segments of the domestic economy and (2) the response of authorities has sometimes been to appreciate the RER or (3) to diminish public expenditure as a compensating mechanism. This problem is related to the questions of what the actual capacity to absorb foreign funds efficiently and how stable the supply is. It is extremely doubtful that these questions can be answered optimally by the market (see chap. 10). What price or direct mechanisms can operate better to manage capital flows in the case of small and medium-sized emerging economies?

Answers to these questions would contribute to further improving the design of a crawling peg policy, with managed flexibility, that would make the evolution of the Chilean external sector much smoother than it was with the jumping peg, a new policy that allowed the economic authorities to devote more effort to other policy areas and contributed to a significant expansion and diversification of exports.

CHAPTER 5

External Debt and Financial Liberalization in the 1970s

During the 1980s, most Latin American countries were facing a dramatic problem of external indebtedness. The sharp deterioration in international markets registered since 1981 affected the developing nations with unusual severity; the drop in export prices and worsening access to the markets of industrialized countries, the rise in international interest rates, and the sharp reduction in capital inflows all contributed to the strongest negative external shock in the last half century.

In addition to a generally recessive character, the effects of the external shock on debtor economies displayed considerable diversity, which was due to the varied bargaining power of each country, the different speeds and magnitudes of indebtedness, and the development strategies adopted in earlier years. The latter was also a determining factor in the level of development that each country had reached when it was hit by the external crisis. In other words, there were nations whose economies stagnated or even contracted during the 1970s, yet others grew vigorously by channeling the abundant external supply of funding in international markets into productive investments.

This chapter focuses on the external debt of Chile. Because of its close relationship with the workings of the domestic capital market and the balance of payments policy, the main features and results recorded in these two areas will be discussed here, too.

As was shown in chapters 1 and 2, the Chilean economy recorded a poor performance during the period 1973–82 (see Arellano and Cortázar 1982; Edwards and Cox-Edwards 1987; Foxley 1983; and Ramos 1986). The failure of this experiment was associated to a significant extent, albeit not exclusively, with the trade and financial policies implemented in the period in question. The way in which these policies were

This chapter is based on "The external debt, financial liberalization, and crisis in Chile," in *Politics and Economics of External Debt Crisis: The Latin American Experience,* M. Wionczek, ed. (Boulder and London: Westview, 1985). I gratefully acknowledge the comments of researchers at CIEPLAN, in particular José Pablo Arellano, and those of Robert Devlin, Rudi Dornbusch, Jaime Estévez, Jorge Marshall, and Carlos Massad. I appreciate the assistance of José de Gregorio.

applied made it possible for the external debt to grow very rapidly. At the same time, instead of supporting domestic capital formation, the increase in debt discouraged it. This outcome had five relevant causes: the rapid and indiscriminate import liberalization (especially of consumer goods), the exchange rate appreciation in combination with the sharp reductions in effective protection (see chap. 2), the persistence of high real interest rates on the domestic capital market, the overwhelming freedom given to the market forces to decide on the use of funds of both domestic and external origin, and the difficulty of identifying the market's comparative advantages or finding attractive opportunities for productive investment.

Finally, great vulnerability in the national economy was generated. Thus, in view of the passive and neutral domestic policies pursued (see chap. 2), the authorities were left with no policy tools with which to deal with external stocks. Furthermore, growing indebtedness and the magnitude of the deficit on the current account as early as 1980 obviously could not have been sustained in the medium term, even had the international financial crisis not taken place. Consequently, the external sector was placed on a course that would inevitably call for a traumatic adjustment process. The seriousness of this situation was exacerbated, of course, by the fact that during the 1970s the national productive base and adjustment capacity were weakened rather than strengthened. Thus, for example, the gross investment rate fell by almost one-fifth compared to the 1970s and the GDP growth rate diminished even more. Correspondingly, Chilean GDP suffered the deepest recession in Latin America in 1982.

The first section presents the main features of the financial liberalization process and supplies a few details of the official conceptual framework, the policies adopted, and the evolution of capital flows and the external debt; special attention is given to bank loans and the behavior of capital flows received by private debtors. Next the macroeconomic impact of external indebtedness is examined, especially the way in which it affected monetary and exchange-rate policies and the disequilibrating adjustment processes to which it gave rise. Then the evolution of interest rates — especially the persistent gap between domestic and foreign rates — is analyzed. There follows a discussion of the various sources of external vulnerability to which Chile was exposed as a result of its financial openness. I argue, contradicting the neoliberal approach, that the problems were concentrated in the private sector segment of the debt. I also attempt to explain why the massive financial inflows were accompanied by a drop in national savings and a decline in the investment ratio. The chapter closes with a brief summary of the lessons provided by the neoliberal experiment for financial relations and foreign debt management.

Financial Liberalization and Foreign Debt

An across the board opening to capital flows and full liberalization of the domestic financial market was the official policy in Chile. This section presents the conceptual framework on which the financial opening was based and then examines the way in which the principles were implemented. Finally, the volume and composition of capital flows and external indebtedness are analyzed.

The Analytical Framework of the Experiment

There are of course some very sophisticated neoliberal versions of how the liberalization of capital markets should work and of its effects compared to those of the so-called financial repression. The essential aspects of the official version can be conveyed by means of a very simple scheme, however.

The liberalization of the domestic financial market and the opening up to capital flows sought to increase overall investment and improve the allocation of resources. It was expected that there would be an increase in the volume of investment and its efficiency, which would provide the basis for vigorous and sustained economic growth.

In simple terms, the conceptual framework may be described in figure 5.1. Curves O and D show the supply and demand for funds in the market, which are identified with saving and investment, respectively. To begin with, there prevails a situation of "financial repression" in the sense that there are restrictions regarding the organization of new banks and the operations they can carry out and there is extensive rationing of the demand. Against this background, the authorities fix an interest rate (r_c) lower than the equilibrium rate for a closed economy (r_e). This determines a volume of savings, V_c, and demand is rationed at the same level (for the sake of simplicity, it is assumed that initially there is no net capital inflow). The volume of savings and investment (V_c) is less than that in a closed market situation with a free interest rate (V_e). At the same time, some nonprofitable investments are made, since rationing means that not all of the most efficient investments take place. Thus, some investments would be made that have returns equal to r_c, whereas others, with a higher yield, would remain without financing (in some of them, the return would exceed r_e since total investment would be V_c).

The domestic financial liberalization would allow a rise of r to its local equilibrium, and savers would face more options for investing their funds. Given the broader variety of options, there would be a larger supply (O_1, to the right of O) replacing the investment in nonproductive assets and supposedly raising the saving propensity by making it more

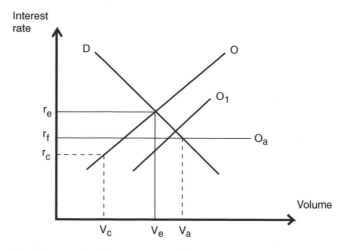

Fig. 5.1. Conventional framework of the liberalization of capital markets

attractive. On the other hand, the financial opening would allow capital inflows, which would complement the domestic funding for investment. With free capital flows, an investment volume of $V_a > V_e$ and an equalization of the interest rate at r_f would be reached.

The savings rate would rise, despite the lower interest rate, if the shift of supply were sufficiently strong, as in figure 5.1. This is a common assumption that is both explicit and implicit in the neoliberal reforms of the financial market.

The exchange rate policy adopted is a determining factor in the final outcome. To reach an equalization of interest rates, there must be no expectations of variation in the real exchange rate (deflated by net inflation). Initially, this was sought through a policy of minidevaluations, as described in chapter 4. Subsequently, a fixed exchange rate was adopted. Official policy assumed that, in a free trade regime such as it was already at work in 1979 with a fiscal surplus and an exchange rate close to the "equilibrium level," freezing the nominal exchange rate would rapidly prevent domestic inflation from exceeding external inflation. Thus, the exchange rate would become the anchor for stabilizing the level of domestic prices. The authorities thus formally adopted the most extreme type of monetarism, that is, the monetary approach to the balance of payments, with its neutral monetary policy.

The official approach assumed that financial liberalization would work efficiently since capital flows were managed by private agents and mostly without official guarantees. Thus, capital would only enter the country if the debtor expected a net return for its use that would allow him or her to service interest payments. Therefore, the growth in the external debt was the reflection of a healthy economy (De la Cuadra 1981, 1025) and private debt would not present the threat of insolvency. This problem would only arise in the case of public debt (Robichek 1981, 172).

A naive vision of the working of private institutions prevailed. Statements by the authorities that users knew how to distinguish between good and bad banks were frequent. The fact is that prudential supervision was very lax in Chile.[1]

The discrepancies between the official approach and the real world were very marked. The volume of national savings and capital formation was less than V_c; that is, instead of growing it decreased sharply. The domestic interest rate stood at unexpectedly high levels and was spectacularly higher than the international rates (table 5.5). Fixing the nominal exchange rate in 1979 led to a significant loss of purchasing power and a growing external deficit. Private indebtedness grew notably, encouraged by the risky assumption that its real cost would remain low and that there would continue to be easy access to loans in the future. Finally, the excessive indebtedness, with the correspondingly rising service, weakened the productive system and the payments capacity instead of strengthening them.

The New Institutional Framework

In this period, three subperiods may be distinguished with regard to the implementation of financial policies.[2] The first ran from 1973 to 1975, when there were no substantial changes in the domestic financial system; banks nationalized under the previous regime remained under state control. On the other hand, various measures undertaken in order to encourage foreign investment and foreign credits had little effect, in the sense that net inflows were negligible.

The second period began in 1975 with the drastic reform of the domestic financial system and the privatization of most of the commercial banks. Together with liberalizing the interest rate in April of the same year, freedom for readjustments (monetary corrections) in operations exceeding ninety days and for interest payments on short-term deposits were granted (see Arellano 1983). On the other hand, quantitative

---

1. Interestingly, something similar occurred in industrial countries with the regulation of loans to developing countries. See Valdés-Prieto 1989 on the relaxation of norms to facilitate the recycling of oil surpluses.

2. For more detailed background on regulations on capital flows, see the appendix to Ffrench-Davis and Arellano 1981.

controls on loans in national currency, which principally aimed at channeling credits into production rather than consumption, were eliminated, and authorized operations as well as their conditions for the different financial institutions were standardized.

The tendency toward uniform treatment also included foreign banks. Their activities had been restricted during the governments of presidents Frei and Allende. In December 1974, restrictions prohibiting their operation in the country were lifted. Nevertheless, the opening to external financing was slower. This gradualism contrasted with the rather abrupt trade liberalization. In the following years, however, there were heavy capital inflows, which grew rapidly between 1977 and 1981. The determining factors were the abundance of funds available on the international market, the low initial bank debt of Chile, the image of creditworthiness that Chile had achieved, and the absence of domestic and external restrictions regarding the use of the funds.

Finally, in the last part of the period, from the end of 1981 onward, despite the further liberalization of capital inflows, the supply shrank drastically, as a result of both the emergence of the international financial crisis and the late recognition by bank creditors of the excessive indebtedness of Chile. When the Mexican debt crisis officially exploded in August 1982, Chile found itself in the midst of a deep crisis. In fact, from the second half of 1981 on, GDP had been decreasing persistently (see Marcel and Meller 1983).

The gradual nature of liberalizing controls on the size and terms of capital flows was meant to ensure control over the money supply, which for several years played the principal role in anti-inflation policy. It was considered that, in view of the sizable difference between the domestic and foreign interest rates, abrupt liberalization of the capital account would attract credit in such volume that it would endanger the price stabilization program.

Official statements insisted on the transitory nature of the restrictions. Indeed, with the passage of time the capital account was liberalized through increases in the quantitative restrictions bounds or their replacement with more flexible or diminished controls.

In 1981, when the net use of foreign savings jumped to 21 percent of GDP,[3] financial inflows (under article 14 of the law on foreign exchange operations) were subject to a minimum stay in the country of twenty-four months and the compulsory deposit of a percentage of the credit (10 or 15 percent, depending on the term) in the case of operations for less than sixty-six months. There were no special restrictions on the volume

3. Figures in 1977 constant prices rescaled with average RER for 1976–78. In current U.S. dollars, the net use of foreign capital was 14.5 percent due to the abnormally increased value of GDP in 1981 as a result of outlier exchange rate appreciation.

of credit that the banks could borrow abroad and lend in foreign currency in Chile, but there was still a limit on the guarantees they could grant. During 1982, in the midst of the crisis of the Chilean economy, the minimum term of twenty-four months was eliminated and the compulsory deposit was set at 5 percent of the foreign loan, which was a rate similar to the reserve requirement for domestic bank deposits.

Financial Capital Flows and Indebtedness: Volume, Sources and Uses

Capital flows grew rapidly from 1977 onward. Even though Chile recorded a large and growing current account deficit in the following years, the net capital inflow was sufficient to allow a significant accumulation of international reserves until 1981. This capital surge took place in a context of dynamic expansion of the external sector, especially of imports of nonessential consumer goods. Inflows were overwhelmingly concentrated in credits to the private sector with no state guarantee. Foreign direct investment and loans to the public sector accounted for less than 20 percent of inflows.

Table 5.1 shows several indicators of annual capital movements. The flows, expressed in constant prices, increased significantly in the second half of the 1970s (cols. 1 and 2). Columns 3 and 4 show that capital movements rose sharply as a share of gross domestic investment and GDP. This was partly a result of the relative stagnation of the latter two variables during the 1970s. External savings (deficit on the current account) and the capital service also grew, with some ups and downs, in relation to exports (cols. 5 and 6), in spite of the dynamic growth of the latter in the early years of the neoliberal experiment. The total debt service in 1982 amounted to 88 percent of exports of goods and services, that is, three times the coefficient of the years 1970–74.

In short, the data show that from 1977 onward capital inflows captured a growing relative weight in the Chilean economy. The coefficients reflecting their incidence show a debt-servicing burden substantially greater than that for Latin America as a whole in the 1970s and early 1980s (Bacha and Díaz-Alejandro 1983; Ffrench-Davis 1983b).

Debt activity (as reflected by the volume of gross transactions and amortization payments) increased faster than net capital flows since the terms of the loans became shorter. This was a direct consequence of the increased share of private creditors in total debt, which operate with shorter maturity terms. The magnitude reached by capital movements is reflected by the fact that, in the two-year period 1980–81, gross inflows were equivalent to 24 percent of GDP.

During the period under analysis, significant changes took place with regard to the agents (creditors and debtors) participating in capital flows. Among creditors, 84 percent of the external debt in 1981 was with banks and financial institutions, which had accounted for only 19 percent in 1974 (see table 5.2). This increased participation by private lenders was reflected in a decline in the nominal amount of bilateral debt with official institutions. This reassignment of borrowing was partly the result of greater use of the supply of foreign banks, which before 1977 had been relatively little used by Chile compared to other semi-industrialized nations. From then on, however, it rapidly caught up. Chile's per capita bank debt in 1982 exceeded U.S.$1,000, compared to a regional average of U.S.$600 and only about U.S.$500 in the case of Brazil (Ffrench-Davis 1983a, table V.5). On the other hand, Chile's bank debt increased by 57 percent per year between 1977 and 1981, compared to an average of 28 percent for developing countries as a whole.

With regard to debtors, after 1975 the growing net capital inflow

TABLE 5.1.   Deficit on the Current Account and Capital Flows, 1970–82

Year	Balance on Current Account (1)	Gross Inflow of Loans (1977 U.S.$ millions) (2)	External Financing of Investment (%) (3)	External Financing and GDP (%) (4)	Export Deficit (%) (5)	Debt Service Coefficient (%) (6)
1970	−166	941	6.8	1.4	6.5	27.0
1971	−367	772	15.5	2.8	16.9	38.4
1972	−690	1,302	36.4	5.4	40.0	27.9
1973	−441	1,106	24.7	3.6	20.7	25.4
1974	−256	1,064	12.0	2.1	8.9	35.1
1975	−534	1,109	32.5	5.0	29.3	55.6
1976	160	1,086	−11.4	−1.4	−6.5	52.7
1977	−551	1,390	34.1	4.6	22.5	52.8
1978	−965	2,559	50.9	7.4	38.5	58.7
1979	−933	2,691	42.2	6.6	27.3	50.8
1980	−1,382	3,270	51.2	9.0	36.8	47.7
1981	−3,348	4,640	108.1	20.7	103.2	70.8
1982	−1,693	2,238	87.2	12.2	53.4	88.5

Sources: Calculated on the basis of Central Bank of Chile, *Balanza de Pagos, Deuda Externa de Chile,* and *Cuentas Nacionales* in 1977 pesos.

Note: All nominal figures were deflated by the external price index (EPI; Ffrench-Davis 1984) in order to convert them into figures at 1977 prices. Column 3 measures the percentage relationship between the deficit on the current account and gross fixed capital formation. Column 4 indicates the relationship between the deficit on the current account and gross domestic product. Column 5 is the relation between the deficit on the current account and exports of nonfinancial goods and services. Column 6 is the gross outflow plus net interest payments as a share of exports of nonfinancial goods and services. For the conversion into U.S. dollars of the figures for GDP and investment, which were originally given in 1977 pesos, the average real exchange rate for the three-year period 1976–78 was used, expressed in 1977 pesos per U.S. dollar of the same year.

was received mostly by the private sector while the government moved toward a budget surplus and amortized its external debt. This situation was in line with a deliberate policy of the government, adopted as part of its program of reducing state participation. This was facilitated by the change that took place in international markets: the loss of weight on the part of official financial institutions, which operated mostly with governments; and the vigorous emergence of private international capital markets, which offered access to both public and private debtors.

Table 5.3 shows the composition of the total outstanding foreign debt of public and private borrowers. Since international reserves grew steadily until 1981, part of the debt was not used. I call this the total "gross debt" and call "net debt" the portion used to finance the deficit on the current account (gross debt minus the increase in reserves). This has implications for determining the origin of the macroeconomic disequilibrium that Chile experienced (exogenous or endogenous) as well as for an examination of the effects of the external debt on domestic purchasing power.

When foreign credit has as its counterpart a higher current account deficit (corresponding, for example, to a similar increase in imports stimulated by a revaluation of the exchange rate or a further import liberalization), the recipient of the loan increases its purchasing power without a direct impact on the liquidity of the rest of the economy. When the external credit ultimately involves an increase in reserves, however, the

TABLE 5.2. Total External Debt and Debt with Private Financial Institutions, 1974–82

Year	Total Debt (U.S.$ millions)[a] (1)	Financial Institutions	
		U.S.$ millions (2)	Share in Total (%) (3)
1974	4,776	923	19.3
1975	5,453	1,352	24.8
1976	5,392	1,506	27.9
1977	5,763	2,144	37.2
1978	7,153	3,723	52.0
1979	8,790	5,885	67.0
1980	11,325	8,579	75.8
1981	15,700	13,169	83.8
1982	17,263	14,986	86.8

Source: Central Bank of Chile, *Deuda Externa de Chile, 1982,* August 1983, tables 1, 3, and 11; Ffrench-Davis and Arellano (1981, table 7).

[a]Total debt refers to the disbursed outstanding stock at the end of the year. In addition to the traditional foreign debt, it includes national currency liabilities, liabilities with the IMF, and short-term debt contracted by sectors other than the monetary system, with the exception of direct foreign-trade operations.

debtor's purchasing power is increased at the expense of the rest of the economy through a reduction of domestic credit or public expenditure or by restrictive monetary open market operations.

An estimate of the impact of capital flows is shown in columns 3 and 4 of table 5.3, which present the total debt minus the international reserves of the respective sectors. As the accumulation of assets was concentrated in the public sector (Central Bank), from 1975 up to 1981 this was reflected in a substantial reduction in its net liabilities. In the case of the private sector, in contrast, net indebtedness grew very rapidly, increasing by a factor of thirteen between 1974 and 1981. These data show clearly that capital inflows contributed substantially to the process of greater private participation in expenditure in the Chilean economy and to its concentration.

It should be noted that most of the private debt was contracted without state guarantee. Thus, in 1981 almost two-thirds of Chile's total debt lacked an official guarantee. That high share could have constituted a decisive bargaining factor in the renegotiations of the external debt.

With regard to the intermediaries, up to 1977 the private sector obtained a significant part of the credits directly abroad because of the quantitative restrictions faced by domestic banks in these operations. Two qualifications should be noted, however. On the one hand, the segment of the nonfinancial private sector with most access to external credit was that with the closest connections to national and foreign

TABLE 5.3.   External Debt, by Borrowers, 1973–82 (U.S.$ millions)

| Year | Gross Debt | | Net Debt | | Private Sector Share in Net Debt (%) |
	Public Sector (1)	Private Sector (2)	Public Sector (3)	Private Sector (4)	(5)
1973	3,276	786	3,063	716	18.9
1974	3,896	879	3,709	773	7.2
1975	4,426	1,027	4,252	931	18.0
1976	4,252	1,140	3,718	1,016	21.5
1977	4,319	1,444	3,763	1,339	26.2
1978	4,858	2,295	3,648	2,147	37.0
1979	5,018	3,772	2,882	3,053	54.9
1980	4,905	6,426	1,569	5,986	79.2
1981	5,145	10,561	1,878	9,761	83.9
1982	5,892	11,371	3,866	10,586	73.2

Sources: Calculations based on Central Bank of Chile, *Boletín Mensual* and *Deuda Externa de Chile.*
Note: Column 1 excludes state-guaranteed debt and external debt contracted by the Banco del Estado de Chile. Column 2 includes state-guaranteed debt and debt contracted by the Banco del Estado de Chile. Columns 3 and 4 represent the gross debt minus the international reserves of the Central Bank and the financial system, respectively. For measuring reserves, holdings of gold were valued at a constant real price of U.S.$42.222 per ounce of fine gold, base 1977.

banking institutions. On the other hand, a substantial share of these loans had bank guarantees. From 1978 onward, the domestic financial sector gained greater importance in the direct intermediation of external private financing. Table 5.4 gives details about the credits that entered the country under the terms of article 14. The private sector captured 94 percent of the gross inflows.

In spite of the expansion of external indebtedness and the increase in the current account deficit, the government did not show much concern in this respect. On the contrary, it maintained that what mattered was the way in which the real net debt evolved, the interest rate paid, and the sector (public or private) indebted.

The official figures for the real net outstanding debt showed a reduction over the five-year period 1976–80: it decreased from U.S.$5.3 billion in 1975 to U.S.$4.3 billion in 1980 (in 1977 dollars). Two external factors explained this reduction in contrast with the high annual rate of indebtedness. The first factor in terms of its importance was the rate of international inflation, which eroded the real value of the debt stock; as a second factor, debt also decreased in response to the rise in the value of reserves maintained in gold. These two factors explain a drop of U.S.$2.7 billion in real net debt during the five-year period (see Ffrench-Davis and Arellano 1981). Thus, instead of having decreased by 18 percent in real terms, the debt would have grown by one-third and would have shown a sharp acceleration toward the end of that period in the absence of these two factors. It was therefore clear that the rapid growth of external indebtedness was dangerous as well as harmful to

TABLE 5.4. Article 14: Gross Annual Flows of Credit by Debtors, 1976–82

			Percentage Breakdown		
			Private Nonfinancial Sector		
Year	Total Flows (U.S.$ millions) (1)	Public Sector (2)	Non-guaranteed (3)	Guaranteed (4)	Financial Institutions (5)
1976	262.6	13.3		86.3	0.4
1977	336.4	13.2		80.1	6.7
1978	780.2	4.2	31.0	26.0	38.8
1979	1,245.2	1.8	34.7	21.6	41.9
1980	2,503.7	3.1	14.5	17.6	64.8
1981	4,516.7	1.9	20.6	4.6	72.9
1982	1,770.8	24.4	24.7	6.1	44.8

Source: Based on data from Central Bank of Chile, "Créditos Liquidados Artículo 14," December 1980; and *Boletín Mensual,* no. 662 (April 1983).

Note: Column 1 shows the gross annual flow of disbursed credits minus compulsory deposits. The breakdown over columns 2 through 5 was estimated on the basis of that for Santiago.

national development, as will be shown later. Nevertheless, the government insisted right up to the end that entering into debt was good business because the real interest rate was very low or negative; furthermore, debtors were in the private sector, which was subject to "free" market laws so that, in the official view, there could be no doubt that borrowing was efficient.

Indebtedness and Macroeconomic Adjustment

The massive process of external indebtedness between 1977 and 1981 had significant effects in many areas of the national economy. The process profoundly affected aggregate demand and its composition, contributed to the spectacular concentration of wealth (see chap. 9 and Dahse 1982), considerably altered the functioning of the savings/investment process, and conditioned to a decisive extent the handling of monetary and exchange rate policies.

The initial impact of external indebtedness involved an increase in the availability of foreign exchange. This gave rise to two possibilities. One was an increase in international reserves, which is usually accompanied by an increase in the money supply; the other consisted of an expansion of the current account deficit. In practice, up to 1981, the growing indebtedness manifested itself in both ways simultaneously, since the net capital inflow was greater than the capacity to absorb it. The current account deficit steadily increased by considerable amounts (see table 5.1, cols. 1 and 4). In 1980, net use of foreign capital was close to the equivalent of 9 percent of GDP, in contrast with an average of 5 percent for Latin America as a whole. The difference between the volume of funds received and those used gave rise to the increase in international reserves registered up to 1980; in that year, Central Bank reserves represented 68 percent of annual imports of goods.

The rapid accumulation of reserves had substantial effects on the country's monetary and foreign exchange policies. Furthermore, the huge capital flows meant that a very high proportion of the total credit available in the national economy had originated from foreign sources. Despite its volume, the substantial gap between domestic and external interest rates persisted. The following section is devoted to these three issues.

Monetary Policy and the Crowding out of
Domestic Credit

From 1975 onward, net purchases of foreign exchange by the Central Bank constituted the main source of expansion of the money supply

(Ffrench-Davis and Arellano 1981, table 13): in the three-year period 1978–80, these operations represented more than 100 percent of the total money issued. As noted, the overwhelming proportion of net purchases of foreign exchange by the Central Bank came from the private sector. Indeed, in some years foreign exchange operations with the public sector even had a contractive effect. With regard to the credit of the Central Bank, the public sector recorded a negative balance from 1975 onward, whereas that of the private sector showed modest expansion throughout the period. This situation continued until 1981, when the serious macroeconomic imbalances that had been building in the Chilean economy began to emerge openly and the loss of international reserves began. Correspondingly, the monetary effect of exchange operations became markedly restrictive.

As indicated earlier, during certain periods direct restrictions on capital inflows were imposed as an instrument of monetary programming. One of these restrictions was directed toward controlling the monetary effect of inflows by limiting the amount of resources that could be changed in the Central Bank each month. This limitation was enforced — with successive modifications in the maximum amounts of exchange operations authorized — in September 1977 and was held up to April 1980 (Ffrench-Davis and Arellano 1981). These restrictions were not sufficient to keep inflows to the private sector down to a volume consistent with the monetary expansion desired by the economic authorities. Consequently, the latter took action over the other sources of money issue and on the exchange rate. In both cases, there was a crowding out of the domestic economy by the sectors associated with foreign financing. Domestic credit to banks was restricted in the face of the increase in high-powered money. The exchange rate, for its part, was revalued in response to the accumulation of reserves, thus crowding out domestic producers of tradables.

Quotas in the expansion of liquidity remained in force as long as the closed economy monetary approach predominated. Subsequently, in 1979 the open economy monetary approach was adopted. Under this approach, the nominal exchange rate was frozen, a "neutral" monetary policy was explicitly adopted, and a process of automatic adjustment of the money supply was scheduled to take place. Thus, changes in the international reserves were to be the determining factors of the degree of liquidity of the domestic economy against the background of a balanced fiscal budget and stable low bank reserve rates.

The monetary approach to the balance of payments survived until mid-1982, with a "neutral" monetary policy based on the dollar standard. During the last year in which it was in force, a contractive "automatic adjustment" began to operate, with disastrous effects on employment and output (see chap. 2 and Arellano and Cortázar 1982).

Foreign Exchange Policy: Instability and Appreciation

Financial inflows were crucial in order to allow the handling of the exchange rate in the light of objectives other than those of efficient resource allocation without bringing about a deterioration in the overall balance of payments (up to 1981).[4] The use of the exchange rate to guide expectations (in 1976–79) and/or to anchor domestic prices (1979–82) did indeed result in lower inflation. Nevertheless, net inflation persistently decreased more slowly than expected by the authorities. The exchange rate was used as a variable to repress inflation, appreciating the peso during the process. This, together with import liberalization and the recovery in economic activity registered between 1977 and 1981, led to a significant current account deficit.[5] At the same time, the gradual real exchange rate appreciation reduced the cost of external indebtedness so that in 1979 and 1980 this cost was negative. Consequently, the flows were encouraged by the evolution of the real exchange rate, accentuating the growing current account deficit and the surplus on the capital account. Some of the quantitative restrictions used to control capital inflows helped to make private capital movements independent of short-term fluctuations in the exchange rate. Mention should be made in particular of the minimum term of two years for indebtedness and the compulsory deposits decreasing with the term of the loan. Typical Eurodollar loans, with long terms, were encouraged strongly by the expectation of continued real revaluation.

Interest Rate Differentials

The official approach anticipated both a sharp tendency toward a drop in financial spreads and the leveling of domestic and foreign interest rates in response to the overall liberalization of the financial system. However, throughout the period large differentials persisted between interest rates for loans and deposits on the domestic financial market. The level of both rates was notably high. Furthermore, in spite of the

---

4. An analysis of foreign exchange policies between 1965 and 1982 can be found in chapter 4.

5. The increase in the deficit was also associated with the rise in interest rates and the deterioration of the copper price. With regard to this latter item, the smaller fiscal income from this source in 1981, compared to the average for 1960–70, was equivalent to 0.7 percent of the 1981 GDP. The current figures for the contribution to fiscal income of the large-scale copper-mining industry have been deflated by the external price index. The deterioration in the copper price was partly compensated for by the improvement in the price of molybdenum, a rise in copper output, and mostly the capture of the economic rent of the copper deposits for Chile due to the nationalization of these activities in 1966, 1969, and 1971 (see Ffrench-Davis and Tironi 1974).

huge capital inflows recorded, especially from 1979 onward, domestic rates were considerably higher than international rates, as shown in table 5.5.

It may be noted that the ex-post gap between the domestic and external rates for loans never dropped below an annual rate of eighteen percentage points. In this respect, the traditional explanation that the differential was due to expectations of a higher devaluation than the effective evolution of the official exchange rate do not seem to have been valid. For example, between 1977 and 1982 the parallel or black market rate was very similar to the official rate (Meller and Solimano 1984). The easy access to the foreign exchange market that existed at that time and the spot nature of the parallel rate do not make it a precise indicator with regard to expectations of devaluation over twenty-four months, which was the minimum term for the entry of capital under article 14, but they do reflect the prevailing atmosphere of a quiet market in which there were continuing sales of foreign exchange by the public over bank counters.

It is quite possible that the market was not aware of the need to make an adjustment for external inflation when measuring the real exchange rate. It is therefore probable that the expected "foreign interest rate," comparable to the real domestic rate on the market, would be closer to its nominal level in dollars than to the ex-post rate given in column 2 of table 5.5. This nominal rate fluctuated between 14 and 23

TABLE 5.5. **Domestic and External Real Interest Rates in Pesos, 1975–82 (annual percentages)**

Year	Domestic (1)	External (2)	Differential (3)
1975[a]	121.0	—	—
1976	51.2	−21.1	72.3
1977	39.4	0.2	39.2
1978	35.1	3.8	−31.3
1979	16.9	−0.9	17.8
1980	12.2	−8.0	20.2
1981	38.8	12.4	26.4
1982	35.2	45.0	−9.8

Sources: Based on data from the Central Bank of Chile; Instituto Nacional de Estadísticas; Cortázar and Marshall 1980; and Ffrench-Davis and Arellano 1981.

Note: In 1982, the "preferential" exchange rate fixed by the government for debtors was used in calculating the external interest rate. This rate reflects the dominant segment of the market, of loans between thirty and eighty-nine days. The international rates paid correspond to the interest rate for bank credits through article 14 plus the cost of compulsory deposits and the financial spread, all converted into their peso equivalents.

[a]Second semester, after the freeing of the interest rate.

percent in 1976–82. Consequently, even using this hypothesis, there would still be a substantial gap with the domestic lending rate.

In addition to the domestic-external gap, there were substantial differentials between the domestic rates for deposits and loans. There were various reasons for these high spreads, and their significance was changing over time. This issue has been dealt with elsewhere (Arellano 1983; Ffrench-Davis and Arellano 1981; Ramos 1986, chap. 8). We shall therefore limit ourselves here to mentioning some of the aspects that have the greatest implications for the focus of this chapter, that is, the external debt and capital flows.

Traditional explanations are as follows: (1) high bank reserve requirements are a determining factor in the gap between domestic interest rates on deposits and loans (the financial spread), (2) the fiscal deficit and the inelastic demand for credit by public enterprises are responsible for the high interest rates on loans, and (3) the restrictions on capital flows are responsible for the differential between r_f and r_e (fig. 5.1). None of these possible causes was of significant importance during the whole period, however. The first of them was of some importance only in 1975–76 because of the high requirements for non-interest-bearing bank reserves and over 300 percent inflation per year. Nevertheless, very large financial spreads, net of the costs of reserves, persisted during most of the period from 1975 to 1982. Second, the fiscal deficit fell rapidly and substantially (reaching equilibrium in 1975) and turned into a solid surplus from 1976 onward (Larraín 1991, table 4.4). Finally, in spite of the persistence of restrictions on capital movements, such flows were huge, as was shown earlier. Consequently, orthodox analysis is not capable of explaining why, with net capital inflows equivalent to an average of 8 percent of GDP in 1978–80, the gap between domestic and external interest rates stood at an average of twenty-three percentage points per year (see table 5.5). In this period, as noted, it was clear that there were still no expectations of a massive devaluation.

Therefore, there are other significant factors that explain the behavior of interest rates and the financial spreads.

1. Various data suggest that the banking system was inefficient and subject to rising operational costs after the reform. One of the reasons for this prior to 1977 was the underutilization of installed capacity. Furthermore, the fact that the system operated with such short terms for both deposits and loans constituted another cause of increased costs. This would seem to explain why in 1978 the operating cost of the system was on the order of 8 percent of total loans, a very high figure in comparison with international standards. Nevertheless, even after discounting the operating costs, the spread still remained very high.

2. The short terms of financing facilitated the prevalence of high

rates.[6] Those who had no access to external credit had to face a severe domestic recession simultaneously with interest rate liberalization. Against the background of heavy propaganda to the effect that the recession would be brief, many businesspersons resorted to expensive short-term credit instead of closing down their operations, expecting a rapid reactivation of demand. Under these circumstances, debtors did not view themselves as taking out a loan at a real interest rate of 40 percent per year but rather as borrowing for thirty days at 2.5 or 3 percent, with the probability of renewing the loan for a few months.

Effective demand, however, remained generally depressed until 1981 (and lagged behind aggregate demand), and interest rates continued to be high and unstable. Remember that only in 1981 did effective GDP reach levels close to the productive frontier (see chap. 1). Given the continuing delay of the expected reactivation, a devaluation for producers of exportables, and a reversal of the trade reform hoped for by producers of importables, entrepreneurs engaged in successive renewals of their bank loans, with the increasing risk that this involved (see Harberger 1985; Held and Jiménez 2001; and Mizala 1992). This phenomenon was further strengthened by the credit requirements of activities that were adversely affected by trade liberalization (see chap. 3). In spite of business expectations that it would be abandoned, the liberalization process was maintained and even — unexpectedly on a number of occasions — further intensified until it culminated in a uniform tariff of 10 percent in 1979.

3. Some opportunities for highly profitable "investments" did arise. Numerous public enterprises were sold at prices significantly below normal market prices. Similar opportunities were offered by investments in real estate and financial assets, whose prices rose notably in real terms: The stock exchange price index increased fivefold in constant prices between 1975 and 1979 and almost doubled in 1980. The elimination of regulations on the use of credit made its rapid redistribution toward these uses possible, which were extremely profitable investments from the private point of view but created no new productive capacity.

4. A noteworthy increase in consumer credit, especially for imported durables was observed. Here, too, the suppression of previous restrictions on bank credit for consumers facilitated the shift in the composition of expenditures. Furthermore, import liberalization promoted an expansion of the demand for credit, to be used for marketing imported consumer goods. Thus, on its way through the financial system the savings of some nationals leaked toward the consumption of

6. On various occasions, it was the falling rate of inflation and the lagging adjustment of the nominal interest rate.

imported goods. This is one explanation for the drop observed in the rate of national savings in contrast to the sharp increase in financial savings, which multiplied by six between 1976 and 1981.[7] In the four-year period 1979–82, which was the period of alleged great success of the economic model, the rate of national saving (measured as gross capital formation minus the utilization of foreign capital, as a share of GDP), reached barely 9 percent of GDP.

5. The gradual recovery of domestic economic activity and wages from the very depressed levels of 1975, together with massive official publicity within the prevailing authoritarian framework, helped to create an image of a dynamic and rapidly growing economy.[8] And as economic recovery on the basis of the utilization of existing installed capacity began to come to an end, aggregate demand was fed with the very large external credits that propped up a consumption boom until far into 1981. The atmosphere of success thus created, together with the consequent expectations of growing permanent income, induced consumers and firms to continue increasing their indebtedness while it prompted the banks to renew and rapidly expand their credit lines. Within this framework, the banking institutions competed with each other, partly by reducing the cost of services (the financial spread) but also by reducing the guarantees demanded from their borrowers.

6. The banks allotted a significant proportion of funds to related companies and individuals. Thus, for example, in 1982 the main private bank, which was controlled by the biggest economic group in Chile, had 42 percent of its portfolio loaned to firms that were openly and directly related to the same group (Harberger 1985; Held and Jiménez 2001). Consequently, financial transactions became mere internal group operations, weakening appraisal criteria and procedures for recovering loans.

7. In a framework of renewal of loans and borrowing to pay interest, the high cost of loans in the domestic capital market helped to increase the demand for them rather than reducing it. Thus, the factors described previously tended to turn the demand for credit more inelastic. At the same time, the high financial costs produced an increase in

---

7. The stock of loans of the banking system in domestic and foreign currencies rose from 9 percent of GDP in 1976 to 55 percent in 1981. Figures that include assets of the Central Bank are 33 and 62 percent, respectively. See Arellano 1983, table 4.

8. As demonstrated by Schmidt-Hebbel, "the explosive rise in consumption of tradables between 1976 and 1981 . . . can be explained, in one half by diminished restrictions on credit or consumer liquidity, and the other half by expectations of higher permanent income and personal wealth, to a large degree stimulated by official euphoria and propaganda" (1988, 178).

the demand for funds in order to pay interest commitments, with this effect predominating over the pure price effect. The magnitude of the effect of financial costs is illustrated by the fact that between 1976 and 1982 an average debtor paid excess interest, over a real "normal" rate of 8 percent per year, amounting to the equivalent of 300 percent of the initial loan. In other words, a borrower who effectively paid 8 percent to the creditor each year, renewed the principal, and capitalized the interest commitments in excess of 8 percent would be liable by the end of 1982 for a debt four times the original amount in money of constant purchasing power.[9] It should be noted that, in contrast, a debtor in foreign currency on similar terms in 1982, just before the devaluation, would be liable for a real debt 44 percent below that contracted in 1976. Consequently, even after a massive real devaluation of 80 percent the debtor would have ended up with a debt just equal to the original amount (and equivalent to only a quarter of the liabilities of a person with a debt expressed in pesos). This calculation is, of course, sensitive to the period taken as a starting point. Thus, for example, "late" debtors who took out credits in foreign currency only in 1981 or the first half of 1982 suffered a serious loss, taking into account the real devaluations registered in the remainder of 1982. This is in sharp contrast to the case of "early" debtors.

8. Finally, foreign credit played a role different from the one traditionally assumed. It is usually supposed that these funds enter into an integrated market characterized by great substitutability between resources of domestic and external origin, so that both types of interest rates would tend to equalize. It is probably true that the external credit did help to relieve the demand for funds on the domestic market. Nevertheless, the effects of the factors mentioned earlier were stronger and therefore pushed up the lending domestic interest rate. This was the result of persistent market segmentation. In effect, only some debtors could borrow directly from abroad or gain access to credit through the intermediation of local banking. As a result, the difference between the domestic and external interest rates reached notably high levels. As already stated, the explanation for this does not lie in the expectations of devaluation, since until far into 1981 these were of no significance, but it is to be found in the significant segmentation that prevailed in the financial market. Of course, this segmentation was not absolute. In the market, there were borrowers

---

9. These calculations were made using the corrected consumer price index. If the official consumer price index had been used, the total amount of the "real" debt would have been 5.3 times greater. The cumulative "error" in the calculation of the official consumer price index in the three-year period 1976–78 was close to 30 percent. See Cortázar and Marshall 1980.

who had simultaneous access to domestic and external sources of funds in diverse proportions.[10]

Credit of external origin was available on a very large scale, representing as much as 40 percent of the total loanable funds of the financial system (including foreign loans) in 1981. The interest rate differentials therefore had substantial effects from both the resource allocation and income distribution points of view. Small- and medium-sized producers were mostly relegated to the segment where high interest rates prevailed. In contrast, entities related to financial institutions and the main economic groups had easy access to external credit, either directly or through the intermediation of national banks. This noteworthy and persistent market segmentation helped to explain the spectacular concentration of income and wealth in these years.

Worsening of the Portfolio and Prudential Supervision

The external debt was associated with a domestic credit boom. Total availability of funding was expanded by nonguaranteed (see table 5.4, col. 3) and guaranteed (col. 4) direct external loans, external credits intermediated by local banks (col. 5), and other loans from these banks. These loans were based on the liquidity generated through foreign exchange operations and the corresponding accumulation of international reserves by the Central Bank.

The credit expansion took place in an environment of very lax prudential supervision. Credits to related parties grew at an accelerated pace, mostly without guarantees. To avoid the prevailing norms, debtors made use of cross credits and turned to dummy firms as well as operating from offshore institutions. In the face of high interest rates, the banks renewed the debts and allowed new credits with the objective of paying the interest commitments (or the capitalization of interest); between 1976 and 1981, loans rose by 38 percent each year in real terms. Nonperforming loans seemed to be low, and the banking system exhibited high profitability on capital, on the order of 17 percent in 1979–80.

Provisioning for risky portfolios, both total and individual, was low. In 1979, total provisioning was reduced from 2 percent of the loans to 0.75 percent, and it was stated that priority would be given to individual provisions but without implementing the latter. When the banking crisis exploded in January 1983, it appeared that 19 percent of outstanding loans had been made to related parties in 1982 and represented 249

---

10. There was also significant dispersion within the domestic market itself. For example, the average publicly offered lending interest rates exceeded the weighted annual average rate calculated by the Central Bank by five and ten percentage points in 1979 and 1980, respectively.

percent of the capital and reserves of all private banks. The profound weakness of the financial system as a result of the neoliberal reforms became evident in the following year, with enormous economic and fiscal costs mounting to nearly one-third of annual GDP (Held and Jiménez 2001; Sanhueza 1999).

External Vulnerability and the Dynamics of Indebtedness

The growing indebtedness generated great vulnerability for the Chilean external sector. In fact, the form assumed by the transfer of external resources and the incentives provided by the economic model led to a crowding out of domestic savings and a decline in productive investment (see table 5.1, col. 3) and, paradoxically, the crowding out of the production of tradables, which lost share as part of GDP (the production of exportables increased less than the reduction in production of importables).

As was shown earlier, for several years the real external debt did not appear to be growing strongly in spite of the rising deficit on the current account. The behavior of real net indebtedness, the ease with which new credits could be obtained, and the low real international interest rates led many countries to take a complacent attitude during the 1970s and early 1980s. This was backed up by the opinion prevailing in domestic official circles and international financial institutions (IFIs) that since indebtedness was predominantly private its use would naturally be efficient (see Robichek 1981, 171–72).

The growing indebtedness made gradual exchange rate appreciation possible. This, in turn, made it still more attractive to resort to external loans; thanks to the appreciation, the real cost of foreign loans was negative during almost the whole period of financial liberalization. At the same time, domestic asset prices rose vigorously. The process was thus self-encouraging, exacerbating capital inflows, which increased aggregate demand and allowed the continued exchange rate appreciation. This led to the growing accommodation of the national economy to a massive financial inflow.

In the productive sector, however, what was taking place was the opposite of what was expected by the government. The savings and investment ratios were notably below the levels reached in the 1960s: the rate of gross fixed capital formation barely reached an average of 15.5 percent of GDP in 1974–82, and in its best year (1981) it did not exceed the average of 20.2 percent of the 1960s. An increasing proportion of inflows was directed toward the consumption of imported goods, crowding out spending on national products and domestic saving. There was a discouragement of investment, especially in the production of tradables. The most obvious "comparative advantages" were located in the purchase of assets on the domestic market from deeply indebted firms at reduced prices. Except for some sectors making intensive use of natural resources — such as fruit production, forestry, and fisheries (which did indeed expand) and luxury construction — investors ran into the difficulty of identifying comparative advantage: exchange rate appreciation, high interest rates, the cutback of public support for productive development, the reduction of public investment, the sharp trade liberalization all combined to provide a discouraging environment for productive investment.

Paradoxically, in spite of the climate of euphoria and the close communication between the government and economic groups, productive investment languished in a context of drastic changes in relative prices and aggregate demand and the absence of an active and complementing role of the state (see articles by Ffrench-Davis, Foxley, and Muñoz in CIEPLAN 1983).

Apart from the poor performance of the productive system, it was obvious that the dynamics imparted to the external sector could not be sustained for long, even if there were no changes in the international environment. Nevertheless the official view was that the process would be self-regulated. It was believed that because there was no fiscal deficit, since the money supply was less than the value of international reserves, and monetary policy was "neutral," a currency crisis could not arise. Several authorities even affirmed that there were some economic arguments in favor of revaluation (De la Cuadra 1981, 1024). It was thought that imports of consumer goods would rapidly reach the saturation level and that the adjustment capacity of the economy had been strengthened by the reforms imposed since 1973. In contrast to these beliefs, when the international financial problems were about to emerge in 1981, the trade deficit amounted to 11 percent of GDP and the current account deficit stood at 21 percent. For a long time, there had been an evident need to reduce the external imbalance and devalue the outlier exchange rate (see Harberger 1985).

The Chilean difficulties in capturing external credits in late 1981 coincided with a domestic situation in which there was a pressing need for fresh resources in order to pay increasing interest and amortizations and cover the huge current account deficit. Regarding the first two items, the composition of external debt showed three strongly negative features. First of all, the prevalence of flexible interest rates amid significant rate increases in the international market together with a climbing outstanding debt led, between 1978 and 1982, to interest payments multiplied by four (to 7 percent of GDP). Second, short-term indebtedness rose from a "normal," sustainable amount of trade credit to 20 percent of the total debt in 1982 (or 13 percent of GDP), thus doubling its share. Third, amortization commitments of private debt increased at an accelerated pace and were projected to triple between 1981 and 1985.

Furthermore, the government had dismantled most economic regulation mechanisms, productive capacity had been weakened, and firms were heavily indebted. Thus, the effects of external shocks were multiplied in the domestic economy, with a decline of GDP of 14 percent in 1982, concentrated in the manufacturing and building sectors (with a combined decline of one-fifth).

In short, the external shock found Chile in a highly vulnerable position, and this multiplied its negative effects on the national economy. As documented in chapter 2, if the value added in financial activities and the trading of imported goods (both based on shaky grounds) is deducted, the per capita national product in 1981, before the effects of the shock, stood only at a level similar to 1974 (see table 2.1). Despite emerging modern sectors in the domestic economy, this is an unmistakable sign of stagnation compared to the growth of the region in the 1970s. Consequently, the abrupt deterioration observed in 1982 came at a time when the economy was already functioning badly.

Some Lessons from This Experience

I would like to emphasize four lessons deriving from the financial opening process. They refer to the distortions caused by indiscriminate opening with regard to equity and allocative efficiency, to the alternative ways in which domestic and foreign financial markets can interrelate, to criteria regarding the regulation of volumes of capital movements, and to the channeling of funds to productive investment.

Financial liberalization is not neutral concerning the allocation of resources, especially during the transition from a closed to an open economy, because of the pressures generated on variables such as the stability of aggregate demand, the composition of the money supply, and the level of the exchange rate. During the transition, it is necessary to adjust the structure of aggregate supply and demand and allow a bigger gap between domestic expenditure and output. The key questions in this respect refer to the optimum path to be followed by the adjustment, how to ensure that inflows are channeled toward investment, and whether access to external funds and their cost will be stable in the future. The financial market operates with very short term horizons and naturally does not take the repercussions on productive activity into account.

Consequently, it is essential that the opening process should be regulated in a manner consistent with macroeconomic sustainability (see Ffrench-Davis 2000, chap. 6).

With respect to the impact on the financial sphere itself, access to external credit is not homogeneous, not only because of domestic regulations but because of the nature of international financial markets. In practice, this type of funding has been available mainly to some segments of the national economy such as large import and export enterprises and firms associated with foreign financial institutions. In the case of credit for importers, for example, the differences in cost analyzed earlier meant that the opening process constituted yet another form of removal of protection from those engaged in import substitution. The differential observed among agents regarding access to and the cost of external credit affects not only allocative efficiency but income distribution. In particular, the opening of the capital account in Chile provided substantial profits for those who were able to obtain external credits (see Zahler 1980). There can be no doubt, however, that the effects and their distribution will depend on the forms of regulation and channels of intermediation used. Thus, for example, the effects on income distribution and the level of investment vary depending on whether the intermediation is carried out by enterprises, by commercial banks, or through the Central Bank or a public institution responsible for promoting productive investment (such as CORFO).

From another point of view, the shift from public to private entities as the destination of foreign funds and the concentration observed in the access to those funds had noteworthy consequences in the political sphere. First, they contributed to the spectacular concentration of economic power observed in these years. Second, they generated powerful antidevaluation forces, which, together with the prevailing economic ideology, gave free rein to the pronounced appreciation up to mid-1982. In this connection, the antidevaluation pressures of importers were reinforced by those of the economic groups growing ever more indebted in foreign currency.

A second lesson that emerges from the Chilean experience and others in the Southern Cone is that indiscriminate liberalization does not lead to rapid integration into a single market of domestic and external funding. Indeed, the opposite occurred. An alternative option leading to an integrated market, functional for national development, would imply: (1) channeling external funds, except for trade and compensatory credit, into a common pool with domestic resources; (2) eliminating the exchange rate risk borne by debtors abroad by denominating the external resources transferred to the domestic market in the domestic currency; (3) explicitly pushing the market toward a maturity structure consistent with productive investment, which calls for long maturity terms; and (4) regulating real interest rates with the objective of avoiding both negative real rates and excessively high rates, since both extremes are prejudicial to the efficiency of investment.

A third lesson is connected with the destabilizing nature of capital flows. In small countries and those where the domestic markets are not fluid and integrated, the instability can be very disturbing in the supply of funding to LDCs for domestic economic activity. A feature of great practical significance is that international financial markets experience sharp fluctuations, which are promptly transmitted to the domestic markets unless there is some form of regulation, principally during the expanding part of the cycle (e.g., in 1977–80). In addition to this overall feature of these markets, the supply of new funds available to each country in particular is subject to abrupt changes in response to variations in the lenders' perception of the countries' creditworthiness or profitability or in connection with the exposition that credit lenders are willing to take in each country. The latter is more closely related to the total amount of the debt than to the net flows in each period. For the debtor countries, however, it is the net transfer (net flow minus interest payments) and the corresponding financing of the current account that is the most relevant variable for their short-term policy and macroeconomic balances.

In the macroeconomic literature, there is a useful discussion on price regulations on capital flows associated with the externalities generated by marginal debtors. The policy recommendation is to apply an ad valorem tax on interest designed to compensate for the *externalities* that rise with the amount of debt (see Harberger 1985). This mechanism makes it possible to tackle the particular problem of a country that faces a stable supply of loans with a positive trend. Likewise, specific taxes can reduce short-term speculative flows by making them more expensive compared to longer term movements (see chap. 10 and Tobin 1978). Nevertheless, the existence of external instability in the supply of funds requires more complex prudential macroeconomic mechanisms, which tend to stabilize the volume of credit recorded in each period. This can be done, for instance, through the introduction of borrowing limits for national banks (a mechanism in widespread use in developed economies), the auction of external debt quotas, ad valorem taxes that fluctuate according to the intensity of the offer of external funds, and compulsory deposits. These will also carry out a fundamentally distributive function, taxing the differentials between domestic and foreign interest rates. When, sometime in the future, an abundant but probably unstable supply of financial credit becomes available again, we should not forget the lessons provided by recent years regarding the huge private and social costs of excessive and disturbing external indebtedness.

A fourth lesson is that, except in the case of flows of a compensatory nature, the regulation of capital flows should consider their channeling toward complementing domestic savings and investment. Insofar as these funds are directed toward the domestic financial market without any clear guidelines as to their destination, they can easily filter through to consumption. The experience of various developing countries suggests that the final use of funds is determined to a significant extent by the way in which capital inflows are regulated and channeled (see Ffrench-Davis and Reisen 1998). Consequently, the effective channeling of external funds toward productive investment represents a necessary condition if external saving is to contribute to capital formation and domestic development.

CHAPTER 6

Debt Crisis and Recovery, 1982-89

In 1982, the external shocks that struck Chile — the cutoff of bank loans, the rise of international interest rates, and falling terms of trade — and the "automatic domestic adjustment" process carried out implied a 14 percent plunge in GDP, the largest drop among Latin American countries in that year. The Chilean economy began to recover in 1984. However, only in 1989 did GDP per capita recover to its precrisis level.

In the early stages, the adjustment followed a rigorous orthodox approach in continuity with previous years. Aggregate demand was curtailed sharply through an automatic adjustment associated with losses in international reserves; most public policies were kept "neutral." Subsequently, due to the severity of the crisis, authorities moved toward more pragmatic policies. In order to ease the external adjustment, tariffs were raised in combination with strong real exchange rate depreciation. Private debt was — directly or indirectly — "nationalized," with the public sector share rising from one-third in 1981 to 86 percent of total debt in 1987. Interest payments were punctually served.

In 1987-88, Chile experienced three positive external shocks — a sharp rise of the price of copper, an agreement with creditor banks to postpone half of the interest payments from 1988 to 1991-93, and other foreign exchange savings resulting from debt swaps. As a result, the economy benefited from the relaxation of binding external restrictions, which allowed a significant aggregate demand expansion in 1988-89. In the productive sector, output was rising, essentially through the use of idle capacity. Therefore, effective growth between the previous peak, in 1981, and the new peak in 1989 averaged only 2.7 percent per year.

The chapter begins by summarizing the causes, uses, and effects of foreign debt accumulation in the period of large positive net transfers in 1977-81; then it focuses on the large negative net transfers in 1982-89.

This chapter is partially based on "Debt and growth in Chile: Trends and prospects," in *Debt and transfiguration? Prospects for Latin America's economic revival,* David Felix, ed. (Armonk, N.Y.: M. E. Sharpe, 1990). Reprinted with permission from M. E. Sharpe, Inc., Armonk, N.Y., 10504. The author appreciates the comments of José Pablo Arellano, Sebastián Edwards, David Felix, Stephany Griffith-Jones, Manuel Marfán, Carlos Massad, and Joaquín Vial and the collaboration of José Miguel Cruz and Andrés Gómez-Lobo.

An analysis of the macroeconomic adjustments in 1982–89 is developed, including an assessment of the relative importance of (1) external shocks, (2) demand-reducing policies, and (3) supply- and demand-switching policies. This is followed by a discussion of debt management after the crisis and a summary of the more pragmatic changes in policy design forced by the crisis. The final section focuses on the macroeconomic performance of the period in terms of GDP growth, investment, and sustainability.

The Debt Crisis

Accumulation of Imbalances in 1977–81

As was discussed in chapter 5, Chile accumulated a large foreign debt in 1977–81.[1] Borrowing was principally by private Chilean firms from foreign banks. The loans carried no guarantee from the Chilean government. Thus, there was major privatization of the sources and uses of debt (see table 6.1).

Until late 1981, net inflows exceeded the absorptive capacity of the domestic economy. Therefore, international reserves accumulated and exerted pressure for real exchange rate appreciation and import expansion. Since the growth of imports outran that of exports, the deficit in the trade balance underwent persistent and substantial increases. The external deficit was led by huge capital inflows, which stimulated aggregate demand and allowed exchange rate appreciation and further trade liberalization. This, in turn, encouraged the increase in imports. A proof of this causality is the accumulation of international reserves during most of that period (see chap. 5 and Ffrench-Davis 1982).

The growing capital inflows, which originated in the fast-rising international supply, were encouraged by the steady capital account liberalization in Chile. Furthermore, a very lax and passive prudential supervision (Held and Jiménez 2001), in combination with a relaxation in the sources of external funds, increasingly eased transfers of oil surpluses from bank lenders to the emerging markets (Valdés-Prieto 1989). The oversupply of external loans, in turn, financed and stimulated higher domestic expenditures, provoking a significant fall in national savings (Zahler 1988). Thus, foreign savings crowded out national savings as a

---

1. For more detailed analyses of domestic financial reforms in Chile, see Arellano 1983; Eyzaguirre 1988; Fontaine 1989; and Zahler 1988. A comparative analysis of Latin American cases in the 1970s and early 1980s is presented in Ffrench-Davis 1983b. The 1980s are examined in Devlin 1989; Feinberg and Ffrench-Davis 1988; Ffrench-Davis 2000, chap. 4; and Griffith-Jones and Rodríguez 1992.

TABLE 6.1.   Foreign Debt of Chile, 1975–89 (in U.S.$ millions and percentages of total)

	Total (1)[a]	Private with Guarantee (2)[b]	Public and Publicly Guaranteed		Private without Guarantee		Capitalized Debt (7)[d]	Total Including Capitalized Debt (1) + (7) (8)[e]
			Amount (3)	% (4)[c]	Amount (5)	% (6)[c]		
1975	5,453	21	4,667	85.6	786	14.4		5,453
1976	5,392	30	4,434	82.2	958	17.8		5,392
1977	5,763	46	4,479	77.7	1,284	22.3		5,763
1978	7,153	48	5,198	72.7	1,955	27.3		7,153
1979	8,790	76	5,369	61.1	3,421	38.9		8,790
1980	11,325	72	5,304	46.8	6,021	53.2		11,325
1981	15,700	69	5,623	35.8	10,077	64.2		15,700
1982	17,263	62	6,770	39.2	10,493	60.8		17,263
1983	18,133	1,815	10,497	57.9	7,636	42.1		18,133
1984	19,746	2,130	13,212	66.9	6,534	33.1	11	19,757
1985	20,607	2,348	15,242	74.0	5,365	26.0	85	20,690
1986	20,898	3,408	17,160	82.1	3,738	17.9	355	21,236
1987	20,722	3,276	17,894	86.4	2,828	13.6	1,187	21,844
1988	19,012	2,829	16,083	84.6	2,929	15.4	2,112	20,965
1989	17,569	2,120	13,568	72.2	4,001	22.8	3,436	20,629

Source: Central Bank of Chile, *External Debt of Chile,* 1990. Figures refer to end-of-year disbursed outstanding debt.

[a]Total including IMF and debt payable in domestic currency and excluding short-term trade credit to nonbank debtors; the latter amounted to U.S.$800 million in 1985 and U.S.$1.1 billion in 1989.

[b]Chilean private debt publicly guaranteed.

[c]Columns 4 and 6 are percentages of column 1.

[d]Face value of debt capitalized through Decree 600 and debt-equity operations through Chapter XIX.

[e]Column 1 plus 100 percent of debt capitalized through Decree 600 plus the redenomination value of capitalized debt through Chapter XIX: averages of 93 percent in 1985–87, 89 percent in 1988, and 84 percent in 1989. See table 7.5.

result of the nature and interaction of the financial and trade reforms carried out in Chile (see chaps. 3 and 5), the overoptimistic environment generated, and the fact that most flows were financial, with a low share of FDI.

Therefore, the national economy became increasingly dependent on massive capital inflows. This was of little concern in official circles, however. It was assumed that a currency crisis was impossible because the debt was mainly private, and thus would be efficiently used (Robichek 1981, 171–72),[2] and the fiscal budget was in surplus, with reserves exceeding the money supply.

2. It was supposed initially that no private loss would be taken over by the public sector. However, after the intervention and rescue of the Banco Osorno, a state guarantee on deposits in domestic currency was established in 1977 (Held and Jiménez 2001).

The foreign currency supplied by loans was used largely to finance an "excess" of imports of consumer and intermediate goods by the private sector (Ffrench-Davis and De Gregorio 1987), in a framework of low capital flight (Arellano and Ramos 1987) but depressed investment. In fact, about three-fourths of the net debt rise in 1977–82 was used to increase the import/GDP coefficient of the Chilean economy. The data suggest that, in net macroterms, none of the loans financed the expansion of productive capacity.[3] Excess imports crowded out domestic manufactures and investment in tradables, while the growing and unsustainable external gap made a future downward adjustment unavoidable.

It is interesting to highlight two contrasts, one positive and one negative, between Chile and other Latin American countries (LACs). On the one hand, capital flight was rather low in Chile, while in Argentina and Venezuela it was notably high (Frenkel 1983). On the other hand, the investment ratio was low in Chile, while Brazil and Colombia exhibited significant productive capital formation as a consequence of more efficient absorption of foreign resources (see Bacha 1983 and Perry and Junguito 1983).

The curtailment of foreign financing in 1982 coincided with notably high real international interest rates and a sizable fall in copper prices. Moreover, the Chilean economy had become particularly vulnerable to external shocks because the government had done away with most of the regulatory mechanisms that coped with external instability (instead relying on the automatism of the dollar standard or currency board) and because the private sector (consumers and figures) was overleveraged (Arellano 1983; Eyzaguirre 1988).

The external shocks, therefore, had an unusually large multiplier effect on the domestic economy. GDP fell by 14 percent in 1982, with manufacturing output falling by 21 percent. Expenditure reducing dominated expenditure switching policies (as will be documented later).

---

3. The fixed investment rate in 1977 constant prices was 20.2 percent in the 1960s. It dropped to 15.5 percent in 1975–81 and to 15.4 percent in 1982–89. This decline can be partly explained by the trade-policy-induced fall in the domestic real prices of imported consumer goods and the role played by the financial system in diverting resources from savings to consumption in a context of lax prudential supervision. See chapter 3; Arellano 1983; and Zahler 1988. But beyond the weaknesses of supervision an important factor was the euphoric attitude of people in the highest income brackets. As a consequence, there appears to have been anticipation of consumption based on overoptimistic expectations of growth capacity. Therefore, there was an intertemporal destabilizing adjustment. See Ffrench-Davis and Reisen 1998 for a similar destabilizing adjustment in Argentina and Mexico in the first half of the 1990s.

Recession in the 1980s

Chile suffered three severe negative external shocks in the early 1980s, which led to a sharp drop in the expenditure capacity of the economy.

The strongest shock was related to gross capital flows. After climbing to 19 percent of GDP, the use of foreign savings fell to one-half of that figure in 1982 and to one-fourth in 1983 (see table 6.2).[4] Clearly, the figure recorded in 1981 reflected a gross policy mistake, which allowed excessive indebtedness. Since 1977, the Chilean economy had been adjusting (in both the productive sector and expenditures) to a unsustainable level of capital inflows. Consequently, aggregate demand was exceeding domestic output, by unsustainable amounts, and even without an international debt crisis a major readjustment would have been needed in the near future. The fact that in the second half of 1981 — long before the Mexican crisis of August 1982 — GDP had begun to fall (Marcel and Meller 1983, table 1) is clear evidence of this.

Adjustment was unavoidable, no matter how well Chile might have managed relations with creditor banks after 1982. The best outcome certainly would have been a zero net transfer, and even that would have implied a huge decline in net capital inflows compared to those of 1977–81.

A second shock was the increase in interest payments that had been associated with growing indebtedness and an impressive jump in the financial cost of foreign debt since late 1979. The third shock was the decline in the terms of trade, which was led by the copper price drop.

Associated with these three external shocks, a serious domestic recession occurred in 1982. In the external sector, the shocks caused sharp reserve losses. Subsequently, an "automatic adjustment," set in motion by the contraction in the supply of foreign currency, exacerbated the reduction in domestic liquidity and aggregate demand. This resulted in a 17.2 percent decline in GDP per capita in 1982–83 and a decrease in investment. Therefore, a large gap soon arose between potential and actual GDP. The productive frontier expansion, in turn, lost speed because of the lower investment ratio.

The ideal adjustment in a perfectly flexible economy would eliminate excess aggregate demand without generating a gap between actual and potential GDP. In an economy with initial underutilization of capacity in the production of tradables, adjustment with an appropriate dose of

---

4. The figures used in this chapter are based on official national accounts, calculated in 1977 relative prices. Naturally, the external sector weight (and its associated shocks) depends on the base year. In 1981 prices, it decreases; in 1976–78 and 1986 prices, it increases.

switching policies could even achieve an increase in resource utilization and output. But, in an economy with price inflexibility, imperfect factor mobility, and limited or confusing information, neutral demand-reducing policies (i.e., policies that affect all expenditure components) can cause a significant drop in output because the demand for both tradables and nontradables diminishes. In the real world, adjustment processes usually involve a drop in output. This causes a lower rate of utilization of installed capacity and subsequently a fall in capacity formation.

Selective policies that facilitate switches in the composition of output and expenditure can dampen output-reducing effects. A good combination of expenditure-reducing and switching policies would tend to allow an outcome closer to a constant rate of utilization of potential GDP (see Ffrench-Davis and Marfán 1989). In fact, if an excess of expenditure prevails, as in 1981, then it is urgent to reduce aggregate demand. However, this can be done in combination with switching policies that are oriented toward reducing the demand for tradables and promoting the supply of exports and domestic investment (see Ffrench-Davis and Reisen 1998; and Ffrench-Davis 2000, chap. 6).

Here follows a brief account of estimates of the external shocks and the paths taken by GDP, aggregate demand, exports, and imports during 1980–89. The purpose is to provide rough estimates of two components of the economic costs of recessive adjustment: underutilization of installed capacity and slackened creation of new capacity.

All variables fluctuated widely in this period, as is shown in table 6.2. Economic activity peaked in 1981. The actual GDP of 1981 is taken as a close indicator of productive capacity as of that year (see chap. 1). In table 6.2, all figures are expressed in per capita terms and as percentages of GDP in 1981. Comparing any figure in a given line to its value in 1981 indicates the change with respect to a situation of constant GDP per capita and constant shares of all other variables in the table. For instance, the 1987 figure for fixed capital formation indicates a fall from 19.5 in 1981 to 15.5. As a share of 1987 GDP (the traditional indicator), the decline was from 19.5 to 16.4 percent. The latter figure, however, does not consider the investment behavior per worker or inhabitant, as is captured in table 6.2.

Actual GDP, in 1983–87, averaged 88.4 percent of 1981 GDP. As in the meantime potential output grew by some points (see chap. 1 and Marfán 1992), the gap between actual and potential GDP was even wider: 14.4 points per annum (table 6.2, lines 1a and1b). Exclusively, only in 1989 did actual and potential GDP converge. The significant underutilization shows that demand-reducing policies had strong negative effects on output, while switching policies (exchange rate and trade policies, the selective fiscal policy, etc.) were weak. This shortcoming was reinforced

TABLE 6.2. Production, Consumption, Investment, and External Shocks per Capita, 1980–89 (per capita variables in 1977 pesos as a share of 1981 actual GDP)

	1980	1981	1982	1983	1984	1985	1986	1987	1988	1989	Average 1983–87	Average 1988–89
1. (a) Actual GDP	96.3	100.0	84.6	82.8	86.7	87.4	90.8	94.4	99.7	107.8	88.4	103.7
(b) Potential GDP	97.1	99.0	102.0	102.7	101.2	102.6	103.4	104.3	105.9	107.8	102.8	106.8
2. Domestic expenditure	102.8	112.9	84.5	79.4	84.7	81.8	84.8	89.5	95.8	105.7	84.1	100.8
3. Consumption	79.7	85.3	75.0	71.7	71.5	69.7	71.1	72.6	77.8	82.2	71.3	80.0
4. Fixed investment	17.0	19.5	12.7	10.7	11.4	12.9	13.6	15.5	16.9	20.1	12.8	18.5
5. Domestic savings	16.5	14.7	9.6	11.1	15.2	17.7	19.7	21.8	21.9	25.6	17.1	23.7
6. Nonfinancial current account	-6.5	-12.9	0.2	3.4	1.9	5.5	6.0	4.9	3.8	2.1	4.4	3.0
(a) Exports	22.8	20.4	21.1	20.9	22.0	23.1	25.0	26.7	27.9	31.7	23.5	29.8
(b) Imports	29.3	33.3	20.9	17.5	20.0	17.6	18.9	21.8	24.0	29.6	19.2	26.8
7. Terms of trade effect	2.0	0.0	-2.1	-1.1	-2.8	-3.4	-3.0	-1.6	1.5	0.9	-2.4	1.2
8. Net interest and profits paid	-3.4	-5.1	-6.7	-6.6	-7.3	-7.3	-7.2	-6.0	-6.4	-6.2	-6.9	-6.3
9. Current account deficit[a]	8.2	18.5	9.3	4.7	8.5	6.0	4.4	2.7	1.1	2.4	5.2	1.8
(a) Capital flows[a]	13.1	18.7	4.8	2.6	9.3	5.6	3.6	2.8	3.2	3.5	4.8	3.3
(b) Change in reserves[b]	4.9	0.3	-4.5	-2.1	0.1	-0.4	-0.8	0.1	2.0	1.1	-0.6	1.6

Source: Author's calculations based on official figures of the Central Bank of Chile and chapter 1.

[a]Unrequited transfers included. Figures based on balance of payments data, which can differ from those of the national accounts.

[b]Figures based on balance of payments data, which can differ from those of the national accounts.

by the structural inflexibility in aggregate demand and supply, given the strength first of positive and then of negative external shocks.[5]

The three external shocks are measured in lines 7, 8, and 9 of the table. Line 9 shows the net use of foreign capital. In the short run, Chile could use its international reserves. That is the reason why this shock appears to be not as intense in 1982 as the cutoff in external financing. The Central Bank lost reserves by 5 percent of GDP to compensate for the foreign capital shortage.

The reserve losses, with a fixed exchange rate and passive monetary policy at the outset of the crisis, gave rise to the sharp reduction in domestic expenditure (line 2) on both consumption and investment. They were transmitted to the external sector (line 6), reducing imports and increasing exportable supply. To reduce the external gap, the indirect tool of an extremely large reduction in aggregate demand was used as the main policy variable.

The 12 percent drop in effective GDP in the quinquennium 1983–87 with respect to 1981 is the "static" output-reducing effect of the combination of external shocks and weak switching policies. In the "dynamic" dimension, investment per capita had fallen 45 percent by 1983 (line 4), reducing both potential GDP growth and the capacity to restructure the composition of supply and demand, which is directly associated with the level of new capital formation. Thus, the low investment rate reduced the possibility of a constructive adjustment of the economy. Furthermore, it was a crucial factor in the poor behavior of real wages in the 1970s and 1980s (see chap. 9).

The other dynamic effect is the impact of the output gap on the creation of new productive capacity. Actually, the drop in capital formation was significantly associated with the large gap between potential and effective GDP (Agosin 1998).

An "automatic adjustment" mechanism, as was used in 1982, relies heavily on the shock effects of demand-reducing policies. After a one-shot endogenous downward adjustment of domestic expenditure, as time goes by, some switching in demand and supply composition gradually takes place spontaneously. That reallocation was assisted additionally by an increase in tariffs and a series of sizable exchange rate devaluations within a crawling peg scheme (see table 6.3).[6]

Notwithstanding the delay and weakness of the switching, there was a gradual recovery of output and expenditure. This was greatly acceler-

---

5. When an economy has been oriented toward becoming more intensive in foreign inputs for a long time (as during the 1970s), it is not easy to reverse the trend without significant real costs.

6. In my view, the strong depreciation was a necessary element, but it was insufficient. The failure was in the lack of other selective switching policies.

ated by a sharp positive shock in the terms of trade in 1988–89 (line 7). However, by 1988, GDP per capita was still below the level achieved in 1981, while investment per capita was 13 percent lower. Only in 1989 did GDP per capita exceed its 1981 level. This was, in addition, the end of a cycle because macroeconomic overheating demanded a major new adjustment in late 1989 and 1990.

In the external sector, the automatic adjustment of 1982 was stronger and came sooner on imports, which are highly responsive to drops in domestic expenditure. Again, time allowed a change in the behavior of these two variables. Encouraged by large exchange rate depreciations, exports grew faster in the latter part of the period (table 6.2). In 1988, the quantum of exports of goods and services per capita was 22 percent above the peak level attained in 1980, while GDP was still below the peak of 1981.

It is interesting to measure the changes in exports and GDP between the peaks of economic activity in 1981 and 1989. Cumulative export growth per capita was significant: 55 percent and nine points as a share of GDP (six points if compared with 1980). However, the cumulative GDP growth was 7.8 percent. This implies that there was negative nonexport GDP growth (as shown in chap. 8).

The behavior of imports is also interesting. A strong recovery ensued following the spectacular drop recorded between 1981 and 1983 and the swings in 1984–86, which were linked to a minirecession experienced in 1985. Per capita imports grew by 57 percent between 1986 and 1989, a twofold increase over the per capita export growth in the triennium (see table 6.2, line 6). In the recovery following an adjustment such as the one carried out in 1982, it is normal for imports to grow faster than exports. Nevertheless, the difference in the rate of growth between both variables was excessive. The rapid increase was not evident in the trade balance at current prices due to a remarkable improvement in the terms of trade — led by the copper price — between 1987 and 1989.

Debt Management in 1982–89

In 1982, external debt was four times the export value and 71 percent of GDP. In the following years, there were five negotiation rounds with creditor banks framed by agreements with the International Monetary Fund (IMF) and the World Bank (three Structural Adjustment Loans [SAL] agreements).[7]

---

7. The five rounds — of 1983, 1984, 1985, 1987, and 1988 — are discussed in Ffrench-Davis 1992. An analysis of the Latin American rounds is provided in Devlin and Ffrench-Davis 1995; and Ffrench-Davis 2000, chap. 4.

Liabilities with banks represented, as mentioned earlier, more than four-fifths of the country's total debt. The negotiations with banks were geared toward rescheduling maturities, maintaining short-term trade credit, and obtaining new loans to finance part of the interest payments. The remaining interest payments were financed with a trade surplus and net transfers from other creditors. Net transfers to bank creditors implied a negative flow of approximately 5 percent of GDP per annum in 1985–87.[8]

On the other hand, official creditors played a crucial role as net suppliers of funds. Multilateral institutions (the World Bank, IDB, and IMF) were the largest lenders. The World Bank and International Development Bank (IDB) with positive net transfers of U.S.$300 million per annum (table 6.3). This was a relatively large figure, as the net transfers from these two institutions to all of Latin America averaged only U.S.$1 billion annually in 1985–87 and turned negative in 1987.[9] As a consequence, private creditor banks reduced their participation to 65 percent of the total debt, while official creditors increased their share from 3 percent in 1982 to 30 percent in 1989. The small outstanding debt with IFIs climbed with an average growth rate of 32 percent per annum.

With regard to transfers by debtors, the state assumed responsibility for an overwhelming share of total debt. In 1987, the public sector share peaked at 86 percent of total debt, if the publicly guaranteed debt is included. This figure was 36 percent in 1981 (table 6.1). This debt "nationalization" was carried out in three ways. The main one was the growing indebtedness incurred by the Central Bank and other public organizations in order to provide foreign currency to cover interest commitments, both to public and private agents.[10] This took place in an environment in which voluntary loans to LDCs had disappeared. Second, the state granted ex post the public guarantee to the foreign debt of domestic banks, under pressure from creditors and some governments of developed nations. Third, the debt swap program mainly reduced private debt (see table 7.3).

Debt kept growing until 1985 (table 6.1, col. 1). Then it remained approximately constant through 1987 at around U.S.$20 billion, though

---

8. Additionally, creditor banks received prepayments in debt swaps, either in cash or in shares of Chilean firms.

9. The "favorable" treatment for Chile is discussed in Felix and Caskey 1990 and Ffrench-Davis 1992. In 1985–87, Chile received 30 percent of the net new loans of the IDB and the World Bank to Latin America, whereas it produced only 3 percent of the GDP of the region (at 1986 exchange rates). It must be recalled that the multilateral Chilean debt was very small in 1982.

10. Furthermore, the Central Bank granted other significant subsidies to private debtors. See Arellano and Marfán 1986, Ffrench-Davis and De Gregorio 1987, and Sanhueza 1999.

with changes in the shares of the various creditors. The drop in bank debt due to debt equity swaps was nearly offset by a rise in debt with multilateral institutions. It was only in 1988 that large swaps produced a net drop in the total debt. That year the Latin American debt also experienced a decrease, though to a lesser extent: only 2 percent in the region compared to 8 percent in Chile (ECLAC 1988).

The government initiated a two-tier system in May 1985 that allowed the prepayment of debt with creditor banks (this is discussed in detail in chap. 7). Later there were prepayment transactions, leading to a reduction of the debt stock and some direct writedowns (Elórtegui 1988; Fontaine 1988; Larraín 1988). The system was based on (1) the debt promissory notes (*pagarés de la deuda externa*) held by creditor banks, which sold them at an average discount of 40 percent of the face value in the international secondary market; and (2) the direct capitalization or conversion of external loans in equities. Until December 1989, U.S.$9 billion were swapped through the different channels, and there were "economic rents" (the difference between the face value and market price of the debt notes) of about U.S.$3.4 billion, which were captured by the agents involved in these operations.

The main benefit accruing from the equity swaps was the reduction of the debt stock; consequently, interest payment commitments were diminished. However, they also generated a series of other benefits and costs, the specifics of which depended on the particular features and management of the swaps. This is analyzed in chapter 7.

TABLE 6.3.   Net Transfers Abroad by Creditor, 1983–89 (in U.S.$ millions)

	1983	1984	1985	1986	1987	1988	1989
Direct foreign investment[a]	51	−51	−56	−139	−57	−102	−5
Multilateral institutions[b]	167	248	349	266	253	109	33
Bilateral official[b]	−57	−101	−69	−60	−38	213	82
Suppliers[b]	−241	−154	−140	−7	131	−30	−19
Banks, MLT[b]	−178	−589	−718	−990	−988	−442	−791
Other MLT[c]	−21	−69	−24	−86	−100	119	104
Short term[d]	−834	906	0	198	−64	−423	405
Total	−1,113	190	−658	−818	−863	−794	−399

Source: Calculations based on data from the Central Bank of Chile.

[a]Net flows of foreign investment are disbursements minus net profits remitted after taxes; they exclude debt swaps, capitalization of credits, and reinvested profits.

[b]Net transfers from multilateral banks of medium- and long-term (MLT) foreign debt minus actual interest payments.

[c]Includes net interest payments to the IMF and medium- and long-term flows other than foreign debt.

[d]Includes credit lines, trade credit, other assets, interest receipts, and errors and omissions. It excludes the counterpart of debt swaps and flows for rolling debts.

TABLE 6.4.   Amortizations, 1987–95 (in U.S.$ millions and annual averages)

Creditors	1987–88	1989–90	1991–93	1994–95
Multilateral institutions	95.8	230.0	338.2	441.8
Bilateral official	25.1	82.5	179.0	185.7
Banks and financial institutions	186.6	244.5	851.5	728.2
Suppliers and others	171.9	242.5	219.0	143.6
Total	479.3	799.2	1,587.7	1,499.2

Source: Central Bank of Chile, *External Debt of Chile,* 1989.
Note: This table includes the effects of debt reductions through debt-equity swaps. It excludes amortizations of future loans required to finance the external deficit after 1989. Therefore, it growingly underestimates amortizations from 1990 on.

After the negotiations with creditor banks in 1987–88, which had relaxed the debt service, the external environment faced by Chile improved notably. The price of copper rose sharply, as did other export prices (cellulose, fish meal, etc.). The terms of trade improvement together with the postponement of capital services for 1991–95 (see table 6.4) implied that the binding external constraint prevailing in 1982–87 had disappeared in 1988. These positive shocks led to a spectacular increase in the amount of foreign exchange available (ECLAC 1988), which allowed the full use of productive capacity and then the overheating of the economy in 1989.

More Pragmatism in Economic Policy

After the first years of adjustment, a more pragmatic macroeconomic policy, aimed at expanding nontraditional exports, increasing domestic savings, and strengthening the corporate and financial sector, was put into practice. There was recognition that there were failures in strategic areas such as the financial and export markets (Larraín and Vergara 2000).

When external funding became scarce, an increase in domestic savings (which in 1982 had faded to 2.1 percent of GDP) turned out to be essential to financing more investment. In order to encourage increased private savings, in 1984 a tax reform was implemented. Several measures were adopted to cope with the weakening of public finances.[11] These included setting wage increases for the public sector below the inflation rate and reductions in several categories of public spending, including social expenditure. As a result, the fiscal deficit improved

---

11. Weakening was caused by the cost to the Treasury of the 1981 social security reform as well as a depression in imports and economic activity.

from 3.5 percent of GDP to a balance in 1987 (Larraín 1991). Given the way in which this balancing was achieved, it had an indisputable regressive bias, as discussed in chapter 9.

With respect to private nonfinancial companies, since 1982 most of them had suffered the effects of the high interest rates, recession, and exchange rate devaluation on their foreign debt. This, together with rather opaque banking practices and a liberal regulatory framework, laid the foundation for an enormous financial crisis, which forced the government to intervene with several financial companies that were experiencing problems, including the two largest private banks.

The government reacted to the financial crisis by implementing an aid program for local debtors and banks (with an estimated cumulative cost of 35 percent of annual GDP), which included, among other measures, a preferential rate for dollar debts, loans at subsidized rates for the financial sector, and the Central Bank's purchase of the banks' nonperforming portfolios, with a commitment from the latter to repurchase them (Sanhueza 1999).

In the mid-1980s, a second round of privatization was carried out. This affected forty-six companies (including financial institutions that had experienced intervention in 1983 and traditional public firms), which were quickly transferred to the private sector (Devlin and Cominetti 1994; Hachette and Lüders 1992).

Among the changes that followed the debt crisis were reforms in trade and exchange rate policies. Some tariff protection was reintroduced, with an increase in the uniform rate from 10 to 35 percent, a 10 percent drawback to minor exports, and other measures discussed in chapter 8. The reshuffling of exchange rate policy was dramatic, with a return to a crawling peg, after bypassing the nominal peg for three years, and a totally flexible rate for a brief period. But the most novel intervention was a series of sharp devaluations that accumulated a real depreciation of 130 percent between 1982 and 1988. Policies were accommodated to the severe shortage of foreign currency in Chile (a more serious shortage than in the rest of the region, as was discussed in chap. 5). These devaluations allowed a better response to external conditions by encouraging exports and a recovery in the production of importables.

The Chilean banking crisis of 1981–86, which followed on the heels of a massive capital surge in the late 1970s, left in its wake a number of valuable lessons that were reflected in Chilean legislation (see Díaz-Alejandro 1985; Held and Jiménez 2001; Renstein and Rosende 2000; Valdés-Prieto 1992; and Aninat and Larraín 1996). Therefore, a deep financial reform was carried out, which was based on rigorous prudential supervision and strengthening of the regulating agency (the Superintendencia de Bancos). The elements of prudential supervision included the continuous monitoring of the quality of bank assets; strict limits on banks' lending to related agents; automatic mechanisms to adjust banks' capital when its market value falls below thresholds set by regulators; and the authority to freeze bank operations, prevent banks in trouble from transferring funds to third parties, and restrict dividend payments by institutions not complying with capital requirements.

Debt and Economic Recovery

Chile fully serviced its debt and came to enjoy rather harmonious relations with its creditors, but the claim that it was able to both service its debt and grow cannot be sustained. That claim relies on the recovery recorded from 1984 on. However, it must be taken into account (1) that there was a huge GDP drop in 1982–83, which implies an artificially low base of comparison; (2) the sizable net transfers from multilateral institutions used to finance part of the payments to creditor banks; and (3) the high copper price that prevailed between 1987 and 1989. Notice that it took six years (up to 1987) for total GDP to overtake the 1981 level, while GDP per capita had to wait until 1989. Furthermore, disposable income was even lower than GDP per capita because of the negative external transfers and only in 1992 did the average wage surpass that of 1981.

The Chilean economy has been very unstable in past decades. In terms of output (GDP), in the 1980s Chile registered the worst drop in 1982 and the greatest expansion in 1989, compared to those of all other Latin American countries. Both changes (i.e., the fall and the expansion) were related to external shocks: deterioration in the terms of trade and foreign debt service, in the first case, and an unexpected improvement in the terms of trade in the second.

Apologetic versions of the economic policy implemented by the Pinochet regime emphasize the evolution of the Chilean economy after the fall, focusing particularly on the 10 percent increase in GDP in 1989. This is misleading for two reasons. In the first place, the greater the fall in economic activity the stronger the subsequent recovery can be. In assessing the results of economic policies, therefore, it is necessary to weigh the overall effects and not just one part of the results (i.e., solely the recovery) because this provides a biased view, particularly in an economy that has had so many ups and downs.

The second reason is that the great expansion of 1989 was not sustainable. It was based on transitory factors that allowed sharp GDP growth, and they could not avoid an overheating of the economy, causing negative effects on macroeconomic and macrosocial balances, which actually required a demand-reducing adjustment in 1990. In fact, the modest investment rate allowed limited sustainable GDP growth of about 4 percent in 1988–89. In reality, the average growth rate in 1981–89 was rather small: only 2.7 percent per annum.

Production Trends and Productive Investment

Beyond short-term fluctuations, trends in GDP are determined by the intensity with which new productive capacity is created. This is related to investment and its productivity.

In the period covered by the Pinochet regime, the average increase of GDP was around 3 percent per year, including drops as deep as 17 percent in 1975 and 14 percent in 1982 and increases of 8 percent in 1977 and 1979 and 10 percent in 1989. The moderate increase of GDP in Chile was accompanied by a strong expansion of exports. The latter experienced a real increase of 10 percent per year between 1974 and 1989.

The main reason why economic growth has been so moderate since 1974 is that investment has been low. Average investment in the sixteen-year period under study was 15.6 percent of GDP. This figure is much lower than the 20.2 percent ratio recorded in the 1960s. This is why, notwithstanding changes in efficiency, productive capacity expanded considerably more in the 1960s: the annual rate was 4.6 percent.

In the 1980s, real wages experienced a significant drop: in 1989, wages were 8 percent lower than in 1981. Three factors can explain why. (1) GDP growth was low (GDP per capita rose barely 0.9 percent per year between 1981 and 1989), (2) a significant portion of production leaked out abroad to service the heavy foreign debt accumulated between 1976 and 1982, and (3) the Chilean economy became much more regressive (see chap. 9).

Low levels of investment were related to the fact that productive capacity was underutilized for many years, as was emphasized in chapter 1. When capacity is underutilized, it tends to reduce the average return on investment, and consequently new capacity creation is deterred.

On the other hand, real interest rates remained very high until 1982 (38 percent in 1975–82), which undermined the financial position of many enterprises and discouraged new projects. After 1982, interest rates were reduced sharply, with some intervention by the authorities, but an additional negative factor was added: the foreign debt service. This implied that a significant share of domestic savings was not invested domestically but was used for interest payments to foreign creditors. Consequently, a much more intense effort was required from domestic savings or other foreign funds to finance investment in Chile.

A last factor that discouraged productive investment was that entrepreneurs devoted a significant portion of their efforts to the purchase of existing assets in a highly active process of property transfers. These were induced by the recessive imbalances that prevailed for many years in the Chilean economy, by an intensive privatization of state-owned enterprises, and later by the government takeover of private enterprises that had gone bankrupt in the early 1980s and were subsequently subjected to reprivatization. But also, in another policy shift toward pragmatism, there were significant incentives for the private sector to invest in exportables and public utilities. As shown in Moguillansky 1999, huge transfers took place, given the form of privatization or reprivatization that was conducted; by means of the rescue of agents caught in the debt crisis; the economic rents involved in debt-equity swaps (see chap. 7); the highly efficient drawback to exporters, and, of course, the much needed dramatic exchange rate devaluation.

The analysis of productivity in chapter 1 showed that the global productivity of investment, corrected by the rate of utilization, was lower than in the 1960s (see table 1.3). How can this be reconciled with the idea that productivity was much higher after the opening of the economy and the liberalization of markets? The answer is that the surviving enterprises tended to be more productive, indeed (Tybout, de Melo, and Corbo 1991), but this was offset by a higher mortality rate among enterprises and a lower rate of utilization of productive capacity.

On the other hand, there was greater heterogeneity among the surviving enterprises, including the new ones, than in previous years. Modernization reached into many economic sectors, but it took a long time to reach the majority of them. For example, there are peasant sectors, small businesses in trade and services, industrial workshops, and self-employed individuals who had serious capitalization difficulties and operated, in part, with lower productivity and income levels than twenty years ago. They managed to stay in business or find a job by scaling down their incomes.

The foregoing coexisted with the benefits of having a growing segment of highly productive and dynamic enterprises, both urban and rural. After the crisis, the surviving firms tended to be stronger than the average firm before the reforms. This was an important and positive legacy for the future. The export-oriented economic policies and the establishment of a market for natural resources and land (which was certainly aided by the previous land reform) provided the favorable breeding ground that enabled entrepreneurial initiative, particularly among members of the younger generation, to venture into risk taking and an exploration of new forms of production.

Macroeconomic Balances

Basic macroeconomic balances relate to the amount of money issued, the gap between export earnings and import expenditures, and the fiscal budget. Excessive and persistent imbalances in all of these areas have caused severe crises, hyperinflation, and recessions in the past. There is a fourth balance, which should be included in macroeconomic equilibria, although it seldom is, consisting of the relationship between the generation of new productive capacity and the increase in actual output (or use of capacity). The magnitude of this gap affects very significantly the level of capital formation and subsequently productive employment.

In general, the Pinochet government was very cautious with regard to monetary expansion and maintained the fiscal budget either balanced or in surplus. A positive consequence of these policies was moderate inflation (by Latin American standards). Nevertheless, there is evidence that such policies are a necessary but insufficient condition for economic stability. In fact, the external sector underwent a prolonged and rising deficit, which was financed with external borrowing for a long period of time (from 1977 to 1981). This led to the 1982 crisis. Furthermore, during most of this period there prevailed a large gap between productive capacity and its utilization (see fig. 1.1).

Following the severe economic recession of 1982 and a few subsequent years marked by uncertainty, a strong and sustained recovery of economic activity began in 1986. In 1986–87, this recovery took place in a relatively stable macroeconomic setting, with a progressive decline in the capacity utilization gap. However, in the following two-year period the situation changed: demand and economic activity expanded at great speed (at more than twice the speed of increase in capacity), and this culminated, in 1989, in an overheated economy when the growth rate of GDP reached 10 percent. The great expansion was led, principally as of late 1987, by an increase in private aggregate demand as a result of a considerable monetary expansion, a significant reduction in taxes, and real exchange rate revaluations, which made imports cheaper. [12]

Real aggregate demand grew very fast in 1988–89, by 22 percent; GDP increased by 18 percent, a deviation from the government's plans, which were aimed at 9 to 10 percent growth in GDP throughout the two

---

12. The private sector's amount of money (M1A) increased by 56 percent in the twelve-month period ending in October 1988 (the same month in which the plebiscite that the Pinochet government was forced to call was carried out). Taxation decreased by approximately 4 percent of GDP in 1988–89, and the real exchange rate underwent a 12 percent revaluation between January 1988 and June 1989, when the Pinochet government was forced to reverse this policy due to the accelerated increase in imports.

years and also contemplated a smaller increase on the demand side. The gap between expenditure and production was covered by the unexpected improvement in the terms of trade (i.e., the price of copper and other items). Productive capacity expanded only by roughly 7 to 8 percent in the biennium. The increase in GDP was based on the existence of installed capacity, which became exhausted in 1989 (see fig. 1.1), when the economy became overheated.

This imbalance became evident with a notorious acceleration of inflation and a strong rise in imports. In fact, on an annualized basis, inflation reached 31 percent between September 1989 and January 1990, a threefold increase over the 10 percent rate recorded by the end of 1988. The volume of exports experienced a vigorous increase of 23 percent during the biennium, but imports grew by 41 percent. The gap was covered by the extraordinary inflow of funds generated by the previously mentioned improved terms of trade. This improvement was centered on the price of copper, which doubled between 1985–86 (U.S.$0.63) and 1988–89 (U.S.$1.24). Copper represented half of Chile's exports, was produced primarily by a state-owned enterprise, and yielded high revenues from taxes and profits to the government.

Due to the existing maladjustments, the Pinochet government was forced to carry out successive adjustments, which included a devaluation in June 1989, adjustments to the financial market in April and September of 1989, and finally a sharp one in January 1990.[13] Thus, in March 1990, when President Aylwin took office, interest rates were notably higher, reaching real levels of over 16 percent for loans.

In short, when the democratic government was inaugurated in 1990 there was a macroeconomic imbalance, and an adjustment process was already under way in order to correct it. On the other hand, actual GDP had reached the productive frontier, and consequently any additional increase of output required, in contrast to the preceding years, a concurrent increase of productive capacity.

---

13. The latter was carried out after the Central Bank had begun operating, according to the tailor-made legal framework established by the Pinochet regime, which was enforced as of December 9, 1989, that is, five days before the presidential election.

CHAPTER 7

Debt-Equity Swaps in Chile

In 1985, the Chilean government set up a program to convert its high foreign debt into Chilean assets. In 1985, the external debt was equivalent to 1.3 times GDP, involving a financial service amounting to net transfers to bank creditors of 5 percent of GDP, much higher than the average for Latin America. The swaps program aimed to reduce the debt volume and its service and as a consequence to resume full access to voluntary lending.

The program was actively supported by the Chilean government and enthusiastically praised by creditors (Central Bank 1988). The latter pointed to the scheme prevailing in Chile as a model for debtor nations. In other circles, however, the official scheme gave rise to various criticisms.

This chapter briefly describes the main features of the more significant forms of debt conversion implemented in Chile and examines the volume and origin of the promissory note transactions recorded. The main effects of the debt-equity swaps are then reviewed, analyzing the costs and benefits involved for Chile. The chapter closes with some conclusions.

Debt-Swap Programs

Proposals for debt conversion have been around for a long time in the academic and applied literature. As a matter of history, in the 1930s many Latin American countries resorted to a form of conversion based on repurchase of their own foreign debt bonds at substantially reduced prices (ECLAC 1965). Chile, for instance, redeemed almost one-third of its debt between 1935 and 1939 at an average discount of 89 percent (Sanfuentes 1987, 29). The present value of all payments (principal and interest), after default had taken place, as a share of principal outstanding

This chapter is based on "Debt-equity swaps in Chile," *Cambridge Journal of Economics* 14, no. 1 (March 1990): 109–26. Reprinted with permission. The author is indebted to Robert Devlin, Felipe Larraín, Manuel Marfán, and Salvador Valdés-Prieto for their valuable comments and to Andrés Gómez-Lobo and Andrea Repetto for their assistance.

at default, was estimated at 31 percent (Jorgensen and Sachs 1988, table 1), a discount of 69 percent.

In the course of the 1980s crisis, such proposals were renewed and several countries conducted conversions, either in the framework of official programs or as isolated operations.[1] There was a rapid rise in the volume of swaps. This was encouraged by high discounts of debt notes in international markets. In fact, the average discount rose from 38 percent in 1986 to 66 percent in 1989 (see table 7.1).

The Chilean program was one of the earlier formal schemes and — given the size of the Chilean economy — was relatively the most significant (see table 7.2).[2] The official scheme was composed of two main elements, one associated with foreign investment and the subject of this chapter. Properly speaking, it was a debt-equity swap program (under Chapter XIX of the Compendium of Rules for International Exchange in Chile). It was available to residents abroad and designed to convert medium- and long-term debt owed by Chilean residents to foreign banks. The latter could use their notes representing loans directly or sell them at a discount to other investors in the international secondary market. The investor then exchanged the debt paper for the debtor's equity capital or with other debtors for cash or notes in Chilean currency. The latter could be sold in the domestic secondary market and then used for equity investment or to purchase productive assets.

When the Central Bank was the debtor involved, it paid with long-term debt notes in Chilean pesos. Hence, it avoided increasing the supply of money. However, it obviously increased the demand for funds on the domestic secondary capital market. This market absorbed the pressure well, both because of its fast growth at this stage of development and because of the emerging surplus in the fiscal budget, leaving space for the additional supply of peso notes from the Central Bank and other debtors. The investor was entitled to buy foreign exchange at the official rate, in order to remit (accumulated and current) dividends abroad after the fourth year following the investment and to repatriate capital after the tenth year.

To promote the dealings of minor investors, the operation of mutual funds by foreigners in Chile under Chapter XIX or Decree 600, which is the legal framework that regulates foreign direct investment (FDI) in Chile, was approved in 1987. These funds were invested in stocks or fixed income assets (which are not really *direct*).

The other formal component of the scheme was not associated with

---

1. Accounts of programs in the 1980s are found in Bouzas and Ffrench-Davis 1990; and Morgan Guaranty Trust 1987.

2. Studies of the Chilean case are presented in Central Bank of Chile 1988; Elórtegui 1988; Fontaine 1988; and Larraín and Velasco 1990.

FDI. Its aim was to reduce foreign debt (via Chapter XVIII), without subsequent access to the official foreign exchange market for remitting profits or capital. The Central Bank periodically auctioned to residents of Chile the right to purchase debt notes abroad. The auction enabled the bank to capture in 1985–89 around 30 percent of the discount of the Chilean debt notes, the remaining 70 percent being captured by other domestic agents. The purchase of debt paper was paid for with foreign currency obtained in the "informal" domestic market, capital that had previously "fled" abroad, or "laundered" money from other foreign sources.

TABLE 7.1. Market Price of Foreign Debt Notes, by Debtor Country, 1986–91 (face value = 100, annual averages)

Country	1986	1987	1988	1989	1990	1991
Argentina	64	48	24	16	15	27
Brazil	74	53	47	30	25	29
Chile	66	62	58	60	67	84
Colombia	81	79	63	59	62	73
Ecuador	65	44	23	13	17	21
Mexico	58	53	48	39	43	53
Peru	20	11	5	4	5	7
Venezuela	75	64	50	37	44	60
Average LDC[a]	62	52	43	34	33	41

Sources: Estimates based on Merril Lynch International Bank and Central Bank of Chile for 1986–88 and Salomon Brothers for 1989–91.

Note: Averages of monthly observations of buyer prices. The buyer-seller differential was 0.5 to 2 points.

[a]Average of buyer-seller prices for 26 developing countries, weighed by their outstanding bank debt.

TABLE 7.2. Bank Debt Swaps and Total Outstanding Debt, in Selected Debtor Countries, 1989

Country	Amount Converted until 1989 (U.S.$ millions) (1)	Share of 1985 Total Debt (%) (2)	Total Debt in 1989 (U.S.$ millions) (3)	Debt/GNP Ratio in 1989 (4)
Argentina	2.5	4.9	65.3	92.9
Bolivia	0.8	16.5	3.6	85.8
Brazil	10.1	9.7	115.9	26.6
Chile	9.0	44.2	18.0	68.8
Mexico	18.3	10.2	28.7	68.3
Philippines	1.4	9.5	93.8	46.9

Sources: Based on World Bank, *World Debt Tables,* various issues.

Other major debt swaps corresponded to loans previously associated with FDI, direct buybacks by the Central Bank, and miscellaneous buybacks, discounts, and debt forgiveness for debtors with financial difficulties. There was broad heterogeneity in the national welfare implications of the diverse swap mechanisms.

Up to December 1989, notes for about 45 percent of the disbursed outstanding debt, amounting to U.S.$20 billion when the program was launched in 1985, had been transacted (see table 7.3). Notwithstanding the U.S.$9 billion (at face value) swapped, total debt was reduced by a much smaller amount: roughly U.S.$2.5 billion, with the drop concentrated in 1988–89. This was the result of new net loans added to the debt stock (see chap. 6), despite the overall negative transfers (new loans and less debt service) from private creditors.[3] In particular, there was a significant increase in liabilities with multilateral creditors (the IDB, IMF, and World Bank).

As a result, a major change took place in debt composition, with a substantial rise in the share of official creditors and a significant drop in liabilities with creditor banks. As it will be discussed later, one-third of these so-called operations of reduction implied only a shift in the form of external liabilities (with a corresponding discount), not their elimination. Thus, the total and capitalized debt in Chile was still comparatively high at 75 percent of GDP in 1989. Moreover, its absolute amount was similar to that of 1985 (table 6.1, col. 8).

Effects of Debt-Equity Swaps

Debt-equity swaps involve a change in the composition of debtor countries' net external accounts; interest payments are replaced with profit remittances and principal repayments by depreciation reserves and potential divestment. Thus, part of the external imbalance moves from "debt accounts" to "FDI accounts" in the balance of payments.

A total U.S.$3.4 billion (equivalent to about 15 percent of annual GDP) was converted under Chapter XIX (U.S.$3.16 billion) and as direct equity conversion arising from loans originally associated with foreign investment under Decree 600 (U.S.$280 million). Operations were approved on a case-by-case basis by the Central Bank, with no commission involved. This did not allow the Central Bank to recover a significant portion of the huge costs incurred in the rescue of private

---

3. The devaluation of the U.S. dollar in 1985–87 contributed to an increase in the dollar value of debt in other currencies, a trend that was reversed in 1988.

TABLE 7.3. Debt Swaps Classified According to Debtor and Channel: Chile, 1985–89 (in U.S.$ millions)

Debtor	Chapter XIX[a]	Capitalized D.L. 600	Chapter XVIII	Portfolio Swaps	Other[b]	Total
I. Public sector	1,308	—	852	70	1,323	3,553
1. Central Bank	925	—	485	27	876	2,313
2. Banco del Estado	281	—	192	5	—	478
3. Public enterprises	102	—	176	38	448	763
II. Private Sector	1,853	276	1,689	85	1,532	5,435
1. Financial	1,852	153	1,600	78	75	3,758
(a) With public guarantee	1,830	2	1,522	78	—	3,433
(b) Without public guarantee	22	151	77	—	75	325
2. Nonfinancial	1	123	89	7	1,457	1,677
III. Total	3,161	276	2,541	156	2,855	8,988

Source: Central Bank of Chile, *Boletín Mensuál* (January 1990). Figures refer to operations already materialized.

[a]Includes U.S.$91 million operated through investment funds.

[b]Includes U.S.$440 million that correspond to two auctions made by the Central Bank; U.S.$357 million that correspond to support for fruit traders affected by the sabotage in the United States of Chilean grape exports; and U.S.$506 million in prepayments in pesos according to the restructuring agreement of the external debt.

debtors. A liberal attitude generally prevailed for authorizing swaps, except in the case of large copper-mining operations and other projects likely to receive contributions in foreign currency.[4] Nonetheless, as will be shown, the value of net cash FDI was low until 1989, which suggests that in practice there was some crowding out by investment financed with notes. In fact, a study by the World Bank revealed that there was substitution in the case of nonbank investors (Bergsman and Edisis 1988). I shall return to this later.

Direct Investment and Debt Response during the Cycle

It has been repeatedly contended that debt-equity conversion improves the country's defense against the dangers of economic cycles. It is worthwhile to examine whether or when this statement is valid. It is useful to distinguish between the capital stock, its flow, and the return on investment.

Undoubtedly, FDI shows a different behavior than do short-term flows. It is led by agents with long horizons of optimization, which

---

4. See Fontaine 1988. In 1989, a step in the opposite direction was taken, allowing operations in the copper mining industry.

implies that FDI determinants respond to variables linked more closely with medium- and long-term fundamentals. Therefore, FDI flows tend to continue in times of recession or crisis while short-term flows tend to do the reverse, mainly for expectations of devaluation. With regard to the outstanding stocks, FDI principally consists of highly irreversible fixed assets, while short-term flows, such as financial credits and stock market investments, are very liquid.[5] Consequently, it is common to observe a falling stock of short-term liabilities in critical situations; that is, a sudden stop and reversal of flows.

When we deal with long-term credits, the difference with FDI diminishes, particularly in the case of credits associated with FDI and long, fixed maturity terms. Also, suppliers' credits for equipment tend to have a stable supply. It is the demand for them, however, that tends to be weakened by the fall in domestic investment during a crisis.

On the other hand, it is claimed that swapping debt for capital has a stabilizing or countercyclical effect because profits are more sensitive to the economic cycle, tending to fall in periods of recession and vice versa. On the contrary, interest rates tend to rise during a recession. Assuming that the decision to borrow or accept FDI was made under "normal" conditions, under unchanged contracts, the debt-equity swap would imply a countercyclical change in capital service during the different stages of the economic cycles in the host country.

Several qualifications can be made to this simple case. One of these reinforces the conclusion in favor of debt capitalization. Several work in the opposite direction.

Capitalization of Self-Loans in Transnational Companies (TNCs)

The case of FDI capitalization of debt with the parent firm is clear-cut. Since it is an exchange of foreign assets within the same firm, the total gross return to capital would tend to remain unaffected. What formerly was distributed as interest payments becomes profits after capitalization. If the same taxes apply to both forms of return on capital, there is no effect on the net capital service for the debtor country. If, for instance, only profits were taxed, the net capital service would be reduced, improving the position of the debtor country. The situation in Chile, with taxation much higher on profits than on interest, comes very close to this case. This helps to explain the scarce conversion of credits associated with FDI.

---

5. In order not to be misled, it is important to control the statistics of FDI for "reinvested profits." These are partly in financial investments; thus, they are not necessarily irreversible and tend to be withdrawn at critical junctures.

Why do creditors capitalize some debt in this case? One reason is that the risk of suffering the rescheduling of capital and interest payments is larger than in the case of "risk capital." This was actually the case in debtor nations in the 1980s. As a matter of fact, there was a restructuring of the debt service, while arrears were common in many countries. Risk capital was hardly risky in this respect.

Variable Share of Profit Remittances
Indeed, not all profits are remitted instantaneously, as they are generated. Investors usually remit abroad a variable proportion of annual profits. Available evidence suggests that the share of total profits that is remitted is procyclical. This, in fact, happened in Latin America in the 1980s: the share of FDI profits that was reinvested in Latin America fell steeply.

The more accessible data for Latin America, which refer to FDI originating from U.S. companies, show that after the 1981–82 shocks FDI profits dropped considerably but remittances increased slightly in current dollars. Thus, the remittance rate (remittances as a percentage of net earnings) rose from 46 percent in 1980–81 to 88 percent in 1984–86.[6] Thus, FDI tended to enjoy more flexibility than the loan's creditor to withdraw remittable profits and reserves for depreciation during the debt crisis.

For short-run macroeconomic stability, it is the net availability of foreign currency that matters. Thus, another important item is the net flow of FDI; in recessions or under otherwise critical conditions, this flow also tends to be procyclical. Actually, during the debt crisis net FDI dropped sharply in Latin America, but the net flow always remained positive.

The same procyclical behavior was exhibited by FDI in Chile (table 7.4). Net FDI experienced a sharp drop from a yearly average of U.S.$332 million in 1980–82 to U.S.$84 million in 1983–86. Additionally, a substantial change can be observed in net transfers between Chile and foreign investors, from a positive figure close to U.S.$217 million per annum in 1980–82 to a negative level of U.S.$32 million in 1983–86. But undoubtedly this behavior was much more favorable than that of creditor banks and short-term flows (see table 6.3). Subsequently, there

---

6. These figures are based on the U.S. Department of Commerce's *Survey of Current Business.* In the period 1980–81, annual remittances averaged U.S.$1.68 billion; they were U.S.$1.92 billion in 1983–86. In 1983, remittances were larger than profits; thus there was a divestment of the undistributed earnings of previous years. As FDI lost relative importance as a result of the accelerated increase of bank debt in the 1970s, the figures involved became small in comparison with interest payments, which amounted to U.S.$30 billion annually.

TABLE 7.4. Capital Flows, Profits, and Net Transfers from FDI, 1974–89 (U.S.$ millions)

	Foreign Direct Investment[a] (1)	Profit Remittances[b] (2)	Net Transfers (1) − (2) (3)
1974	−16.7	8.9	−25.6
1975	−4.2	7.5	−11.7
1976	−1.2	5.3	−6.5
1977	21.4	23.9	−2.5
1978	181.1	35.3	145.8
1979	244.5	41.1	203.4
1980	213.2	85.7	127.5
1981	383.0	126.0	257.0
1982	400.8	134.0	266.8
1983	131.8	90.7	41.1
1984	71.8	116.8	−45.0
1985	72.1	129.2	−57.1
1986	60.3	126.2	−65.9
1987	105.0	151.8	−46.8
1988	124.2	206.5	−82.3
1989	269.2	261.3	7.9

Source: Central Bank of Chile, *Balanza de Pagos,* various issues.
Note: Figures differ notoriously from those of the Foreign Investment Committee owing to different definitions.
[a]Column 1, net investment. Excludes investment financed with debt-equity swaps and loans.
[b]Column 2, profit remittances after taxes.

was some recovery of net FDI, but profit remittances grew notably faster, as shown in table 7.4.[7]

*Old Debt Is Riskier for the Supplier than
"Risk Capital"*
Under "normal" circumstances, the present value of profit flows tends to exceed that of interest flows if both are calculated with the same pure interest rate; the difference would be associated with the larger risk taken by "risk capital." Under the abnormal circumstances following 1982, however, it seems likely that captive bank credit was more risky for creditors than typical FDI.

Creditors recognized that the hopes for normalization of relations with the debtor countries were unrealistic.[8] The prevailing perception

7. In the 1980s, the Central Bank only recorded distributed profits, disregarding undistributed profits. Notice that a sizable portion of investment by TNCs was financed with loans from parent or other sources. These are not included in the FDI figures. They were included in the foreign debt of Chile, although they were excluded from debt renegotiations.

8. The radical changes in market sentiment took place in the early 1990s, though predominantly with nonbank creditors. See Ffrench-Davis 2000, chap. 5.

was that bank debt was facing a high probability of one of two alternatives. The first was the long-term rescheduling of outstanding debt, with interest capping or "involuntary" financing of interest payments. The other was the "involuntary swapping" of old for new debt with a discount in favor of debtors. The discount could be related to the market discounts, which in 1989 averaged 66 percent for LDCs' debt notes. On the other hand, it appears to be more troublesome for the debtor nation (or less "worthy" since FDI was much smaller than debt) to modify the rules that apply to FDI remittances. In fact, debt service was "subordinated" to the service of FDI.

Consequently, leaving aside the capital gain implied by the note discount captured by the investor, it is likely that in order to reach an "indifference point" the expected rate of profit should be lower than the interest rate. The evidence suggests that the opposite was the case in debt-equity swaps. The domestic stock of productive capital was offered at prices punished by the recession and at additional discounts for investors under Chapter XIX. Therefore, for investors it turned out to be more profitable to operate through this channel than through direct credits.

Table 7.5 shows that Chilean debtors captured, through Chapter XIX, roughly only twelve percentage points of the 39.5 percent average discount on the international secondary market in 1985–89. If market trends are taken into account, a growing discount, and the mounting proposals by international authorities to give way to some form of replacement of old debt for discounted new debt, the twelve percentage points of discount captured by Chile seem to be a remarkable underestimate of potential discounts in the period under study. In fact, the Central Bank received a discount between 42 and 50 percent in two buyback payment operations in 1988 and 1989.

TABLE 7.5. Debt-Equity Swaps: Volume and Prices, 1985–89

	1985	1986	1987	1988	1989	Total
I. Debt-equity swaps (U.S.$ billions)						
1. At face value	32.3	213.5	707.3	885.9	1,321.8	3,160.8
2. At international prices	21.3	143.6	436.0	515.7	796.4	1,913.0
3. At redenominating prices in Chile	30.0	198.9	659.3	791.3	1,105.1	2,784.8
II. Prices (% of face value)						
1. International secondary market (I.2/I.1)	65.9	67.3	61.6	58.2	60.2	60.5
2. Redenomination in Chile (I.3/I.1)	93.0	93.2	93.2	89.3	83.6	88.1

Sources: I.1 are the Chapter XIX swaps recorded by the Central Bank from June 1985 to December 1989. I.2 was calculated with monthly figures of volume of swaps and prices in the international secondary market. I.3 is based on monthly estimates of redenomination in the domestic market.

If the real rate of return for the investor after taxes of equity swapped happened to exceed 7 percent (for a redenominated value of 88 percent), this would have implied that equity capital servicing for Chile was to become larger than real interest payments saved at prevailing high rates (10 percent nominal and 6 percent real, including spreads). Evidence suggests that profits doubled that benchmark. Later on, however, we will refer to the positive implications of the chronological sequence.

The Pricing of Swapped Equity

A third effect operating in the same direction — in favor of the foreign investor converting debt into equity capital in the debtor country — is that in periods of recession the price of domestic productive assets declines; stock prices in fact tend to be very procyclical. Table 7.6 shows the strong real fluctuations of the stock price index (in pesos) in the Santiago Stock Exchange in the 1980s.[9] These fluctuations become more intensive when the index is expressed in its U.S. dollar equivalent (which allows us to cross it with equity swap figures). Adjustment by the real exchange rate shows a notably depressed index apart from its instability. Between the second half of 1980 and 1985, for instance, real prices in pesos dropped by 64 percent. If the recession involves an exchange rate devaluation as an adjustment mechanism, in the face of an external shock, this trend is enhanced when stock market prices are expressed in U.S. dollars, showing an even larger real price drop of 77 percent. Therefore, when debt-equity swaps were initiated in 1985 the space for recovery was enormous. In fact, until 1989 the real index in U.S. dollars recovered by 187 percent. If these prices are used as a reference for an evaluation of FDI, which was concentrated in the purchase of existing local enterprises, the differential between the expected present value of profit rates and the interest rate, which is negative for the host country, will jump.

A strong increase in stock market prices in 1989 involved a substantial capital gain for "early" investors and a smaller one for "late" investors. This rise in prices was partly stimulated by the overheating of the Chilean economy (see chap. 6) but also by the intensity of debt-equity swaps, including the initiation of "foreign investment funds." Nevertheless, in 1989 it was still possible to buy 38 percent more shares with a real U.S. dollar than in 1980.

Devaluation is the best switching mechanism in an adjustment program facing external restrictions. Naturally, this also implies that the country's assets in U.S. dollars become cheaper for foreign buyers. This

---

9. I am aware of the problems of making comparisons of the index over time. Aside from the dividends policy and new stock issues, the Chilean economy did suffer dramatic changes of firm ownership, firm boundaries, and asset and liability structures.

means that, hypothetically, many debtor countries could be "bought up" easily by their creditors. A significant share of debt-equity conversions was associated with privatization of public enterprises or firms temporarily under government administration as a result of the economic crisis of 1982. Consistent with the government's desire to privatize as quickly as possible, with either local or foreign buyers, the rates of return on converted capital were considerably higher than interest rates.

The creditor banks, which made some of the largest transactions directly and held 40 percent of the gross capitalization, thus converted "bad" (risky) loans into "good" equity capital (Dornbusch 1988). Increasingly, nonbank firms became involved, too. After acquiring debt notes in the international secondary market, they also acquired existing local private companies and initiated some new ventures.

TABLE 7.6.   Indexes of Stock Prices in Pesos and Converted to U.S. Dollars of 1980 (1980 = 100)

		Real Exchange Rate[a] (1)	Stock Price Index		
			In Pesos, Nominal (2)	In Pesos, Real[b] (3)	Converted to U.S.$, Real[c] (4)
1980	I	104.2	87.5	93.1	89.4
	II	95.8	112.5	105.6	110.2
1981	I	87.2	102.9	88.0	100.9
	II	82.4	87.2	71.3	86.6
1982	I	81.4	79.9	64.4	79.2
	II	111.5	78.3	56.5	50.7
1983	I	120.8	65.3	41.5	34.4
	II	116.1	63.0	35.6	30.7
1984	I	119.6	78.7	41.5	34.7
	II	127.0	77.4	36.8	29.0
1985	I	140.4	87.3	35.1	25.0
	II	161.9	113.1	40.9	25.3
1986	I	164.7	164.0	54.1	32.8
	II	168.1	229.1	70.6	42.0
1987	I	170.9	318.7	89.2	52.2
	II	176.2	394.8	100.4	57.0
1988	I	186.5	407.8	97.2	52.1
	II	183.5	461.9	104.5	56.9
1989	I	176.0	629.7	131.5	74.7
	II	185.0	686.3	129.2	69.8

Sources: Based on data from the Central Bank of Chile and the Santiago Stock Exchange, average per semester of monthly figures.

[a]Nominal rate deflated by the CPI and inflated by the index of external prices faced by Chile.

[b]General stock price index deflated by the CPI.

[c]Equivalent to (3) × 100/(1).

The Multiple Preferential Exchange Rate: An Implicit
Subsidy for Foreign Investors

Given the discounts in the international secondary market, there was an inherent economic rent to be distributed among agents participating in swaps. Potentially, the discount could have been captured by debtor nations. It would have been a counterpart of or compensation for the sizable costs involved in the adjustment process since the early 1980s.

Chapter XIX implied a considerable capital gain or implicit subsidy to creditors or investors operating with debt notes. As a consequence, the note discount tended to crowd out foreign investment in cash for investment with notes. The first four and a half years during which Chapter XIX had been in force, the foreign debt notes were recognized in Chile at an average of 88 percent of their face value. The discount, therefore, was captured to a substantial extent by the foreign investor. In fact, only between one-fifth and one-third of the market discount went to the Central Bank or other debtors (table 7.5), with an average of 30 percent (i.e., twelve of thirty-nine percentage points). The remaining 70 percent was captured by creditors or foreign investors. This economic rent, which was distributed without an auctioning process or any other transparent allocation mechanism, amounted to U.S.$870 million (table 7.5, lines I.2 and I.3).

The same result, observed from the foreign exchange market standpoint, implies that the investor swapping debt notes under Chapter XIX benefited from the equivalent of an exchange rate substantially higher than the official, and even the "informal," market rate (Gemines 1987). On average, for the whole period the seller of the notes received, on a peso basis, 88 percent of the face value.[10] Since notes had been acquired at 60.5 percent of the face value, the peso amount received per U.S. dollar spent was 46 percent higher than the official rate. Why was there a preferential exchange rate for foreign investment that arrived in notes?[11]

---

10. Initially, the notes delivered by the Central Bank were quoted at approximately 93 percent. Commercial bank notes were priced between 92 and 98 percent (Gemines 1987, 22). The domestic secondary market discount was associated with the interest rate that the Central Bank paid on its notes, which initially was 0.5 percent less than the market rate (90 to 365 days maturity). The Central Bank modified the discount on several occasions according to the market rate. On demand by operators, the bank also issued notes in U.S. dollars.

11. The Pinochet government contended that "the present provisions allow the domestic debtor to capture the corresponding portion of the benefit" for the country. As a share of 70 percent of the benefits in favor of the creditor bank or investor was difficult to justify as an appropriate distribution, it was then pointed out that the investor resigned the state guarantee offered under Decree 600 and became submitted to restrictions not applicable to nationals, which—in the government view—allowed the conclusion that "the

Of course, an implicit exchange rate differential of 46 percent had significant distributive and allocative implications. It should be recalled that later, upon the withdrawal of capital and profits, investors would be entitled to the official exchange rate.

Justifiably, some representatives of the Chilean entrepreneurs complained about this notorious discrimination against domestic investors in areas in which their activities competed with foreign investors benefiting from financing with foreign debt notes at a significantly preferential implicit exchange rate.

The Net Flow of Actual Foreign Investment

The issue of the crowding out of FDI with fresh money is more difficult to tackle. How much FDI would have occurred in the absence of debt-equity swaps? There are direct and indirect effects and a variety of chronological sequencings.

One sort of information, obviously incomplete, is the data on FDI flows. The total recorded flow (of investment in cash plus that financed with notes) grew notably after Chapter XIX went into effect. However, an overwhelming share was covered by debt-equity swaps. In fact, the net FDI financed in cash was *still* significantly lower in 1989 than levels reached in the early 1980s.

Obviously, the option of financing investment with debt notes transacted at a substantial discount in international markets and then redeemed in Chile at close to face value tends to be more profitable for the foreign investor than cash direct investment in Chile. Net cash FDI averaged U.S.\$97 million per year in 1986–88, down from U.S.\$332 million in 1980–82 (see table 7.4) and substantially below the official estimate of U.S.\$315 million per year that had been projected in mid-1985 for 1986–88 (Ministry of Finance 1985).

Net FDI recovered in 1989, reaching U.S.\$270 million; a significant new component, with U.S.\$87 million corresponding to investment funds that were authorized to operate in the stock market at a reduced tax rate on profit remittances (a distortion that rewarded "financial" investment instead of the creation of productive capacity).

The gap between projections and the actual results was partly the result of a possible overestimation of the flow of FDI in government projections and of the negative effects of other variables influencing FDI behavior, but it could also reflect cash investments that were crowded out by debt notes.

operation is balanced." See the statement of Minister of Finance Hernán Büchi in *El Mercurio,* December 10, 1987. The huge amount swapped in 1987–88 and the low FDI, in cash, suggest that this statement was mistaken.

In some cases, the implicit subsidy was undoubtedly the determining factor in the investment decision. In other cases, the existence of the implicit subsidy was an incentive for any foreign investor to change the form of the financial investment it had intended to make in any event. Instead of financing it with fresh money, which would be subject to the official exchange rate, the investor naturally preferred to cover it with notes bought at a discount. Given the fact that operations under Chapter XIX were launched simultaneously with privatization of Chilean enterprises, under weak local acquisition capacity and a depreciated exchange rate, the price of the companies turned out to be low for foreign investors and expected profitability was high.

The tendency to crowd out cash investment could have been counterbalanced by provisions requiring a specific contribution in cash for every conversion of notes. In Chile, some important operations comprised both forms of foreign investment. This is one way to encourage cash contributions, conditioning to them the transferring of part of the implicit subsidy or preferential exchange rate (see Bouzas and Ffrench-Davis 1990).

There is a second piece of information, at the microeconomic level, which is drawn from a survey conducted by the International Finance Corporation (IFC) (Bergsman and Edisis 1988) among swap investors in Argentina, Brazil, Chile, and Mexico. The data presented here are aggregated for the four countries but differentiate between bank and nonbank investors. In the case of the former, the survey reveals that none of the investments made by banks would have occurred without a swap program (8), that is, what is denominated 100 percent "additionality." In the case of nonbanks, 33 percent of the transactions studied were additional and 10 percent were partly additional; consequently, more than half were not. The latter reveals a significant degree of crowding out of FDI in cash.

What would 100 percent additionality imply? Frequently, there is a misunderstanding about the contribution of swaps to the financing of capital formation. If there is zero crowding out (100 percent additionality), this implies that there are no net capital inflows resulting from the swaps: cash FDI remains constant, and debt-equity swaps do not contribute fresh funds. Additionality below 100 percent implies a negative net capital inflow for the debtor country.

Hence, swaps by themselves reduce debt but do not provide net financing in the capital account. The standard literature mistakenly tends to associate the volume of swaps with additional capital inflows that contribute to increasing net domestic investment (see several essays in Central Bank 1988).

If there is a debt-equity swap over an already existing domestic firm, there is no direct effect on overall domestic investment. It is only a transfer of productive assets. If the swap is used to create new productive capacity directly, ceteris paribus there is a rise in capital formation. However, this is in fact not financed by net capital inflows but by the domestic capital market — as, for instance, with the proceeds received by the investor that sells, in the domestic secondary market, the peso notes delivered by the Central Bank. The sale of these notes tends to put upward pressure on interest rates and crowd out domestic investment. To save space, we will not examine all the other effects that are set in motion. What matters here is that swaps do not directly provide foreign financing, and in many cases they are limited to the purchase of existing assets. But they could contribute to changing the mood of the market.

Other Effects

Direct effects on the balance of payments are extremely important in a debt crisis, but there are other major effects as well. A few of these are outlined here.

One of the most significant is the relation between FDI and national productive development and the ability to sustain an autonomous national economic policy. Can FDI be reconciled with national development and a national policy? Of course it can be reconciled, and it may even be a significant complement. FDI can contribute financing, technology, and improved market access for exports.

The last argument is more valid when, instead of denationalization of existing firms, the FDI principally contributes to an increase of productive capacity along with vigorous investment by local firms. What happened to domestic investment pari passu with debt-equity swaps? The gross investment ratio in 1987–89 was consistent with around a 4 percent growth of productive capacity (chap. 1; Marfán 1992, table 5). We will consider two alternative interpretations for the increase in the investment ratio from 14.8 percent in 1985 to 17.4 percent of GDP in 1987–89 (all figures in 1977 prices).

An extremely conservative interpretation assumes that the capital formation ratio in 1985 reflected a stable trend value.[12] Obviously, the assumption that a capital formation ratio of 14.8 percent was a stable value is hard to justify. This rate was only capable of supporting a capacity growth of 2.5 percent per annum (see chap. 1). Therefore, the investment ratio in 1985 was notably lower than that of the 1960s, when growth and investment rates of 4.6 and 20.2 percent, respectively, were recorded.

Given the exposed background information together with the information that FDI also rose under Decree 600, it is easy to deduce that

---

12. Agosin 1998 empirically tests the behavior of the investment ratio for Chile. The macroeconomic atmosphere and the right alignment of macroprices are determinants of investment performance. All were recessive outliers in 1985. See also Servén and Solimano 1993.

gross investment in fixed capital under the control of local investors (less assets transferred to foreigners) diminished between 1985 and 1987–89. This reflects the massive transfer of existing firms to foreign debt swappers without sufficient creation of new capacity by national producers. It is definitely clear that in spite of a considerable quantity of conversions and the recovery of FDI overall investment continued at levels significantly below historical achievements (see chap. 1).

The verification that a high percentage of the initial operations was merely a transfer of existing assets and to producers of nontradables proves to be quite illustrative. According to Central Bank records, less than half of the amount operated prior to July 1990 corresponded to new projects or extensions. This average changed eventually with time, achieving an expansion in the production of exportables.

The transfer of assets producing nontradables implies that there is no contribution to better access to export markets and that profit remittances will not be compensated for by an increase in the foreign exchange supply. Naturally, the same would be true in the case of operations with the existing exportables if export volume did not increase considerably afterward.

At the beginning of the 1990s, the Central Bank announced a more selective policy for operations under Chapter XIX. The following investments were excluded: investment in real estate, insurance, private social security, investment funds, stock dealers, and financial services. Priority was given to the creation and expansion of firms specialized in the production of tradables (Garcés 1990). Following the resurgence of the private capital supply in the early 1990s, prices of notes increased rapidly, especially for Chilean paper. Thanks to the quality of the democratization process and macroeconomic policy, they rose above 90 percent in 1992.[13] Thus, the official conversion mechanism had a natural end between 1990 and 1991.

Some Conclusions for Debtor Nations

It was frequently said that reducing creditors' exposure with debt-equity swaps would contribute to the resumption of voluntary lending. First, it should be understood what the assertion refers to. There was no voluntary refinancing of old debt.[14] On the one hand, in the late 1980s several

---

13. In 1990, U.S.$1.1 billion were reconverted, of which U.S.$418 million corresponded to Chapter XIX, with an average price of 67 percent and a redenomination of 81 percent. This way, the economic rent captured by intermediating agents diminished from twenty-three points in 1989 to fourteen in 1990.

14. Due to herd behavior among bankers, countries with improved fundamentals continued to be negatively affected by the high exposure of the remaining debtors (Devlin

LACs enjoyed some access to the voluntary financing of profitable investment projects, as happened increasingly in Chile. How much did this depend on Chapter XIX or investment opportunities, improved macroeconomic balances after seven years of highly recessive adjustment, and the export strategy in the debtor country? It is likely that the latter three were determinant. On the other hand, the decisive role of high copper prices cannot be ignored. In 1988–89, they contributed greatly to the balance of payments, with an unexpected inflow equivalent to about 8 percent of (the 1989) GDP. Given that exceptional inflow of foreign currency, the binding external restriction in the Chilean economy dissappeared.

Second, debt-equity swaps were stimulated by the discounts in the secondary debt market. Nonetheless, the discount itself discouraged the renewal of voluntary credits, for once granted their market value would fall below parity. From 1985 on, a rising volume of debt-equity swaps took place pari passu with a drop in note prices in secondary markets; average prices fell from 62 percent in 1986 to 34 percent in 1989 (see table 7.1). Still, in 1989 the perception that the debt problem was not being solved prevailed over the demand pressure exerted by swappers.

Third, in the case of Chapter XVIII the capital service was clearly reduced. However, under Chapter XIX the future capital service tended to increase, with a higher risc for profit remittances than the drop in interest payments.

The positive effects of the debt-equity swap were mainly concentrated in the savings of interest payments in a framework of extreme scarcity of external financing; it also contributed to a better knowledge of the national economy by foreign investors and as a variable for negotiation with creditors. At the same time, there were a variety of disadvantages and risks, as described in this chapter. This means that there were positive and negative conversions. It has been shown throughout the chapter that this diversity was present in the Chilean experience.

Debt-equity swaps could play a positive role whenever the following rules were enforced. First, the discount should be retained by the debtor country, either through negotiation or by auction. This involves a note price rather similar to the quotation in the international market, as happened in debt prepayments by the Central Bank, and not at a price substantially higher, as happened under Chapter XIX. It cannot be justified that foreign investors receive a preferential exchange rate in contrast with the remaining national and foreign investors. Second, priority should be given to increasing productive capacity, principally in exportables, in order to relieve future external restrictions.

1989). This herd effect was harmful even for countries such as Colombia, which had made moderate and efficient use of foreign capital (Bacha 1983).

CHAPTER 8

Export Dynamism and Growth since the 1980s

The development of the export sector arises as an outstanding feature of the Chilean economic reforms. The early trade liberalization carried out in the 1970s, the high rates of growth of exports, and the recovery of GDP recorded by the Chilean economy after the crisis of 1975 would seem to indicate a successful trade reform. However, that assertion is misleading. The import-led nature of the reform of the 1970s (the first trade reform), exchange rate appreciation after the mid-1970s, and the wrong intensity and sequencing of economic changes built up a discouraging environment for exports. The consequences became evident in the early 1980s, despite the positive effects at the beginning of the process (see chap. 3).

A second export takeoff emerged after the debt crisis of 1982 as a result of new conditions, such as a sharply depreciated real exchange rate in the 1980s and specific public policies, including a rather pragmatic second trade reform that reintroduced some protection to importables and to nontraditional exportables. Then, in the 1990s, the export dynamism was encouraged by a more comprehensive policy that combined both the principles of an open economy and processes of selective integration with some strategic trade areas, all in an environment of high investment and growing productivity until 1998.

Trade Policy in the 1980s: A Departure from Orthodoxy

In response to the deep recession of 1982, Chile had to adjust its policies to face the severe external constraint and stimulate domestic recovery. As a consequence, there was a change from the orthodox model implemented in the 1970s to a rather pragmatic economic approach that included some significant setbacks, from an orthodox perspective, with respect to the first reforms (see chap. 6 and Moguillansky 1999). In this new context, the generation of a trade surplus as a means of serving the foreign debt was given top priority. The strategy implied both the reduction of imports and the promotion of exports, which were done through three actions: an increase in the uniform import tariff, the use of a battery of instruments to encourage exports, and an active exchange rate policy to ensure external competitiveness for the Chilean economy.

Export Promotion and the Second Trade Reform

Chile's trade liberalization scheme is the oldest and longest continuously applied program in Latin America. In 1973, before the introduction of reforms, trade was subject to a great deal of government interventionism.[1] As was seen in chapter 3, in late 1973 trade policy reforms were launched that covered the elimination of all nontariff trade barriers, a sharp process of tariff reduction, and the establishment of a single exchange rate. Although it was not one of the program's initial goals, by June 1979 a uniform tariff of 10 percent had been established.

During the first trade liberalization program, sharp tariff reductions and the dismantling of quantitative controls appear to have had a great impact on export growth. The point of departure was one in which the large majority of domestic prices of current (consumer and intermediate) importables was not tied to international prices; consequently, there was enormous room for the reduction of costs by substituting imported inputs for domestic ones, and there also were broad opportunities for improving productivity. Additionally, in late 1973 there was a significant underutilization of installed export capacity, due to the huge distortions then prevailing in the Chilean economy; that is the more significant reason for the spectacular increase and diversification of exports during 1974. The fact remains, however, that because of the recessionary situation in which most of the reform was implemented, its abruptness, and the trends exhibited by the exchange rate and interest rates, the dynamism from the strong export performance was transmitted too weakly to the rest of the economy; indeed, fixed investment was far below its historical levels, and the economy exhibited a sharp deindustrialization (see chap. 2).

Rapid trade liberalization, in combination with exchange rate appreciation after the mid-1970s and early 1980s, provoked a great external imbalance, which multiplied the effects of the negative shocks associated with the debt crisis. Thus, the domestic and balance-of-payments crises that hit Chile in 1982, as a result of a combination of errors in economic management and negative external shocks (see chap. 6), caused aggregate demand to fall by 30 percent and GDP to shrink by over 14 percent

---

1. Notice that this was the situation in 1973. However, in the second half of the 1960s, there was a comprehensive reform in process that included the gradual rationalization of the import regime, the enhancement of mechanisms of export promotion, and a consistent implementation of a crawling peg exchange rate policy (Ffrench-Davis, 1973).

between 1981 and 1983. In an effort to cope with the crisis, a number of discrete devaluations were applied since mid-1982, and later a crawling peg was reintroduced. At the same time, the uniform tariff was raised in stages up to 35 percent in September 1984 (with annual averages of 24 percent in 1984 and 26 percent in 1985). As the severe shortage of foreign exchange began to ease, the tariff was gradually lowered again, first to 30 percent in March 1985, then to 20 percent in June, to 15 percent in 1988, and to 11 percent by mid-1991.

Following the 1982 crisis, trade policy became more flexible in several respects. The government began to make somewhat active use of antidumping measures to protect the economy from unfair trade practices. To this end, the total tariff (the uniform rate plus compensatory surcharges) was raised to a maximum of 35 percent — the level to which Chile had committed itself under the terms of GATT in 1979 — on imports that Chile could prove were being dumped. In addition, price bands, supposedly consistent with international price medium-term trends, were set for three main agricultural products (wheat, sugar, and oil seeds); given the then depressed international prices, this had significant encouraging effects on agriculture and also constituted a departure from the uniform tariff. With regard to exports, the drawback was extended to a simplified system for minor exports; under this system, many nontraditional exports became eligible for a refund of up to 10 percent of their foreign currency proceeds so long as total sales of the corresponding item did not exceed a given annual maximum. Box 8.1 summarizes the main mechanisms used to promote exports.

One of the outstanding initiatives of export promotion was developed by the Chile Foundation, a semipublic institution. The foundation's first efforts were directed mainly at providing technical assistance to a number of projects. Few of these early projects got beyond the pilot stage. In view of this problem, the foundation decided it needed to gain more experience by launching business projects of its own. The idea was to determine which activities might benefit from new technologies and then to acquire and adapt these technologies. Once a technology was assimilated, the foundation would take charge of commercial production and marketing through a subsidiary. When the subsidiary became profitable, it would be sold, thereby completing the technology-transfer process.

Salmon farming is one example of a very successful initiative. In 1981, the foundation decided to carry out a pilot project using a cage-based technique of freshwater salmon farming. Commercial production began in the period 1986–87, and output doubled in the following period. The project began to turn a profit in 1988, and the technology-transfer cycle was completed that same year when the foundation sold

Box 8.1. Export Incentives by the Late 1980s

Exemption from the value-added tax on exports and the refund of taxes paid on inputs incorporated into exports. This mechanism is designed to avoid double taxation on final products (Decree Law of 1974).

Simplified tax rebates or drawbacks on minor export items (nontraditional products) in the form of refunds of 10 or 5 percent of the *fob* value of exports (Act of 1985).

Waiver of duties and value-added tax (VAT) on imputs imported for use in production of goods for exports on premises designated for that purpose (Fiscal Decree of 1986).

Deferred payment of customs duty on imports of capital goods. This provision is of general applicability and is not confined to exporters (Act of 1987).

Rebate of customs duties paid on imported inputs incorporated into export products (Act of 1988).

Source: Ffrench-Davis, Leiva, and Madrid 1992.

the project to a Japanese fish and shellfish company. This project gave a definite boost to overall salmon output in Chile, which became one of the top Chilean exports and the main nontraditional one in the 1990s (ECLAC 1998).

In summary, Chile carried out a "second trade reform," with a mix of restrictions, liberalization, and intervention, after 1983. While it is true that the basic characteristics of the country's trade policy — in terms of the dismissal of nontariff barriers and the adoption of a uniform tariff — had not changed since 1979, it must be recognized that the tariff had once again become relatively high by 1984 and was accompanied by antidumping measures and the price bands mentioned previously. In fact, the tariff level averaged 20 percent in 1984–89, which was double the average rate for 1979–82. The greatest difference, however, was that during the first liberalization drive the exchange rate had appreciated steadily in the second half of the 1970s and in the early 1980s. During the 1980s, on the other hand, the reduction of the tariff from its maximum level of 35 percent in 1984 to 15 percent by 1988 was accompanied by a sharp real depreciation, under the pressure of the debt crisis (see table 8.1). This sent out powerful signals to exporters while at the same time encouraging the production of import-competing goods. Moreover, the tariff rate all along was higher than it had been in 1979–82. Unlike the first liberalization effort, the increase in exports was also coupled with a strong upturn in the output of import substitutes, especially between 1984 and the late 1980s.

If we are to draw any conclusions from the trade reform processes experienced by Chile, one of them must certainly be that the second reform program yielded better results than the first (chap. 3; ECLAC 1998, chap. 5; Ffrench-Davis, Leiva, and Madrid 1992).

The Evolution of Exchange Rate Policy

Exchange rate policy has experienced substantial change over time. Beginning in 1976, the nominal rate began to be used to fight inflation (see chap. 4). This was because inflation stubbornly refused to slow down in reaction to the deep economic recession, which also caused a surplus on current account in 1976. The real revaluation that usually results from using the exchange rate as an anchor was intensified in 1979, when the rate was fixed in current pesos, at a nominal parity of 39 pesos that was maintained until the crisis of 1982; a significant real appreciation took place during this triennium. After a period of experimentation with

TABLE 8.1.   Average Tariff and the Real Exchange Rate, 1973–2000 (annual averages)

Year	Average Tariff[a] (%)	Real Exchange Rate[b] (1986 = 100)
1973	94.0[c]	65.1[c]
1974–79	35.3	73.2
1980–82	10.1	57.6
1983–85	22.7	79.1
1986–89	17.6	106.6
1990–95	12.0	99.5
1996–98	11.0	80.3
1999–2000	9.5	84.1

Sources: Ffrench-Davis, Leiva, and Madrid 1992; Central Bank of Chile.

[a]Simple average, excluding exemptions and preferential arrangements negotiated with LACs.

[b]Annual averages. The nominal exchange rate was deflated by the Chilean Consumer Price Index (CPI; duly corrected in 1973–78) and inflated by an external price index. This index was constructed on the basis of the index of wholesale prices, weighted by the share in Chilean trade of Argentina, Brazil, Canada, France, Germany, Italy, Japan, Peru, Korea, Spain, the United Kingdom, and the United States, from 1986 on; it was obtained from the Central Bank of Chile. For the years up to 1985, the information was taken from Ffrench-Davis, Leiva, and Madrid 1992 and includes France, Germany, Japan, the United Kingdom, and the United States.

[c]As of December 1973.

successive policy changes, a crawling peg exchange rate was again adopted in 1983 and used thereafter. Basically, the Central Bank fixed a benchmark price for the dollar on the official market (called the "agreed" exchange rate), with a floating band initially of ±2 percent. The "official" rate was devalued daily, in line with the differential between domestic inflation and an estimate of external inflation. On a number of occasions, discrete real devaluations were added, helping to achieve the spectacular real depreciation following the 1982 crisis (130 percent between 1982 and 1988).

Because various foreign exchange controls remained in force (except for a few weeks in 1982), there also operated in parallel an illegal (but openly tolerated) foreign currency market. This was legalized as the "informal" foreign exchange market only in April 1990, under the provisions of the Central Bank Autonomy Act issued in the last days of the Pinochet government.

In 1988, revaluations together with tax and tariff reductions managed to reconcile a reduction in inflation with a sharp recovery in aggregate demand and economic activity. The recovery was completed in 1989, with economic activity then climbing up to the production frontier (see chap. 1). The tax and tariff reductions and exchange rate appreciation in 1988 were directly associated with the additional income generated by a sudden jump in the copper price in 1987–89; the improvement in the terms of trade in 1988 with respect to 1986 was equivalent to 6 percent of GDP (measured at 1986 constant prices). A sizable increase in imports and in the current-account deficit in 1989 (if the current account is recalculated using the "normalized" price of the Copper Stabilization Fund), together with new inflationary pressures, led the Central Bank to reverse earlier reductions in interest rates.

By mid-1989, the dollar floating band was widened further to ±5 percent. The Central Bank's action was accompanied by a shift in the foreign currency market expectations, which led the market to move quickly to the ceiling of the band (the depreciated corner). Thus, with no great trauma, a significant depreciation was achieved without modifying the "official" rate. For about a year, which included the return to a democratic regime, presidential elections (in December 1989), and the inauguration of President Aylwin (in March 1990), the observed exchange rate remained at the ceiling of the band. This occurred despite the fact that the adjustment process was tightened in January 1990 to control the jump in inflation (which had reached an annualized rate of 31 percent in the five preceding months). The downward adjustment in economic activity was based on a sharp rise in interest rates, which was led by a Central Bank ten-year paper, offered at the high real annual rate of 9.7 percent.

Trade Policies since 1990

The economic team that took office in 1990 maintained the basic principles of the past trade policy, except for the introduction of reciprocated trade agreements with several partners, mostly in Latin America. The economy remained open to trade, and there was continuity in terms of maintaining a uniform import tariff rate for the rest of the world; the rate of 11 percent was retained from 1991 up to 1999, when a gradual reduction of five points for 1999–2003 was initiated. The macroeconomic policies, however, were substantially modified, in a significant *reform to the reforms* (see chaps. 1 and 10).

Toward a "Reciprocated" Trade Policy

Undoubtedly, the most important feature of the Chilean trade policy of the 1990s was the search for arrangements to expand access to export markets. The new political conditions allowed a clear turning point in the Chilean approach, moving from an across-the-board unilateral openness toward a strategy that also included preferential free trade agreements (FTA) subject to reciprocity.

Since the Chilean economy already showed advanced trade liberalization, the benefits from further unilateral openness were estimated to be small in a world where trade areas and economic blocks were increasingly important (Ffrench-Davis 2000, chap. 8). Advancing in economic integration in Latin American was seen as a form of *open regionalism.*

As a result of the active policy, economic complementarity agreements were signed with countries of the Andean Community, that is, Bolivia (1993), Venezuela (1993), Colombia (1994), Ecuador (1995), and Peru (1998), and with the Central American Common Market (1999). In the case of MERCOSUR (Mercado Común del Sur) — the main Latin American market, including Argentina, Brazil, Paraguay, and Uruguay — an agreement was signed in 1996 and a free trade area was scheduled for 2004.

Deep integration was reached with Mexico (1991 and 1999) and Canada (1997) through free trade agreements that are quite comprehensive. For instance, the agreement with Canada included a special clause to allow the use of capital controls by Chile.

The Chilean policy also has included the intensification of linkages with other regions. As a result, a cooperation agreement was signed with the European Union (1999), and several negotiations have been developed with the United States and with Asian-Pacific countries.

At the national level, Chilean trade policies in the 1990s had to face a quite different context than that of the 1980s. GATT rounds and the subsequent rules of the World Trade Organization restricted the use of subsidies to exports in developing countries. Therefore, both the use of simplified tax rebates and the deferred payments of customs duties on imports of capital goods — instruments of great effectiveness and efficiency in the 1980s and early 1990s — were limited and scheduled to end by January 2003.

Thus, during the 1990s authorities focused their efforts to promote exports on instruments aimed at more directly correcting some market failures. The main programs, managed by the Chilean export promoting institution, PROCHILE, provided information to exporters and support in activities fostering Chilean products in new markets. These policies were effective in terms of easing market access to participant firms (Álvarez and Crespi 2000) but were far removed from the strength of the somewhat heterodox export strategy of the 1980s.

The Exchange Rate Policy and the New Capital Surge

During most of the 1990s, the system of crawling bands was maintained. In line with the experience of other Latin American and emerging countries, Chilean authorities had to deal with the return of the private capital flows that heavily influenced their exchange rate policy. Chile's real exchange rate tended to appreciate as a result of large capital inflows, mostly FDI (see fig. 10.1). However, the appreciation of the exchange rate was more moderate in Chile than in other countries; in broad terms, as witnessed by the moderate deficit on the current account (2.5 percent of GDP in 1990–95), appreciation was equilibrating (consistent with the net increases in productivity and the improvement in the terms of the external debt). As analyzed in chapter 10, significant modifications were introduced to the exchange rate policy to resist the appreciating trend; among them, the official exchange rate became pegged to a basket of currencies, rather than just the U.S. dollar, in order to deter speculative capital inflows predominantly in dollars, and the Central Bank actively intervened in the foreign exchange market, including intramarginal intervention (within the band). Furthermore, taxes and reserve requirements were applied to foreign credits and deposits to soften the external capital supply in face of capital surges and to reduce the share of short-term capital inflows. One explicit goal was protecting the export model by avoiding an excessive exchange rate appreciation and instability (Ffrench-Davis, Agosin, and Uthoff 1995; Zahler 1998).

However, prudential macroeconomic policies lost their strength in the second part of the decade, when a larger capital surge was not followed by a timely and adequate reaction of the Central Bank. Therefore, the overabundance of capital inflows led to a real appreciation of 16 percent between 1995 and October 1997 (see chap. 10).

The Asian crisis meant a new capital flight and the subsequent depreciating pressures. The Central Bank resisted them by narrowing the band and raising interest rates up to September 1999, when the exchange rate was allowed to float freely. This change of regime eased the correction of the then too appreciated real exchange rate, but it has implied a higher volatility subsequently.[2]

Export Performance

Export Dynamism

Since the 1970s, it has been possible to distinguish two growth cycles of exports in Chile that represent a clear departure from previous historical performance. The first one extended from 1974 to the late 1970s. Between 1974 and 1981, the average annual growth of the volume of exports was 8.7 percent, but for noncopper exports it reached 16 percent. As discussed in chapter 3, there was stagnation in total and manufacturing exports in the early 1980s because of the significant appreciation of the real exchange rate and the slowdown of the world economy. In fact, in 1981 total quantum export fell by 3.3 percent, led by a 7 percent drop in noncopper exports (Sáez 1991).

The second cycle of high export growth rates began after 1982 when the real exchange rate was sharply devalued. Total export quantum grew 10 percent per year in 1982–89. Table 8.2 shows that, in the second part of the decade, the volume of copper exports expanded slowly, but this was compensated for by a spectacular growth of noncopper exports: noncopper traditional export quantum grew 9 percent a year in 1986–89, but the most dynamic group was nontraditional exports, with an annual quantum growth of 22 percent in that period.

Exports quantum continued to grow strongly in the 1990s, averaging 9.1 percent a year in 1990–2000. This expansion was mainly explained by nontraditional exports, with an annual increase that averaged 12.7 percent throughout the decade, while copper and noncopper traditional exports grew 9.5 and 5 percent, respectively. The value of primary commodity exports remained largely unchanged in the first part of the 1990s, reflecting the copper price drop. In 1994–95 the prices of these major exports recovered, which contributed to the large increase in

---

2. Caballero and Corbo (1989) show empirically that real exchange rate volatility has strong negative effects on export performance.

TABLE 8.2.   Export Quantum Growth, 1961–2000

	1961–70	1971–73	1974–85	1986–89	1990–94	1995–2000
Copper	3.9	−2.3	5.0	3.3	5.1	13.4
Noncopper	7.8	−8.5	15.8	13.1	11.4	6.8
Traditional				9.0	7.1	3.3
Nontraditional				21.7	16.3	9.7
Total exports	4.9	−4.5	9.3	8.8	8.7	9.4

Source: Sáez 1991 for 1960–85; Central Bank of Chile for 1985–2000. According to *fob* exports of goods.

exports that occurred in that biennum. This boom was interrupted by the Asian crisis that hit the Latin American economies in 1998–99. It implied sharp negative terms of trade shock, which strongly reduced the export value, especially of traditional items. The value of nontraditional exports, on the other hand, exhibited a greater strength during the crisis, contributing to the economic recovery in 2000. The vigorous growth recorded by this group of exports, from their takeoff in 1984, explains why this set of products has equaled the share of copper in total export value in the late 1990s (fig. 8.1).

Although the Chilean export model looks healthy, there is a point of concern that deserves attention. Despite the exceptional growth of the quantum of nontraditional exports since the 1980s, their dynamism has experienced a gradual deceleration: annual growth was 21.7 percent in 1986–89, 16.3 percent in 1990–94, and 9.7 percent in 1995–2000 (table 8.2). That implies that their quantum has tended to converge to the average rate of total exports. Given the slow growth of traditional noncopper exports in 1995–2000, copper exports have counterweighted them with an annual quantum growth of 13.4 percent. However, as documented by Moguillansky (1999) and Sachs, Larraín, and Warner (1999), those impressive growth rates appear unsustainable due both to investment constraints and to the fact that markets are limited.[3]

The real exchange rate appreciation during the second half of the 1990s and its consequences in the export sector competitiveness appear as the main cause of the declining trend in nontraditional growth (Díaz and Ramos 1998). Econometric estimates by Moguillansky and Titelman (1993) of the price elasticity of the export supply of Chile with respect to the real exchange rate across industries support this hypothesis. The estimates indicate that variations in the real exchange rate have differentiated effects, depending on the type of good exported, and that

---

3. Even though a quarter of world copper reserves belongs to Chile (Sachs, Larraín, and Warner 1999).

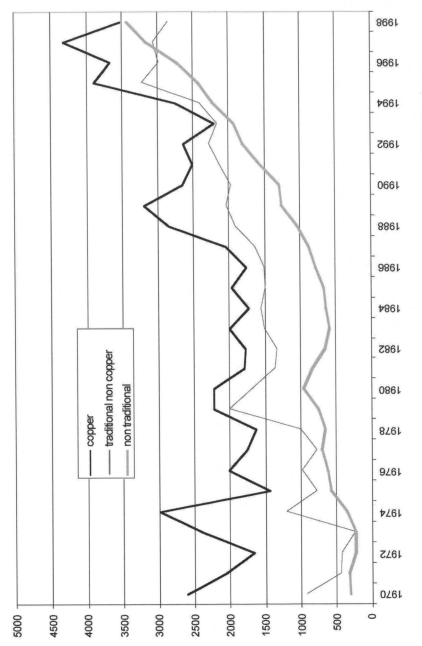

Fig. 8.1. Value of exports of goods, 1970–98 (1986 U.S.$millions). (Based on BADECEL figures.)

a persistent real depreciation (appreciation) tends to have a positive (negative) impact on the volume and the diversification toward intensity in value added. Thus, a depreciated and stable real exchange rate is likely to crowd in investment in exportables and the diversification of exports.

The trade pattern of the 1990s has been strongly affected by FDI because of its dual role in the sense that it affects both export capacity and the exchange rate. In fact, FDI has significantly contributed to the Chilean export development. A conservative estimate indicates that in 1990–2000 approximately 30 percent of the funds invested in exportables were channeled through FDI, going mostly to copper production.[4] This enormous contribution of FDI to export capacity, however, lost dynamism in the second half of the decade. In 1990–95 FDI in export sectors represented 75 percent of total inflows, while in 1996–2000, that share fell to 35 percent.

The loss of participation was compensated for by a sharp increase in total FDI. These larger inflows, in turn, were responsible for part of the peso overvaluation in 1996–97. This process had not only negative macroeconomic consequences, such as those analyzed in chapter 10, but also productive effects because of the resulting "Dutch disease" for most exporting sectors, especially the nontraditional ones, which are more elastic to the level and stability of the real exchange rate. Furthermore, the imbalance was intensified since most FDI was not directed to create export capacity but was channeled to nontradable sectors.[5] These facts are consistent with the boom of copper exports and the slower growth of noncopper exports. They highlight the importance of a comprehensive set of policies to ensure sound export development.

The Composition of Exports

Chilean exports have become increasingly diversified but remain strongly resource intensive. The share of copper exports decreased from 70 percent in 1970 to about 45 percent in the early 1980s and remained around that level until the 1990s, when their share fell below 40 percent.[6] The fall in their share is partly explained by the declining price of copper during

---

4. However, the value added of this copper output is notably lower than that of CODELCO, because privately produced copper is less elaborated and effective taxes on profits are lower.

5. Moreover, a high share of FDI during the late 1990s included merges and acquisitions of existing assets, which do not generate new productive capacity directly.

6. It should be borne in mind that there were significant reductions in copper production costs in most of the main world copper producers during the 1980s. For this reason, the expected "normal price" for copper for the following years tended to be much lower than in the previous decades. See Bande and Ffrench-Davis 1989 and Vial 1988.

the first half of the 1990s. The number of products, on the other hand, grew from 200 in 1970 to 2,800 in 1990 and to around 3,900 in 1996 and then stabilized at that level.

Noncopper traditional exports — composed of fresh fruit and natural-resource-based manufacturing, such as fish meal, wood pulp, and paper — grew vigorously in the 1970s, jumping from 24 percent in 1970 of total exports of goods to 40 percent in 1979. In the early 1980s their real value declined as a result of the antiexport bias of the exchange rate appreciation (see chap. 3), and their share in total exports dropped to about one-third in the 1980s. From 1987 on, their real value resumed growth but at a slower pace than the rest of goods and with important swings. As a consequence, their share decreased below 30 percent in the late 1990s.

Nontraditional exports — which include manufacturing exports other than those based on natural resources and new resource-based prod-ucts — initially expanded during the first trade reform. Their share in-creased from less than 10 percent in 1970 to around 20 percent in the second half of the decade, but they lost dynamism in the early 1980s. As mentioned earlier, from the mid-1980s on, this group again exhibited strong and sustainable growth, and consequently their share climbed to 35 percent in the second half of the 1990s, matching the value of copper exports during 1998–99.

The first column of table 8.3 shows that, despite diversifying in the last years, Chile's exports continue to rely heavily on natural resources, notwithstanding a tendency to export more manufactured goods. In fact, nontraditional exports also include a high share of goods intensive in natural resources (see line b for each year). The classification of table 8.3 indicates that the percentage of natural-resource-based exports was over 85 percent in 1998. This feature is not surprising because Chile has a rich endowment of natural resources combined with geographical fac-tors that condition high static comparative advantages. Moreover, in the last decades, dynamic competitive advantages also have been developed through clusters around forestry products, wine, salmon, and fresh fruit. These successful experiences, according to some analysts, could give support to a "Nordic" strategy of development for Chile, based on the manufacturing of natural resources (Díaz and Ramos 1998).

However, there are other arguments in favor of further diversifica-tion toward more manufactured goods and services, and less to purely natural-resource-intensive products. Achievements in this area are im-portant because, first, the fact that a large share of Chile's exports are still in their primary forms means that the economy remains subject to the large and erratic fluctuations that characterize commodity prices. Second, the long-term dynamism of these products is limited, which can

TABLE 8.3. Geographic Distribution of Chilean Exports, According to Technological Content, 1970–98

Year	Product	Composition (% of total)	Geographic Distribution (%)					
			Latin America	European Union	United States	Japan	Asia	Other
1970	a. Nonprocessed natural resources	12.9	10.6	33.0	14.9	39.8	0.1	1.6
	b. Processed natural resources	84.5	10.3	67.1	14.2	7.8	0.4	0.2
	c. Manufactures	2.2	62.6	2.2	10.1	13.0	1.0	11.1
	d. Total	100.0	11.5	61.1	14.1	12.1	0.4	0.8
1983	a. Nonprocessed natural resources	27.2	9.2	25.0	26.7	25.7	8.4	5.0
	b. Processed natural resources	66.8	11.3	43.1	27.8	3.1	7.7	7.0
	c. Manufactures	6.0	33.2	17.1	35.7	2.3	4.1	7.6
	d. Total	100.0	12.0	36.6	28.0	9.2	7.7	6.5
1989	a. Nonprocessed natural resources	26.3	13.2	27.4	20.9	19.3	15.4	3.8
	b. Processed natural resources	66.3	10.8	43.6	14.2	12.7	13.5	5.2
	c. Manufactures	7.5	21.2	20.2	36.8	3.6	3.5	14.7
	d. Total	100.0	12.2	37.6	17.7	13.7	13.2	5.6
1998	a. Nonprocessed natural resources	30.5	17.2	19.1	21.8	27.4	11.4	3.1
	b. Processed natural resources	55.5	19.4	36.0	13.1	10.0	18.7	2.8
	c. Manufactures	14.0	55.7	17.3	14.2	0.6	1.1	11.1
	d. Total	100.0	23.8	28.2	15.9	14.0	14.0	4.1

Source: Based on BADECEL (Base de datos del comercio exterior de América Latina y el Caribe) figures in current U.S. dollars, classified according to ECLAC 1992.

become a negative factor in future economic growth for the whole economy (Sachs, Larraín, and Warner 1999). Third, the production of more manufactured products involves positive externalities for the rest of the economy, through learning by doing processes and gains by dynamic competitive advantages (see chap. 1; ECLAC 1998, chaps. 3 and 4).

The Diversification of Export Markets

Exports have become more diversified not only in terms of products but also in terms of markets of destination. A first indicator, the number of markets, rose from 31 in 1970 to 120 in 1987 and to 174 in 1999.

Traditionally, the European Union (EU) was the most important destination for Chilean exports. In 1970, for instance, 61 percent of total exports went to Europe, while the rest was principally distributed between the United States (14 percent), Japan, and Latin America (12 percent each) (see table 8.3).

After the first trade liberalization, the geographical distribution experienced some changes, mainly due to the growing importance of Latin and North American markets at the expense of the participation of the EU. The debt crisis and its strong impact on Latin America, however, implied a setback in that trend, with a return in its share to 12 percent in 1983. The United States received 28 percent of exports, while the quantity of exports to the EU was reduced by nearly half (to a total share of one-third), and Asian countries other than Japan had emerged as relevant partners.

When the military rule expired in 1989, both Latin American and European markets had held their shares. The U.S. participation had fallen to 18 percent, while Asian markets now received 27 percent of Chilean exports.

In the 1990s the U.S. markets stabilized their share while the EU lost importance but remained a major destination. Asian markets expanded their weight, becoming the main destination in 1997, with 35 percent of Chilean exports. Exports to Latin American countries, on the other hand, also expanded rapidly in response to trade agreements covering most markets in the region and to their trade liberalization, renewed economic activity, and appreciation of their real exchange rate relative to other regions. Therefore, the regional markets reached a share of 24 percent in 1998.

The growing share of the Asian markets was reversed in 1998 as a result of the Asian crisis. The collapse of that market contributed to the strong export contraction in 1998–99, and consequently its share diminished by seven points. The EU, on the other hand, recovered the position of main export market with a share of 28 percent.

The basket compositions of Chilean exports vary hugely according to their geographical destination. Table 8.3 shows that unprocessed and processed natural resources represent a much higher percentage of exports directed to industrialized countries than to the Latin American markets. In contrast, a notorious difference between these markets appears in manufactured products. In 1998 these goods represented 56 percent of total exports to Latin America, much more than the 21 percent of 1989, compared with 17 percent to the EU, 14 percent to the United States, and 2 percent to Asia. The great importance of Latin American markets in the marketing of manufactured products can be crucial for future Chilean exports development because, as mentioned before, this segment has been highly dynamic, doubling its participation between 1989 and 1998.

At the intraregional level, MERCOSUR is the main trade partner of Chile. The participation of this market in total Chilean exports (relative to Latin American markets) diminished during the 1990s; however, it gained share as importer of Chilean non-natural-resources-based manufactured products, from around 40 percent in the 1980s to nearly 50 percent in the 1990s, which highlights its strategic importance for diversifying exports. Among the Latin American markets, Mexico is the most dynamic, with a growing share both in total exports and manufactured exports.

Thus, Latin American countries are playing an increasingly important role in the diversification of Chile's exports toward manufactured products. This diversification has been closely associated with the trade liberalization of the region, including regional trade arrangements.

The question remains, however, as to the sustainability of Chile's manufacturing export growth. On the one hand, much of the demand for these products continues to depend on the Latin American region's economic growth performance, macroeconomic sustainability, and exchange rates favoring intraregional trade. On the other, it also depends on the strengthening of productive capacity in output intensive in value added and innovation.

Exports and Growth

Exports have been frequently called the engine of Chilean economic growth. The growing share of exports in GDP has been a channel of transmission of externalities resulting from exposure to foreign markets. Here, however, I will concentrate on another relation that has been extremely significant in Chile: the influence of domestic policies—principally the changing macroeconomic environment—on the association of exports with GDP. In fact, the correlation between export growth and actual GDP growth has been high after the debt crisis in the second half of the 1980s and the 1990s (Meller 1996). During these periods, the export sector was one of the most dynamic of the economy, while Chilean GDP recovered in the 1980s and then entered the highest continued growth period in its history in the 1990s. Actually, the volume of exports grew notably faster than GDP (table 8.4). Most econometric studies on this issue find a significant positive effect of exports (and especially noncopper exports) on GDP growth (Agosin 1999; Coeymans 1999; Meller 1996).

However, to be the engine of growth, a sector's expansion must be linked to the creation of new productive capacity in the rest of the economy, a feature present only in the 1990s. As discussed in chapter 6, the external debt crisis and the subsequent automatic adjustment carried out meant a generalized fall in domestic output in 1982–83 (recall the drop of 14 percent of GDP), where demand-reducing policies caused a high underutilization of productive capacity; naturally, given a sizable devaluation, underutilization was totally concentrated in nonexportables.

The export-promoting measures of the 1980s, summarized earlier, functioned as supply-switching policies, reallocating available resources against the background of a very low overall investment rate (and, as a consequence, low creation of new capacity). Depressed domestic demand and the increased export profitability, as a result of the exchange rate depreciation, provided the conditions that encouraged investment and output in exportables. Consequently, it was not exactly a case of export-led growth but rather one of an export drive led by the binding external constraint and a recessionary domestic adjustment. Evidently, strong export expansion, which averaged 8 percent per annum in 1982–89 (and 28 percent of GDP), was a factor contributing to the recovery of economic activity; however, it could not compensate for the near stagnation in nonexport GDP, which grew only 1.0 percent, as compared to the 1.6 percent growth of population, and thus exports were unable to transmit its dynamism to total GDP, which expanded modestly by 2.6 percent per annum (see table 8.4).

In the 1990s, the story was different. The capital formation ratio rose to unprecedented levels, and this process was intense not only in the export sector. Nontradables exhibited notably higher rates of expansion: for instance, infrastructure works and telecommunications showed an annual growth of 18.3 percent and 32.4 percent, respectively, in 1990–97 (Moguillansky 1999).[7]

---

7. These figures must be compared with an annual growth in infrastructure of 2.6 percent in 1982–89.

TABLE 8.4.   Exports and Economic Growth, 1960–2000

	GDP Growth	Export Growth[a]	Nonexport GDP Growth[b]	Exports/GDP (constant prices)	Exports/GDP (current prices)
1960–70	4.2	3.6	4.3	11.9	14.0
1971–73	0.5	−4.1	0.9	9.9	11.8
1974–81	3.3	13.6	1.4	20.7	21.8
1982–89	2.6	7.8	1.0	28.3	28.3
1990–94	7.3	10.0	6.3	34.6	31.0
1995–2000	5.5	8.7	4.0	39.3	29.1

Source: Based on official figures from National Accounts of the Central Bank of Chile at 1986 constant prices and rates of change; exports include goods and nonfinancial services.

[a]Different sources and methodologies explain differences from figures in table 8.2.

[b]Nonexport GDP is equal to GDP minus the domestic content or value added in exports. Imported inputs in exports were assumed to be equal to the share of nonconsumer imports in GDP.

In parallel, export dynamism remained high despite the real exchange rate appreciation recorded during part of the decade (see fig. 10.2). Three factors contributed to this outcome. First, world trade was more dynamic during the 1990s. In 1980–89 the volume of world trade expanded by 3.7 percent annually, while in 1990–99 the rate was 6.2 percent. Second, Chile gained access to new markets under preferential conditions thanks to several trade agreements. Third, the record investment ratio of the period allowed a great increase in productivity and external competitiveness. Furthermore, it must be kept in mind, on the one hand, that a major part of the appreciation of the first half of the 1990s was an equilibrating movement following the currency drought of the 1980s and, on the other, that during those years there was a deliberate policy of protecting the export development through prudential management of the capital account (see chap. 10; Ffrench-Davis, Agosin, and Uthoff 1995; Zahler 1998).

Therefore, in the 1990s global GDP growth was led by both the tradable and nontradable sectors. Actually exports and nonexports grew 9.3 and 5.1 percent a year, respectively, in 1990–2000 (see table 8.4).[8] This, accompanied by an environment of full utilization of productive capacity, macroeconomic stability, and prudence, accounts for the high growth rate of the Chilean economy during most of the decade.

In the second half of the 1990s, however, real exchange rates appreciated excessively, led by an excessive capital inflow (see chap. 10),

8. These averages include the record, full employment years, 1991–97, and the downward adjustment years, 1990 and 1998–2000. Given that 2000 was a year with a recessive gap, annual growth of potential non-X GDP was 6.3 percent in 1990–2000, above the 5.1 percent of effective non-X GDP.

provoking a distortion in resource allocation and the trade balance. Therefore, there was some overinvestment in nontradables (particularly in construction and commerce) with a weakening of the output of tradables (particularly manufactures).

Concluding Remarks

In all, during the three last decades Chile witnessed a period of exceptional export growth. This outstanding performance was associated, during the last two decades, with active heterodox policies aimed at sustaining a competitive real exchange rate and generating export capacity rather than associated solely with the orthodox economic reforms of the 1970s.

Four reciprocally reinforcing groups of factors appear to be significant for explaining the behavior of exports. First, a depreciated real exchange rate has proven to be a determinant variable of the overall performance of exports. Second, the diversification toward goods and services with value added is crucial for enhancing the quality of exports, in the sense of benefiting from more dynamic demand and better international prices; the stability of the real exchange rate, incentives such as the simplified drawback for nontraditional exports, and intraregional integration are significant variables at hand. Third, in order to upgrade the quality of exports, there is a need for an intensive national effort to *complete* domestic markets for technology, labor training, and long-term segments of the capital market; all these are crucial ingredients for achieving systemic competitiveness. Fourth, the export drive needs to be accompanied by a domestic macroeconomic environment, sustainable and with *right* macroprices, adequate for productive development in order to contribute to export-led growth.

CHAPTER 9

Changes in Income Distribution and Poverty from the 1970s to the 1990s

Income distribution has once again become a major issue in Chile. This is healthy because problems cannot be understood and solved unless their existence is acknowledged. Despite effective efforts made in the 1990s to reverse the deterioration of the 1970s and 1980s, poverty is still a fact of life for one in every five Chileans, and inequality in opportunities and income is still manifest. Lack of equity is a marked feature of the Chilean economy and society.

Distribution has changed significantly over the last thirty years. There is clear evidence that the situation worsened markedly in the 1970s and 1980s, with both inequality and poverty rising. In the 1990s, poverty fell sharply. The information regarding distribution, however, is less conclusive. Some data, such as those from the National Socio-Economic Survey (CASEN), show some improvement in income distribution in the early 1990s, compared to the late 1980s, which remained relatively stable during the rest of the decade. Other information, such as the National Bureau of Statistics (INE) household budget survey, shows a substantial improvement between 1988 and 1997. What all the information signals, though, is a significantly worse distribution than in the late 1960s and a continuing high level of poverty. It can be said with certainty, then, that in the 1990s (1) the deteriorating trend seen during the Pinochet regime was brought to a halt, (2) poverty was reduced sharply, and (3) income distribution became less unequal than in the 1980s. But despite this, the net balance indicates that Chile lost ground over the last thirty years rather than progressing toward greater equity. Equity is an essential ingredient of modernization.

In this chapter, we shall review the most important developments in

I am grateful for the helpful comments of David Bravo, Juan Carlos Feres, Osvaldo Larrañaga, Carlos Massad, and Jaime Ruiz-Tagle; the exchange of views with Harald Beyer, Guillermo García-Huidobro, Gunther Hinze, Dagmar Raczynski, Pilar Romaguera, Jaime Ruiz-Tagle, Jr., Daniel Titelman, Arístides Torche, Andras Uthoff, and Humberto Vega; and the efficient assistance of Heriberto Tapia. I especially appreciate the authorization of Juan Carlos Feres to use information prepared for Feres 2001. Of course, the responsibility for interpretations is mine alone.

distribution over recent decades. We shall concentrate on three aspects. Two of them are structural: the need to improve the quality and quantity of investment in people, or human capital; and the need to enhance productive investment and its link to productive employment. Both factors contribute to raising productivity across all sectors of society and thus to spreading opportunities to larger segments of the labor force. The third aspect, to which I attach enormous importance, is the attainment of sustainable macroeconomic balances.

The efficient approach for obtaining both growth and equity implies a comprehensive definition of macroeconomic equilibria. This includes far more than low inflation and structural fiscal balance (though both are necessary and convenient). It also requires real economy equilibrium, that is, making full use of available productive capacity, avoiding excessively fluctuating and outlier interest and exchange rates, and securing a favorable macroeconomic environment for productive investment.[1]

The biggest setbacks in distribution and poverty have been caused by critical macroeconomic imbalances: the hyperinflation of 1973 and the recessions of 1975 and 1982. To these should be added the cases in which macroeconomic "balances" have been achieved at the expense of other balances, such as the cases of macrosocial imbalance in 1985–87 and external imbalance in 1997. During the last episode, the subsequent recession in 1998–2001 — though notably mild compared to those of 1975 and 1982 — represented a severe setback with social, economic, and political costs. The distribution of household income per capita worsened in 1999–2001 with respect to the 1990s, even though it was somewhat less uneven than it had been in the 1980s (Larrañaga 2001). I argue that consistency between different objectives is essential if macroeconomic balances are to be sustainable over time and provide the required environment for socioeconomic development (see Ffrench-Davis 2000, chap. 6).

Trends in Income Distribution and Poverty

Good measurements are important because they provide information on the effectiveness of socioeconomic policies aimed at reducing the inequalities and poverty characteristic of underdevelopment. Nonetheless, the measurement of poverty and income distribution is beset with great difficulties.

The definition of *poverty* is a conventional one. The generally accepted definition of *the poor* is that they are "those whose income per

---

1. As illustrated in Ffrench-Davis 2000, Latin America was characterized in the 1990s by strong macroeconomic disequilibria, in their real meaning. Chile was an outstanding exception in the first half of the 1990s, but the quality of its environment began deteriorating to some degree in the following years (see chap. 10).

capita is lower than the cost of two baskets of food and basic nonfood needs" (ECLAC 1997, box 1). This is the dividing line between the poor and the nonpoor used in the CASEN survey in Chile. The definition does not tell us anything about how far the many people who ceased to be numbered among the poor between 1987 and 1998 have risen above the poverty line or about the previous position of those who might have returned to poverty in 1999. It is not an indicator of distribution, although CASEN obviously provides a great deal of valuable information for a number of distributive indicators and for an understanding of poverty and the strategic points from which to combat it.

Income distribution is much harder to measure, particularly at the poorest and richest extremes. Again, even if the figures available are correct, there are still many alternative ways of organizing the information, for example, by income or expenditure per household or per household member, and the differences are substantial.[2] Once the information has been classified, there are also different ways of measuring distribution; indicators range from the more cryptic (such as the traditional Gini indicator) to simpler ones such as the ratio between the shares of the richest and poorest decile or quintile. This latter indicator is quite widely used; its drawback is that it does not take into account the 60 or 80 percent in the middle and it gives great weight to the richest income bracket, where measurements are very defective.

There are different sources of information on distribution in Chile. The one of longest standing is the employment survey of the University of Chile, which has been collecting information on incomes in Greater Santiago once a year since 1958. The CASEN survey is conducted by the Ministry of Planning (MIDEPLAN), with data available for 1987 and then every two years since 1990 for all Chile; both the coverage and the survey itself were improved in the 1990s, so that comparability with 1987 is limited. Once a decade or so, the INE carries out a detailed survey of household budgets in Greater Santiago, which represents 40 percent of the population of Chile. Data are available for 1969, 1978, 1988, and 1997. INE also collects income data in a survey that supplements the employment study. Some results differ radically between the various sources, and there is considerable disagreement among specialists about the merits of each one.

The debate over which variables best determine distribution patterns and developments is also open. The information provided by the surveys themselves has been used as a basis for recent research, interpretations, and policy proposals. Here I shall mention four strong variables,

---

2. It would seem advisable to adjust for the number of household members, but two problems need to be dealt with first: (1) spending needs vary by age (one way of attempting to correct this would be by working with an "adult equivalent" as the unit of account); and (2) there are "economies of scale" in the household (Contreras and Ruiz-Tagle 1997).

which are ultimately the result of socioeconomic structures and public policies.

First, income levels have a highly positive relationship with years of schooling. Nonetheless, this relationship is subject to two qualifications, which have deep implications for public policy in this specific area. On the one hand, the quality of education and the matching of supply and the demand for skills are essential (Bravo and Contreras 1999; Larrañaga 2001). This is illustrated by the fact that, although the average worker had 3.5 years more schooling in 1992 than in 1970 (Hofman 1999), the average wage was similar, having been depressed in the intermediate years. Furthermore, schooling is measured on the basis of the number of years of traditional education, without taking the training accrued during people's working lives into account. Training is essential as a way of enhancing the productivity of workers with little education or schooling whose quality does not match the current demand for labor.

Second, increasing the participation of women in the labor force is a key factor in reducing the number of households in poverty. Data produced by Beyer (1997) on the basis of the CASEN survey of 1994 and the 1992 population census show that in the poorest quintile of households only a fifth of all women are in the labor force; in households in the fifth, or richest, quintile, half of all women participate. Of women with thirteen or more years of education, 57 percent participate in the labor force, while less than 14 percent of those with three or fewer years of schooling are reported as being active. The extent to which women participate in the labor market determines which proportion of household members receive pay, the figure being 22 percent in the bottom quintile and 51 percent in the top one, with an almost linear progression in the intermediate brackets. Improving opportunities and facilities (such as day nurseries) for working women with lower incomes is a key factor in increasing equity.

Third, unemployment is another very influential factor. In the CASEN survey of 1998, the unemployment rate was ten times as high in the first quintile as in the fifth, and its sensitivity to the economic cycle, and even to slight fluctuations such as those of the 1990s, is very high. In the first quintile, unemployment fell from 22 percent in 1990 to 14 and 15 percent in 1992 and 1996, respectively, rising to 28 percent in 1998 (MIDEPLAN 1999). Unemployment is also substantially higher among young people and those with less schooling. Consequently, policies intended to strengthen the demand for labor and make the supply more flexible and better able to adapt to technological changes — with sustainable macroeconomic stability, vigorous physical capital formation, and increasing investment in people — play a very significant role in improving the distribution of opportunities.

Fourth, social expenditure has a progressive incidence, representing a rising share of the access of the poor to goods and services in the 1990s.

The Historical Record up to 1973

By 1970, social development in Chile was among the highest of all Latin American countries. The level of education, the national health system, the system for constructing low-rent housing, and the massive school meals program were among the most advanced in the region. A large middle class had also emerged, although it was concentrated initially in urban areas. Progress also extended to unionized workers and the rural sector, where it was associated with the land reform carried out between 1965 and 1973 (Ffrench-Davis 1973).

These advances were the result of a continuous process that had become entrenched in the 1920s and had accelerated under the social democratic (Radical Party) governments that held office between 1939 and 1952 and then under presidents Ibáñez, Alessandri, Frei, and Allende (1952–73).

Notwithstanding the social gains made in the 1950s and 1960s, the distribution pattern that existed around 1970 was regarded as highly unsatisfactory. Consequently, a number of proposals for improving the situation were put forward by the parties of the Center and Left. Several of these were put into practice during the administration of President Allende. As a result, income from labor (minimum and average wages) and social spending (pensions, family allowances, the education and health budgets, etc.) increased massively in 1971, although in a way that was obviously unsustainable. The inflationary surge of 1972–73, with annual rates in excess of 200 and 600 percent, respectively, led to drastic reversals in the pattern of distribution on a number of these fronts in comparison with 1970 (see chap. 1).

Progress and Setbacks during the Pinochet Regime (1973–89)

Some social indicators continued to improve during the Pinochet regime, while others went sharply into reverse.

The illiteracy rate, already down to 20 percent in 1952, fell to 10 percent around 1973 and to less than 6 percent in 1989, while the number of students enrolled in primary schools, as a percentage of the population aged six to fourteen, rose from 65 percent to almost 100 percent in 1973 and remained at this level until the early 1980s. In the second half of the 1980s, however, coverage fell to 95 percent, which suggests that a dropout problem arose as a result of the 1982 crisis. As for secondary education, the proportion of fifteen to eighteen year olds enrolled rose from 10 percent in 1952 to 51 percent in 1973 and 75 percent in 1989.[3]

Developments were very positive with regard to life expectancy and general and infant mortality, improving yet further the trend these indicators were showing in the 1950s and 1960s. In particular, infant mortality fell markedly, showing for Chile the lowest level in Latin America in the 1980s, along with Costa Rica, Cuba, and the English-speaking Caribbean. This good performance was the result of public efforts to improve mother and child care, including nutrition programs for children at the nursing stage; to a decline in the number of births; and to irreversible factors such as improvement in the education of mothers (Monckeberg 1998; Raczynski and Oyarzo 1981).

Nonetheless, the performance of other indicators was negative (see table 9.1). This was essentially a reflection of great macroeconomic instability, a low rate of gross investment per member of the labor force (involving a negative impact on productivity per worker) and laws that were biased against labor, as a result of which average earnings in 1989 were 8 percent below their 1970 level. In other words, over nearly two decades average wages, rather than increasing as is natural, fell, and something similar happened with pensions. The minimum wage declined by a similar percentage over the period, and its coverage narrowed considerably, with lower levels being applied to workers under twenty-one (later to those under eighteen) and over sixty-five (Cortázar 1983). Similarly, family allowances, which had played a progressive role, growing continuously in importance until the early 1970s (Ffrench-Davis 1973), went into a steady decline after 1974, until by 1989 they were 72 percent below their 1970 level.

Public spending per capita on health, education, and housing also fell. The decline in these three components reached around 22 percent in comparison with 1970.[4] Spending on the National Health Service dropped substantially. Only social security spending increased, owing to a rising number of pensioners. However, some social spending (though not the bulk of it) was targeted at the poorest members of society, which would appear to have partly offset the decline in their work income.[5]

---

3. Figures are from ECLAC, *Statistical Yearbook,* based on official Chilean information.

4. Public spending is financed by fiscal funds, the contributions of beneficiaries, and changes in liabilities. A large discrepancy between the official and "corrected" figures for social spending in the 1970s is discussed in Marshall 1981.

5. Sometimes faulty targeting implied the crowding out of the middle class or even the poor, for example, from the university after the elimination of free access without a comprehensive system of scholarships. As a consequence, public expenditure in higher education is concentrated in quintile 5.

TABLE 9.1. Wages, Family Allowance, and Public Social Expenditure, 1970–2000 (real indices, 1970 = 100)

	Average Wages (1)	Minimum Wage (2)	Family Allowance (3)	Per Capita Public Social Expenditure		
				Education (4)	Health (5)	Total (6)
1970	100.0	100.0	100.0	100.0	100.0	100.0
1980	89.0	130.0	81.6	88.6	82.3	90.1
1981	96.8	135.7	80.9	92.1	74.7	97.5
1985	83.2	86.1	54.6	76.0	64.0	90.5
1986	84.6	82.1	45.7	71.5	62.5	86.9
1987	84.3	77.1	38.1	65.7	61.5	84.7
1988	89.8	82.3	33.2	64.1	70.4	86.0
1989	91.6	91.8	28.4	62.5	69.6	83.7
1990	93.3	98.0	33.7	58.8	65.3	81.6
1991	97.8	107.2	41.4	64.7	75.7	87.8
1992	102.2	112.2	42.4	73.1	87.0	95.4
1993	105.9	117.7	43.2	78.2	95.9	102.9
1994	110.7	122.1	43.9	83.9	104.0	107.4
1995	118.3	127.5	45.3	92.3	106.7	113.9
1996	123.2	133.0	47.2	102.7	114.3	123.2
1997	126.1	137.8	49.7	111.6	119.4	128.1
1998	129.5	146.2	51.9	122.6	127.5	135.7
1999	132.6	159.6	53.3	129.4	129.6	144.3
2000	134.4	170.4	53.7	138.4	138.5	151.0

Sources: Instituto Nacional de Estadística and Jadresić 1990 for wages; Cortázar and Marshall 1980 for corrected CPI; Cabezas 1988 and Budget Office (since 1986) for social expenditure.

Note: Column 1, general wage index until April 1993 and later hourly wage index. Column 2 represents liquid income. Column 3 is family allowance of blue-collar workers in 1970, then the uniform allowance, and later that for the low-income bracket. Column 6 includes expenditures on education, health, housing, and pensions. All are average figures for each year.

Many of these indicators deteriorated during the 1970s, made a partial recovery in 1979–81, and worsened again between 1982 and the end of the decade (Ffrench-Davis and Raczynski 1990); average and minimum wages began to rise only in 1988, family allowances in 1990, and public social spending in 1991.

The decline in labor income and monetary social expenditure, as well as the regressive bias of the tax reforms in those years, were reflected in a worsening distribution of consumer spending. The most systematic and highest quality information available is from the household budget surveys conducted in Santiago.[6] The figures for 1969, 1978, and 1988

6. We have made efforts to seek a possible bias in the EFP associated with the facts that Santiago includes only 40 percent of Chile's population and that it is essentially urban. After comparing the results of the CASEN surveys for Santiago and the entire country, we find that concentration coefficients are relatively similar in the five surveys recorded

TABLE 9.2.   Distribution of Expenditure per Household, 1969, 1978, and 1988 (percentages of total)

Quintile	1969	1978	1988
1	7.6	5.2	4.4
2	11.8	9.3	8.2
3	15.6	13.6	12.6
4	20.6	21.0	20.0
5	44.5	51.0	54.9
Total	100.0	100.0	100.0
Q5/Q1	5.9	9.8	12.5

Source: Instituto Nacional de Estadísticas, *Encuestas de Presupuestos Familiares,* for Greater Santiago.

Note: Households are ranked according to household expenditures.

show a steady decline in household spending in the three lowest expenditure quintiles. Furthermore, the poorer the sector of the population the greater is the decline (see table 9.2). For example, the share of the poorest 40 percent of households (the first and second quintiles) fell from 19.4 percent in 1969 to just 12.6 percent in 1988; in other words, their share of total expenditure in Santiago dropped by a third. By contrast, the relative situation of the richest quintile improved consistently, with its share rising from 44.5 percent in 1969 to 51.0 percent in 1978 and 54.9 percent in 1988. Furthermore, this is the only quintile in which spending per family rose in real terms between 1969 and 1988.

This information on the distribution of spending shows that the second stage of the Pinochet government (1982–89) was also regressive, so that the concentration of wealth and income observed during the first stage, from 1974 to 1981, was accentuated.[7] Information from the University of Chile employment survey, which is also for Greater Santiago, likewise shows deterioration in income distribution, though differing in scale and with large fluctuations from year to year. Between 1974 and 1987, the situation worsened steadily, stabilizing temporarily during the upswing of 1977–80 only to deteriorate again afterward. The bottom was reached in 1987, whether measured by the Gini coefficient or the ratio between the first and fifth quintiles (Ruiz-Tagle 1999).

In chapter 2, we examined the role that a number of the reforms and policies of the military government played in exacerbating the severe crises that Chile faced. The dogmatic approach, particularly during the first half of its rule, increased the country's vulnerability to external

during the 1990s, with an average Gini coefficient of 57.2 percent and 57.4 percent for Santiago and for Chile, respectively (Feres 2001).

7. The years of the surveys do not exactly match those of the economic cycles.

shocks and worsened the ensuing losses. Among the worst consequences of the resulting recessions was the chronic unemployment that prevailed in the country (see fig. 9.1). By 1975, the percentage of unemployed already stood at 15.7 percent, a figure that rises to 17.6 percent if those working in the PEM (minimum employment program) and the POJH (employment program for heads of households) are included. By 1983, the number of unemployed stood at 740,000 (around 19 percent of the labor force); emergency job programs absorbed another 500,000 (nearly 13 percent of the labor force),[8] for a total of 31.3 percent. The problem was later alleviated by the economic activity recovery, but only in 1989 was there a return to single-digit unemployment rates, with open unemployment of 8 percent. In a situation in which unemployment hit the lowest income groups the hardest, with a lack of adequate unemployment insurance and weakened public social networks, the decline in the welfare of largest sectors of the population is easily explained.

Income Distribution and Poverty after the Return to Democracy (1990–2000)

Since 1990, three periods with different socioeconomic results can be distinguished. During the first years, there were noticeable improvements in the average and minimum wages and social expenditure, which meant a recovery from the depressed levels of prior decades. Then, from 1996 onward, progress in poverty reduction slowed and wages experienced smaller increases, while other social indicators kept improving. Finally, the environment worsened dramatically in 1999–2000, with a sharp rise in unemployment. However, the minimum wage — which is set by the government — rose significantly with the establishment of a triannual program for 1998–2000. Similarly, wages of teachers and workers in the National Health Service and public pensions experienced special raises. The associated higher fiscal expenditure was duly financed.

The return to democracy brought with it greater concern on the part of the state for equity and poverty issues and an understanding that efforts to achieve macroeconomic balance needed to be accompanied by the pursuit of macrosocial balance, whence the goal of "growth with equity." Consequently, in the 1990s the authorities began to make systematic efforts to improve the social situation and introduce *reforms to*

---

8. Although the job creation programs were originally designed for a work week of only fifteen hours, in practice full-time work was required. The wage paid, meanwhile, was only a fraction of the minimum wage; it eventually fell to less than a third with no social security coverage. Unemployment benefits were virtually nonexistent, although the PEM performed partly as a subsidy in exchange for work. Earnings from the POJH varied between 1.6 and 2 times those from PEM (Ffrench-Davis and Raczynski 1990, table A.13).

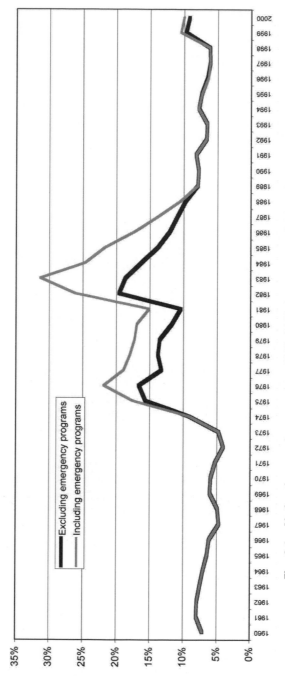

Fig. 9.1. National unemployment rate, 1960–2000 (percentage of labor force). (Data from National Bureau of Statistics and Jadresić 1986, annual averages.)

the reforms (Ffrench-Davis 2000, chap. 7). Public spending was restructured to provide more funds in social areas, and tax revenues were increased for this purpose by means of a fiscal reform that raised the VAT rate and progressive taxation. In the labor market, important agreements were reached, leading to a substantial improvement in the minimum wage and to *reforms to the reforms* that reduced the imbalance of power between workers and employers. Again, significant reforms concerning macroeconomic management had major effects on productive employment and the sustainability of macroeconomic balances. The introduction of the unremunerated reserve requirement and other prudential mechanisms for regulating volatile capital inflows played a key role (see chap. 10; and Ffrench-Davis 2000, chap. 10).

The result of this set of policies was substantial growth in real average earnings, which in 2000 were 34 percent higher than in 1970 (the 1970 level was never attained during the Pinochet regime) and 47 percent higher than in 1989, a minimum wage that was 86 percent higher than in 1989, and family allowance increases that have made up some of the ground lost during the 1980s (see table 9.1). The unemployment rate also improved considerably, averaging 7.3 percent in the 1990s compared to 18.1 percent in 1974–89 (see table 1.1 and fig. 9.1). Naturally, the macroeconomic conjuncture has had a significant impact on the unemployment rate. This is revealed in the rate of 6.1 percent during the 1997 boom compared to 10.2 percent in the depressed 1999–2000 period.

These policies, together with more efficient macroeconomic management for most of the decade — which laid the foundations for faster growth and large-scale job creation — enabled a drastic reduction of poverty and indigence up to 1998. In 1987, 45 percent of the Chilean population was living in poverty.[9] Subsequent measurements by the CASEN survey, summarized in table 9.3, show the steady progress that was made in this area, the figure having fallen to 21 percent by 2000.

It is clear that poverty was reduced in the 1990s. What is the outcome in income distribution? It is less clear-cut and in some ways contradictory. Some data show an improvement while others suggest no change; according to several sources, the picture was significantly better in the earlier years, with subsequent reversals in some sources. In any case, while the information available generally points to an improvement compared to the 1980s, it is clear that distribution is still very

9. Previous studies that had the same poverty indicator but used methodologies that are not totally comparable reveal that in 1969 some 17 percent of households were poor, a figure that stood at 45 percent in 1985 and 38 percent in 1987 (Altimir 1982; ECLAC 1991). The figure for poor households in 1987 is consistent with the 45 percent of the population shown in the CASEN survey of 1987 to be living in poverty.

**TABLE 9.3.   The "Indigent" and Other "Poor" Populations,
1987–2000 (percentages)**

	1987	1990	1992	1994	1996	1998	2000
Indigent	17.4	12.9	8.8	7.6	5.8	5.6	5.7
Other poor	27.7	25.7	23.8	19.9	17.4	16.1	14.9
Total poor	45.1	38.6	32.6	27.5	23.3	21.7	20.6

Source: MIDEPLAN and national data from the CASEN surveys.

regressive. A major national effort will be required, then, to correct this sharp inequity.

The most consistent source of information on income distribution is the INE's household budget survey (HBS). The results of the HBS for 1997 are not directly comparable with the three prior surveys because of methodological differences, which highlights the difficulties of processing and comparing surveys.[10] For instance, the 1997 survey shows that quintile 1 concentrates 3.93 percent of household expenditure, if imputed rent is excluded and the data are ranked by household, while it concentrates 8.80 percent of expenditure if imputed rent is included and data are ranked by per capita income. Likewise, the Gini index can vary by up to nine points, depending on which criteria are used to order and aggregate the data (Feres 2001). This sizable sensitivity is not significant when one is analyzing sharp changes in income distribution, such as the strong regressive setbacks of the 1970s and 1980s. On the contrary, when changes are rather slight, different methodologies can diverge in the sign of the results.

The availability of estimates of imputed rent for homeowners is a remarkable advance recorded from the 1988 survey on. The significant progress in housing programs attained by Chile has had a growing effect on quintile 1 by raising its share in total expenditure by 0.5 to 1.5 percentage points between the 1988 and 1997 surveys. This effect reinforces a progressive distributive change between the two surveys (table 9.4). Thus, the lack of this imputation represents a clear shortcoming in accurately estimating the welfare of poor households that became owners of their homes.

Demography also has played an important role that must not be ignored. The average number of members of households fell in all quintiles between 1988 and 1997, with a 6 percent drop in the total average (from 4.09 to 3.84 persons). In general, this change has been stronger

10. These three surveys rank households by expenditures, excluding imputed housing rent. The 1997 survey records acquired expenditures and generated disaggregated data on imputed housing rent.

in quintile 1 than in quintile 5. Consequently, operating with per capita data is much more accurate than using total household income or expenditure.[11] Therefore, I have opted to use per capita data, including imputed rent figures. Among the six different methods of classifying information with imputed rent, presented in table 9.4, the Gini index shows an improvement in distribution between 1988 and 1997. The table presented also presents six cases in which figures are not corrected by imputed rent; in two cases the Gini index and the quintile 5/quintile 1 ratio indicate a worsening while in the remaining four cases they show an improvement in 1997.[12] Therefore, the entire set of information strongly supports the hypothesis of distributive improvement between both surveys.

The income data from the University of Chile employment survey for Greater Santiago are consistent with those from the INE household expenditure survey. The ratio between the first and fifth quintiles shows a statistically significant improvement in the 1990s (an average of 16.3 in 1991–97) compared to the 1980s (an average of 20.3 in 1982–90). It is also better than it was in the 1970s (17.1 percent in 1976–81), although the difference is not statistically significant. Despite the improvement in the 1990s, however, income distribution is still significantly more concentrated than it was in the 1960s (at 13.4).[13]

These data suggest that the deterioration of the 1980s was partially repaired in the 1990s, the distribution being close to that recorded in the late 1970s. Consequently, the sharp deterioration generated in the 1970s has not yet been reversed.

Prior to 1992, most indicators pointed to an improvement. The best-known one, the CASEN survey, shows an increase in the share of monetary income received by the poorest quintile of households between 1987 and 1992 and a decrease in the share of the richest quintile. From that time onward, however, the survey depicts stagnation and even some deterioration. But, still in 1996, all available data, both original and

---

11. We are aware that it would be more accurate methodologically to use "adult equivalent" (see footnote 2), but available data from the HBS survey do not allow it.

12. Other information, collected in the 1997 survey, shows very high indebtedness in the first quintile, with spending exceeding income by a third. Quintiles 1 to 7 register indebtedness, while quintiles 8 to 10 reveal savings (INE 1999, table 11).

13. The figures are based on a classification by household income per capita. The source (Ruiz-Tagle 1999) also provides data for total family income and income per capita adjusted by economies of scale and per adult equivalent. The ranking for the averages of the subperiods into which I have grouped the information is similar among the three categories. The results are also similar if the Gini coefficient is used. Nonetheless, the annual observations suffer from a great deal of "noise." Likewise, there are major differences in the levels of the coefficients depending on the criteria used to rank the information. This reminds us how careful we should be when drawing comparisons among different sources, methodologies, and stages of the economic cycle.

TABLE 9.4. Greater Santiago: Expenditure and Income Distribution per Household, 1987–88 and 1996–97 (percentages per quintile)

| | Distribution of Expenditure per Household | | | | Distribution of Income per Household | | | | Distribution of Expenditures per Household | | | |
| | Ranked According to Household Expenditure | | Ranked According to per Capita Expenditure | | Ranked According to Household Income | | Ranked According to per Capita Income | | Ranked According to Household Income | | Ranked According to per Capita Income | |
Quintile	Without IR	With IR	Without IR	With IR	Without IR	With IR	Without IR	With IR	Without IR	With IR	Without IR	With IR
Household Budget Survey												
1987–88												
1	4.3	4.9	5.9	6.4	3.1	3.8	4.0	4.8	6.5	6.3	7.7	7.6
2	8.2	8.6	9.6	10.2	6.4	7.0	7.9	8.6	9.0	9.3	10.7	10.8
3	12.6	12.8	13.5	13.6	10.6	11.1	11.2	11.8	13.2	13.2	13.5	13.9
4	20.2	20.1	19.9	19.8	18.4	18.6	18.3	18.6	20.3	20.0	19.8	19.4
5	54.8	53.6	51.2	50.0	61.6	59.5	58.6	56.2	51.0	51.1	48.4	48.4
Total	100.0	100.0	100.0	100.0	100.0	100.0	100.0	100.0	100.0	100.0	100.0	100.0
Q5/Q1	12.7	10.9	8.7	7.8	19.9	15.7	14.7	11.7	7.9	8.1	6.3	6.4
Gini (1)	0.45	0.44	0.40	0.39	0.52	0.49	0.48	0.45	0.40	0.40	0.36	0.36

Household Budget Survey

1996–97												
1	3.9	5.1	5.4	6.7	3.8	4.8	5.2	6.3	6.4	6.7	8.3	8.8
2	7.9	8.9	9.1	10.4	7.7	8.5	8.8	10.0	10.2	10.6	11.6	12.3
3	12.4	13.1	13.4	14.2	11.9	12.5	12.7	13.6	13.6	14.0	14.1	14.7
4	20.1	20.2	20.9	20.4	19.5	19.7	19.7	19.5	20.4	20.4	20.2	19.9
5	55.6	52.8	51.2	48.4	57.1	54.5	53.6	50.6	49.5	48.2	45.9	44.3
Total	100.0	100.0	100.0	100.0	100.0	100.0	100.0	100.0	100.0	100.0	100.0	100.0
Q5/Q1	14.3	10.4	9.5	7.2	15.0	11.4	10.3	8.0	7.7	7.2	5.5	5.0
Gini (2)	0.46	0.43	0.41	0.37	0.47	0.44	0.43	0.39	0.39	0.37	0.34	0.31
Ratio of Gini (2)/(1)	1.02	0.98	1.03	0.97	0.92	0.90	0.90	0.87	0.96	0.92	0.93	0.87

Source: ECLAC, based on special tabulations of the fourth and fifth Household Budget Surveys. Taken from Feres 2001.

[a]IR = imputed rent for homeowners.

adjusted, ranked both by household and by per capita income, show an improvement in the poorest 40 percent of households (in most cases in quintile 1) and a worsening in the richest 20 percent of households. That year, the Gini index had improved in all cases with respect to 1987 (see Feres 2001). In 1998, when the recessive adjustment began—it was already evident in November, the month when the survey was applied—a worsening in some indicators can be identified with respect to the 1996 survey. Nonetheless, these changes have low statistical significance. In summary, generally the 1990s perform better in terms of equity than did the 1987 sample.

The trend reversal in income distribution is also seen in the University of Chile employment survey for Santiago, with a worsening in 1994 and 1996–97 after improvements in the early 1990s. The deterioration in 1994 is partly accounted for by the fact that there was a minor contractive adjustment in this year (see Cowan and De Gregorio 1996), but 1996–97 were years of overexpansion (with the external deficit more than doubling that of the first half of the 1990s). We can interpret this overexpansion as an unsustainable surge in spending, with macroprices out of line, driven by an unsustainable volume of capital inflows. A great deal of such capital naturally goes to high-income sectors, including "wage earners" in these brackets; "trickle down" is never progressive. It is interesting to note that the (spectacularly large) spending boom in 1980–81 was also associated with a regressive impact on income (see Larrañaga 2001, figs. 1 and 2).

Thus, improvements in distribution took place mainly in the early years, when the *reforms of the reforms* were carried out; these injected a dose of equity into the regressive neoliberal inheritance. In the second five-year period, wage improvements moderated (with annual rises averaging 3.1 percent in 1996–98 as opposed to 4.9 percent in 1991–95), and the unemployment figures were already showing some deterioration in 1998.[14]

The main variable accounting for the lack of sustained progress would appear to be the labor market, with rises in the level of employment and social expenditure being offset by increasing wage inequality, which was mainly associated with differences in education (Beyer 1997; Bravo and Marinovic 1998; Larrañaga 2001).

---

14. Against this, there were substantial improvements in pensions and the minimum wage in 1998–2000, reflecting a growing awareness of the distribution problem but also coinciding with recessive years. Nonetheless, pensions and the minimum wage experienced strong improvements in 1998–2000, which reflected the public concern over social issues, on the one hand, and the frustrated expectation that investment and GDP would keep growing at around 7 percent per annum on the other. In the three-year period, actual GDP growth averaged 2.7 percent per annum, while fixed investment fell 14 percent between 1998 and 2000 (approximately 5 points of GDP). This deviation from the productive trend of the 1990s caused persistent regressive damage in the labor market.

The Concertación governments have pursued long-term policies of "investment in people," including a major reform of education. Nonetheless, the effects of the *reforms of the reforms* in the 1990s have been short of the target for three reasons. On the one hand, the main bills put forward by the two democratic governments faced opposition in the Senate, which meant that they had to be negotiated, and the reforms ultimately achieved were downsized (see Cortázar and Vial 1998; Ffrench-Davis 2000, chap. 7). Second, the institutional structure — the installed capacity of the state for spearheading actions against poverty and inequality — had been run down, as in the case of public health and education. Third, the policy was sometimes contradictory, being swept along at times by neoliberal fashion, an example being the setback in macroeconomic policy in 1996–97. Macroeconomic sustainability deteriorated since 1996 (see chap. 10). Chile became more vulnerable again, and it is in this condition that the country had to cope with the Asian crisis, with its patently regressive effects on employment and poverty, in 1999–2001.

Finally, the effects of investments in people take time to make themselves felt. Consequently, it is interesting to observe what happens to distribution when the free services provided by the state, whose benefits emerge in the long term, are added to people's monetary incomes.

As can be seen in table 9.1, there has been a substantial rise in per capita public spending delivered in the form of services such as education and health care, aimed essentially at the poorest quintiles. When corrected for these nonmonetary items, income distribution improves considerably, bringing down the difference between the richest and poorest quintile from 15.5 to 8.5 times for the CASEN survey of 1998. As social spending rose in the 1990s and was better targeted, its contribution to reducing inequality increased. This can be concluded from data produced by Bravo and Contreras (1999, table 7); these authors show that in 1990 the public sector provision of monetary income plus goods and services to the first quintile represented an addition of 49 percent to net per capita income, a figure that rose to 59 percent in 1994 and 75 percent in 1996. These large figures reflect the importance of free health care and the provision of education. A key variable is whether higher social spending actually leads to an increase in the volume and/or quality of services or whether the same services are merely provided at greater cost.[15] To ensure that spending produces results, effective pressure needs

---

15. It needs to be borne in mind that a substantial proportion of the increase in social spending in the 1990s was used to raise the wages of teachers and National Health System personnel. It is clear that in 1990 their salaries were notably out of line with the market and below the minimum required for efficient functioning. Unfortunately, while the quality of services fell as a result of the decline in pay and in the social status of these public services in the 1980s, improved incomes are not immediately followed by a recovery in quality.

to be applied to ensure high standards of productivity and better service to beneficiaries.

It will be recalled that at the beginning of this chapter and in chapter 1 I noted the dissatisfaction that was felt regarding the macrosocial imbalances prevailing around 1970. Although income distribution improved in the 1990s, the available data indicates that the situation is even worse now than it was then. This is a cause for greater dissatisfaction, and it means that more vigorous and effective efforts need to be made.

Factors Underlying Poverty and Income Concentration

The Role of the Neoliberal Reforms

The economic reforms applied in Chile in the 1970s and 1980s have had significant repercussions in the social field. Changing structural conditions, which meant a shift from an economy in which the state had a sizable presence to one driven by the free market forces, led to many changes in the distribution of well-being among the population. On the one hand, there were large, direct, negative effects on various social indicators owing to the move away from a model that treated income distribution and the struggle against poverty as top priority objectives to one that focused on the neutrality of policies. On the other hand, the extreme implementation of neoliberal principles and failure to take account of the heterogeneity of agents, combined with significant market failures and segmentation, translated into costly adjustment processes and severe recessions and generated a background of low productive investment and high unemployment (see chap. 1 and Ffrench-Davis 2000, chap. 1). Thus, indirectly these policies had a negative impact on an unprotected population. For this reason, the worsening of income distribution and the high levels of poverty that prevailed during the Pinochet government should come as no surprise.

As far as the reforms are concerned, one of the greatest changes was in the fiscal sphere. Reforms to the tax system, in 1975, included the abolition of wealth and capital gains taxes and a substantial reduction in the burden on profits. On the other hand, a value added tax was adopted and exemptions that existed for basic consumer goods were abolished.[16] The objective of these changes was to reduce the tax burden and concentrate it

16. There can be no doubt that the replacement of progressive taxes with VAT without exemptions was regressive in itself, and this was compounded by drops in social spending. This should not lead us to overlook the efficiency and high yield of VAT or the fact that a rate rise that has the purpose of increasing social spending is clearly progressive.

on taxes that were "neutral and efficient," the criterion of progressiveness being relegated to the background.

Public spending, as a percentage of GDP, was reduced by more than a quarter, in comparison with the late 1960s, after having spiraled out of control in 1972–73. There was a dramatic fall in public sector investment, which declined by more than half between 1970 and 1979 as a share of GDP. Public support for private productive activities, in the form of subsidies and infrastructure, also fell. Social spending increased as a share of all public spending, although, as has been noted, it fell in per capita terms. In 1981, it was lower than it had been in 1970, with a drop of 8 percent for education, 25 percent for health, and 30 percent for housing, all measured in real terms (Ffrench-Davis and Raczynski 1990). The decline continued until 1990.

The privatization of many of the means of production owned by the state took place in the mid-1970s. The process was conducted against the background of a domestic recession and extremely high interest rates. For this reason, only a few private groups were in a position to buy the privatized enterprises, mainly those that had greater access to external credit. Therefore, the concentration of wealth and power was strengthened still further (see chaps. 2 and 5; Dahse 1979; and Dahse 1982).

Chapter 5 analyzed the way in which the reforms in the financial market, far from enhancing productive investment, were characterized by extremely high real interest rates and a great deal of financial activity but contributed little to the generation of new productive capacity and were associated with crowded out domestic savings. Increasing financial inflows led the economy through a path of unsustainable expenditure, which ended in the deep crisis of 1982. The state had to intervene in the financial system to avoid a worse collapse; the high cost of subsidies to the financial system and borrowers contributed to a markedly regressive redistribution of wealth, which involved reductions in social spending and public sector investment in the 1980s and the long-lasting recession in the years following the crisis. Recall that only during 1988 was the 1981 level of GDP per capita restored.

Labor legislation also underwent major changes that had a negative impact on workers: the coverage of the minimum wage was reduced, the dismissal of workers was made easier, and the labor tribunals were abolished (they were restored in 1986). The unions were suspended in September 1973; later, in 1979, they were authorized again but with limited powers that excluded collective negotiation with unions of other companies, restricted the rights of union leaders, and fomented the segmentation of these groups (Campero and Valenzuela 1981; Cortázar 1983). In combination with political repression and economic depression, the legislation was effective in reducing the power of social organizations and their ability to defend their rights. These institutional factors emerge as a significant cause of the drift toward informal working and, for long periods, the deterioration in income distribution, which characterized the years of the dictatorship (Bravo and Marinović 1998).

In the early 1980s, deep reforms in the architecture of social security were introduced, affecting the health and pension systems. There were two structural reforms of great significance, which had a major impact on the fiscal budget, and distributive effects at the time the reforms were implemented. The structural changes to health care culminated in the creation of a dual system, with a public component acting through a National Common Fund (the Fondo Nacional de Salud or FONASA) and a private component consisting of a network of health care institutions (ISAPRES), which compete among themselves, acting as insurance companies.

To a large extent, health care was being financed by a payroll tax. The reform initially meant that 11 percent of the beneficiaries moved to the new ISAPRES system with 48 percent of the yield from health contributions (Titelman 2001). Regardless of the quality of the reform, this effect evidently constituted a regressive form of "targeting," and it helped to deepen the crisis in the public health system. Most people in the four poorest quintiles are covered by the public health system, and only in the richest quintile do ISAPRES cover a higher proportion of people than FONASA.[17]

Similarly, private pension fund management companies (the Administradoras de Fondos Previsionales [AFPs]) began to operate in 1981, in what marked the transition from a pay as you go system (which remained in existence for a decreasing number of people) to an individual capitalization one. This has a number of consequences for distribution. On the one hand, with fewer people retiring early (only white-collar workers had the option) and with higher pensions conditional on larger contributions beforehand, there were clearly progressive effects. On the other hand, the reform led to a decline in public revenue as payments were transferred to the AFPs in 1981. As the public sector was left with responsibility for covering the financing of existing pensions and the pensions of those due to retire in the coming years, the public social

---

17. Another important point, with regard to distribution, is the risk discrimination applied in the private system in the way that the insurance premium is linked to the health risk of the person concerned. This discriminates greatly against the elderly, the young, women, and in general those who are most in need of health services. It is noteworthy, for example, that if we limit the analysis to those aged sixty-five or over we find that even in the fifth quintile most people, some 56 percent, are treated in the public sector (Titelman 2001).

security deficit rose from 2 percent of GDP in 1980 to 7 percent in 1983–86. In a time of recession, this increased the strain on the fiscal accounts and was one of the factors behind social spending constraints and the unraveling of investment in human capital. As can be seen in table 9.1, the cuts in social spending on education and health between 1980 (before the reforms were implemented) and 1987 were spectacular. The reform did not succeed in including lower income informal or self-employed workers. Whereas 60 percent of the labor force was actively contributing to the social security system in 1974 (some 79 percent were affiliated), in 1988 the figure was just 55 percent; between these two years, the rate had fallen spectacularly, to a point as low as 40 percent in 1982 (Arellano 1989). Another important distributive implication is the concentration of power in the hands of AFP owners, who use the funds of workers to buy shares and thus have a strong say in appointing the boards of companies.

Finally, the trade reforms introduced since the mid-1970s have proved to be a key factor in explaining factorial income behavior. On the one hand, they had a great impact on the production structure of the country (see chap. 3), which led to a significant relative decline (and often an absolute one) in employment in some sectors (this was particularly steep in manufacturing) accompanied by a weaker dynamism in expanding sectors (Valdés 1992). This negative balance was strengthened by the exchange rate appreciation of 1979–82 and by the procyclical bias of macroeconomic policies.

Since the economy was opened up, there has been a marked increase in the rate of return to higher education, with the wage income distribution worsening, as has been noted. The forces behind this change in relative prices are rooted in the relative decline in the demand for unskilled labor accelerated by abrupt import liberalization and low investment, acting in tandem with greater human capital requirements in the economy since the reforms. But this tendency toward a growing wage gap would appear to be partly the result of an exogenous increase in demand for qualified workers (resulting from the direction of technological change and transmitted by growing trade links with the rest of the world, where wage inequality is also on the rise), vis-à-vis a rather inflexible composition of supply in terms of human capital.[18] At the same time, the productive structure in the 1980s was dominated by a natural-resource-intensive export sector using little unskilled labor,

---

18. Labor training can contribute significantly to making the labor supply more flexible. There was some progress in this field in the 1990s. The percentage of the labor force trained under the tax-exempt National Training and Employment Service (SENCE) scheme increased from 4 percent in 1990 to nearly 8 percent in 1998. Nonetheless, only 20 percent of companies made full use of this benefit and the distribution of their spending was highly regressive (Benavente and Crespi 1998).

which kept demand for this group low and accentuated the inequality of wage distribution.[19]

The concentration of human capital investment opportunities, with only a minority of the labor force attaining more than 12 years of schooling (which is the threshold that denotes a break in the yield curve to school years), depicts an inadequate training effort and a regressive system of higher education. This became even more regressive when public funding for the universities was cut back in the 1980s and public institutions yielded in importance to private ones, which has acted as a mechanism that perpetuates historical inequities across generations.

Crucial Factors

The regressive trends of the 1980s were not exclusive to Chile. In general, income distribution worsened, real wages fell, and the level and quality of employment declined throughout Latin America. Something similar happened in the United States and Great Britain in that decade, with the ratio between the richest and poorest quintiles rising. In the United States, the family incomes of the poor fell, while those of the richest 10 percent improved substantially in the 1980s (Krugman 1990).

Poverty and income distribution are determined essentially by the production process itself,[20] whence the great importance of ensuring that the transformation of production is accompanied by equity. For this, growth is essential. It is clear that the choice is not between growth and equity. It is not simply a matter of choosing growth, since to achieve this, and make it sustainable, is no easy matter: Chile has only managed it in exceptional periods, one of which was 1990–97. Consequently, the most crucial thing is to identify the determinants of growth, and at the stage of development that Chile is now going through there are crucial complementarities between the sources of growth and equity, between macroeconomic and macrosocial balances.

The creation of productive employment is the main channel through which economic and social progress is transmitted. This depends on supply and demand, and both are affected by public policies.

For there to be demand, productive investment must be high, much

---

19. Like other countries in Latin America, Chile has comparative advantages in the production of natural-resource-intensive goods. The use of non-labor-intensive methods to produce them was to entail a worsening of income distribution, in contrast to what would happen in other developing countries that concentrate on the production of labor-intensive goods, such as the Asian ones (Fischer 1999).

20. Inequality is also the result of a demographic factor. Higher fertility rates that continue to be a feature of low-income sectors and the relatively low market participation of women from the lower strata reinforce the regressive trend of income distribution.

higher than it was during the neoliberal regime. Larger capital formation makes it possible to have higher growth with greater job creation and better wages. The fact that average wages were still lower in 1989 than in 1970 is principally due to the low investment ratio recorded in the 1970s and 1980s. Similarly, the high rate of investment between 1992 and 1998 helps to explain the sustained although still insufficient improvement in wages that occurred under the two democratic governments.

But physical investment is not enough. There is also a need to increase human capital, to invest in people, given the dynamics of innovation and technological progress (an issue discussed later). Investment in people, one of the two components of social spending, is a factor of production. An even more important feature, though, is that investment in people — particularly in education and health care — prepares them to participate more effectively in the market and is instrumental in bringing the perpetuation of poverty, whereby the children of the poor are condemned to be poor themselves, to a halt. Better nutrition and more education of higher quality are key inputs for a more flexible labor supply, which permits a more effective adjustment to the demand requirements, within a globalization environment. The other component is continuous redistributive spending, aimed at compensating the losers with modernization, those who cannot earn a better living in the market or those who have ended their working lives and have insufficient pensions or none at all.

Stability, Investment, and Distribution

Comprehensive stability is essential to equity and economic growth. If we look at what happened to wages and employment during recessive periods in the last quarter of the century, we can see that in all of them the fall in labor income was disproportionately high and informal working increased. Given the regressive effect that adjustment processes normally have on lower income sectors and wage earners, it is clear that efforts need to be made to remove the factors that cause instability and uncertainty (Rodrik 2001).

The definition of stability is crucial. CPI stability is essential, but it is only one ingredient of comprehensive stability, of which the stability of the *real* economy is the most significant. That implies using productive capacity (potential GDP) with *right* macroeconomic prices (see Ffrench-Davis 2000, chaps. 1 and 6).

This conclusion is even more compelling when we observe the performance of investment, since instability is also a disincentive to invest. When firms are producing below capacity and land is underused, it is obvious that there are fewer market incentives to invest in the creation of new productive capacity (Ffrench-Davis and Reisen 1998; Agosin 1998). Empirical evidence shows that one of the most common tendencies during recessive adjustment is a sharp drop in investment: if aggregate demand is adjusting downward, some installed capacity will be underused, and the potential investor will therefore wonder what point there is in continuing to create additional productive capacity. Since capital formation is not a priority for short-termish thinking, public investment is generally cut as well, and this discourages private investment still further.[21]

The result is a negative effect on the link between the present and the future, a link that is strengthened with investment and productivity increases.

There are two ways of looking at productivity. One considers how much the output of a given set of resources increases or decreases as its utilization rate changes. When in the course of an economic cycle output falls sharply by 14 percent, as happened in Chile in 1982, what is really falling is the rate of resource utilization. Against a background of instability, this way of measuring productivity indicates that the same labor and capital that existed before are now producing 14 percent less than they were. But this kind of productivity is restored by bringing what already exists back into use once the recessionary stage of the cycle has given way to the expansionary one, even when the volume of resources and potential productivity remain unchanged. The other view of productivity is concerned with efforts to innovate, with new combinations of productive resources and improvements in their quality. This second type of productivity is one of the determinants of long-term growth. Frequently, research mixes up these two components (see essays by several authors in Morandé and Vergara 1997).

Economies with large fluctuations tend to discourage technological innovation, as instability leads both to large losses and great opportunities for easy profit. In such periods, the profits of some are generally made at the expense of others (in a negative sum game). If a business periodically has the opportunity to earn 10 or 20 percent on invested capital in a short-term operation, it is obvious that it will be less concerned with improving productivity at a rate of 2 or 3 percent a year by means of complex technological innovations. During upswings in the economic cycle, there are great opportunities to generate disproportionate profits as a result of sudden changes in the relative prices of both

---

21. Another consequence has been underinvestment by domestic SMEs. Correcting this imbalance takes time, and progress has been slowed by downward adjustment processes, as increases in interest rates above "normal" levels and domestic demand restriction affect such companies more severely than large ones, which are more diversified and can obtain financing through other channels.

products and assets, without the need for a managerial effort for long-term innovation. What happens, therefore, is that cyclical instability processes tend to result in neglect of medium and long-term productivity: what is the point of worrying about improving the quality of what you produce and the way it is produced, and the design of products and new production lines, when other opportunities are available?

Instability clearly creates an environment that is prone to speculative investment rather than technological innovation and productive investment.

Environments of great instability, like those seen in Chile during the 1970s and 1980s, tend to be accompanied by two other phenomena whose effects on society as a whole are negative. On the one hand, as we have seen across virtually all of Latin America, there are cuts in social spending during cyclical downturns. Public sector social spending on education, health, and housing has tended to "overadjust," falling proportionately more than GDP, even though needs increase during periods of recessive adjustment (ECLAC 2000).

Second, in these situations of instability losses tend to emerge in productive or financial sectors, with an inclination to sustain them by public sector subsidies. One case at hand is that of the Chilean banking system after the 1983 crisis, as discussed earlier, with a total final cost equivalent to 35 percent of a year's GDP (Sanhueza 1999). Thus, over the course of a few years, the equivalent of a third of national output (or public expenditure on education during a full decade) was transferred from some sectors to others in order to cope with this banking crisis. The magnitude of the problems in the banking sector accounts for the need to act, but it in no way justifies the specific policies imposed. Similarly, there can be no doubt that transfers as large as these could have been designed to have a very different distributive impact. Most of the large transfers of wealth that took place in the 1970s and 1980s were only possible in the framework of great instability, reinforced by the arbitrary and ideology-driven approach of the authoritarian regime in power.

Technological Innovation

The last two decades have been a time of great technological innovation in the world, particularly in areas such as communications, information technology, and electronics. These innovations unquestionably have served to improve productivity. What has happened to world growth over recent years? Paradoxically, the world is growing more slowly. The average expansion rate has sunk from 4 percent a year in 1965–80 to 3 percent in 1980–2000; the good performance of 2000 (over 4 percent) was rather exceptional and not the new trend rate.

This in no way means that technological progress has not been helpful to growth. Rather, it shows that some requirements of quality and proportion must be met. For one, technological innovation cannot be significantly introduced on a large scale in isolation. Much of it is embodied in machinery and equipment and the capabilities of people. This means that much higher productive, physical, and human investment will be needed in order to incorporate technological development and thus improve national total factor productivity.

Meanwhile, a high rate of technical progress requires flexible and increasingly highly qualified labor if excessive "technological unemployment" — where the dynamics of innovation displace workers who are unable to adapt to the requirements of the new technologies — is to be avoided. In order to countervail the expanding gap between low and high wages, an increase in physical investment and investment in people is essential. High investment can compensate for labor-saving techniques and easier restructuring. Other crucial aspects are improving the skills of labor and providing better training for workers during the course of their working lives, whence the importance of reforming education and redoubling labor training efforts.

Recently, however, the trend in the world at large has been a reduction in investment and savings ratios (Schmidt-Hebbel and Servén 1999). This is closely related to the declining effectiveness of macroeconomic policies and the nature of innovation in capital markets, which have brought about a dizzying increase in the speed at which speculative capital can move from one country to another; this has led to great instability in exchange rates, interest rates, and economic activity.

Thus, a downward trend can be seen in world productive investment, together with a spectacular increase in international capital flows. This contradiction is explained by the fact that most of these funds are not tied to productive investment, but are of a speculative nature. These movements are guided by expectations about differentials in interest rates, exchange rates and stock market prices in different countries. There are too many agents dedicated to the capture of capital gains rather than generating productivity gains. This financierism appears to be one of the reasons for the weakening of productive investment and economic growth.

Concluding Remarks

The regressive trends in Chile in the years prior to 1990 were generally reversed by the active policies of the two democratic governments. Although considerable progress was made in reducing poverty and indigence during the decade, after an initial improvement income distribution fell back into stagnation, which raises major challenges for the authorities.

The 1990 tax reform made it possible to finance increased social spending and initiate the long process of restoring and raising the quality of education and health care. The labor reform helped unions to gather strength and workers to better defend themselves. Nonetheless, it should be borne in mind that neither reform went as far than the democratic government intended, although progress was achieved in the desired direction.

Improvements in the minimum wage and family allowances in the 1990s directly benefited Chileans in the poorest quintile. The same result was achieved by means of innovative targeted programs such as primary schools in poor areas and labor training for youngsters (Raczynski 1996).

There is overwhelming evidence that macroeconomic balances are of crucial importance for the success of any development strategy. The price that has to be paid when balances are lost is very high. Not only do countries forfeit any initial improvement in growth or equity that might have been achieved, but experience shows that there are also very high political costs for governments that succumb to populist temptations, whether on the Left or the Right. The methods used to achieve macroeconomic equilibria can be very diverse (Ramos 1993; Ffrench-Davis 2000, chap. 6): they may be more focused or dispersed, more cyclical or stable. They depend, among other things, on the relative weight given to variables such as the composition of public spending and revenue, the structure of financial institutions and capital flows, exchange rate policy, and public sector initiatives that contribute to the skills and organization of lower income sectors. These features make the difference between a government for the minority and one that serves the majority.

A significant change has taken place in macroeconomic policy since 1990. As a result, major imbalances like those recorded in 1975 and 1982–83 were avoided. For example, Chile could have persisted with the neoliberal approach by adopting a passive policy toward inflows of speculative capital, as Argentina and Mexico did. In that case, it would have suffered an acute recession and a marked deterioration in income distribution once again in 1995, which is what happened in those two countries.[22] However, Chile implemented fairly efficient regulations on short-term financial flows, thanks to which the "Tequila effect" reached the country in diluted form.

---

22. In Mexico, for example, real wages were on average 15 percent lower in 2000 than in 1994.

As is discussed in chapter 10, after 1995 the peso was allowed to appreciate excessively and the current account deficit was allowed to expand in 1996–97. What lay behind this policy reversal? Chile showed itself to be immune to the 1995 crisis in Mexico and Argentina, which enhanced perceptions of the country's strength. What was not understood is that this was primarily due to the deep change that had taken place in macroeconomic management in the first half of the 1990s; a key instrument was clearly the unremunerated reserve requirement, which discouraged inflows of short-term liquid and speculative capital. In the international financial media, meanwhile, wide support was given to the dangerously mistaken idea that financial crises were a matter of the past.

Finally, inflation reduction targets were given priority over the other objectives of Chilean economic policy; a 16 percent appreciation in the real exchange rate between 1995 and October 1997, resulting from a dangerous move toward a quasi-free-floating exchange rate policy in that period, was largely instrumental in reducing inflation from 8.2 percent in 1995 to 2.6 percent in 1997 (and to 1.9 percent in the wholesale price index [WPI], which has a large tradables component). This was not so much the result of a deliberate policy as of a more passive approach toward the capital surge into Chile over those two years and its impact on the exchange rate (see chap. 10). These imbalances in 1996–97 made Chile more vulnerable to the Asian crisis of 1998. Once again, as adjustment took place across the economy, and despite government efforts to increase social spending the least affluent sectors suffered most. The result in 1999–2001 was an increase in unemployment, stagnation in the reduction of poverty, and a worsening of income distribution. Recent data on the distribution of household per capita income in Santiago shows a worsening in 1999–2001 (Gini 55.3) in comparison to 1991–98 (Gini 52.5) but still somewhat less uneven than in 1987–90 (Gini 57.0) (Larrañaga 2001).

Securing structural improvements in distribution is a long-term task. It has been addressed willingly since the return to democracy but with some inconsistencies. Among other macro- and mesoeconomic aspects, the approach that needs to be taken includes:

1. Improving active macroeconomic management to make the economy less vulnerable to external shocks, the effects of which are always regressive; reactivating and improving regulation of flows in the face of the next capital surge; rebuilding an active exchange rate policy in order to provide greater predictability for the export sector; avoiding the two extremes of a fixed or totally free-floating exchange rate; and establishing a systematically anticyclical fiscal policy.

2. Continuing to reduce legal tax elusion and illegal evasion, which are detrimental to fiscal equity.
3. Implementing a systematic educational reform and improving and standardizing educational quality, and upgrading programs and teaching staff, with the financing these require.
4. Making a real push toward an increase in the quantity, functionality, and efficiency of labor training, in order to enhance the flexibility and adaptability of the labor supply.
5. Providing SMEs with significantly greater access to long-term domestic financing, modern technology, entrepreneurial and labor training, and more stable domestic markets and to enhance the ability to search for foreign markets.
6. Strengthening the dynamism of nontraditional exports with greater value added. The essential ingredients for renewed momentum of exports, more closely associated with domestic productive development, are as follows: consolidating Latin American integration processes, promoting an active exchange rate policy, an ambitious national program for labor training, and the productive development of SMEs.

CHAPTER 10

Managing Capital Inflows in the 1990s

Toward the end of the 1980s, private capital inflows began to return to Latin America (see Calvo et al. 1993 and Ffrench-Davis and Griffith-Jones 1995). The reversal of the drought in capital inflows of the 1980s undoubtedly had positive effects. It relaxed the binding foreign exchange constraint under which most countries labored during the debt crisis. However, both the large magnitude of the new capital flows and their composition, which is prone to volatility, have caused disequilibria for which the recipient countries have been, by and large, ill prepared.

In the first place, if they are to contribute to long-term development, capital inflows should lead to a significant increase in the investment rate, something that, with the exception of Chile, has not taken place in most countries in the region. Chile was one of the first countries to attract the renewed flows of foreign capital and one that faced the largest supply in relation to its size. It will be argued that one reason for the greater degree of success in channeling foreign capital to investment has been the discouragement of short-term flows and the large share of foreign direct investment in capital inflows in the 1990s. The Chilean experience does indeed suggest that, when capital inflows take the form of FDI, there is a greater likelihood that the investment rate will rise than when foreign capital takes more liquid or short-term forms.

Second, large inflows pose difficult dilemmas to policymakers. Without intervention on foreign exchange markets and in the absence of regulations on capital inflows, the real exchange rate will appreciate, which may be undesirable from the point of view of other important policy objectives (e.g., encouraging export growth and diversification, attaining higher domestic investment rates, or meeting targets for the

This chapter is based on a paper coauthored with Manuel Agosin (Professor of Economics, Universidad de Chile), in *Short-Term Capital Flows and Economic Crises,* Stephany Griffith-Jones, Manuel Montes, and Answar Nasution, eds. (London: Oxford University Press and United Nations University, 2001). Reprinted with permission from Oxford University Press and United Nations University/the World Institute for Development Economic Research.

current account deficit consistent with sustainable capital inflows). On the other hand, intervention in the foreign exchange market tends to swell the domestic money supply and increases the difficulties of controlling inflation.

Third, a significant proportion of the recent inflow to emerging markets has taken the form of short-term or liquid capital. Two components of capital inflows are clearly of a short-term nature: short-term credits and deposits, on the one hand, and portfolio flows on the other.

Portfolio inflows, defined here as financial investment mostly in Chilean equity, are not usually thought of as short-term capital, but in practice they are. Portfolio investments can be liquidated at any moment at the market price of the moment and therefore may be just as short term in nature as short-term indebtedness. Typically, portfolio investors operate with imperfect information, they seek short-term capital appreciation, and they are prone to bandwagon effects, either in taking positions or in liquidating them. This has been clearly evident in the financial crises that have stricken first Mexico (December 1994) and more recently the Asian economies since mid-1997 and Latin America since 1998. In both cases, the original crisis spread to other "emerging market" countries, as investors lost confidence not only in the economy, where the crisis had started, but in those of other developing countries that had received large financial capital inflows. Large portfolio inflows were thus followed by large outflows, with sharp reversals of initial appreciation in exchange rates and stock market prices.[1]

During the capital surge of the 1970s, Chile had maintained a fairly open capital account, pioneering the neoliberal fashion. However, policies in the 1990s represented a significant move toward greater pragmatism. In a nutshell, the policy response during the 1990s surges in the supply of foreign capital can be described as an attempt to discourage short-term inflows while maintaining liberal policies toward long-term inflows. Particularly, policies were directed toward increasing the cost of short-term inflows via non-interest-bearing reserve requirements; it is a price-based policy tool intended to modify relative costs in the market. The authorities also resorted to the introduction of uncertainty in the spot exchange rate (with intramarginal intervention) and had sterilized intervention in order to slow down real exchange rate appreciation (in face of inflows that surpassed the barrier of the reserve requirement)

---

1. Nationals of the countries concerned have been observed to behave much in the same way as foreign portfolio investors when they are allowed to do so. Thus, the ultimate cause of exchange rate and asset price volatility appears to be the openness of the capital account and the ease of moving into and out of assets denominated in foreign currency rather than just the behavior of foreign investors.

and compensate for the monetary effects of reserve accumulation. With this set of policies, the government sought to protect a development strategy whose main elements are export growth and diversification. In parallel, the fiscal budget was in surplus and prudential supervision of the financial sector was enhanced.

Policy was effective in achieving its targets during most of the 1990s. However, in 1996–97 this policy mix and the intensity with which it was applied remained unchanged, in spite of a new vigorous surge in capital flows to most countries in the region. This surge should have been met with increased restrictions.

As a consequence of the lack of stronger action on capital inflows during 1996–97, and despite heavy intervention in foreign exchange markets, the Central Bank was unable to prevent a sharp real exchange rate appreciation and a worrisome rise of the deficit on the current account. Undoubtedly, this problem could have been met with a higher reserve requirement or other similar policy tools. Nonetheless, as will be discussed, the benefits of the active regulation implemented in previous years had left large international reserves, a rather low stock of foreign liabilities, and a small share of volatile inflows.

By 1998–99, the contagion effects of the Asian currency crisis had made themselves felt. The large inflows of financial capital of 1996–97 gave way to outflows, and the nominal exchange rate began to depreciate. By late 1999 the real exchange rate had returned to its 1995 average level but in the process the Central Bank had lost international reserves, with the corresponding significant impact on domestic liquidity. For the first time in the decade, in 1999 the Chilean economy experienced a significant gap between effective GDP and productive capacity; as a consequence, unemployment rose and the investment ratio dropped sharply and remained recessed in 1999–2001. Naturally, the extent of recessive adjustment was partly associated with the boom in 1996–97.

Thus, there is a need to reassess the policy options to further improve the management of financial flows and exchange rate policy in the future, so as to discourage excessive inflows and protect the economy from excessive exchange rate volatility. A more active and flexible use of a comprehensive policy mix, matching the intensity of surges, should be adopted.

This chapter studies the phenomenon of massive capital inflows in Chile in the 1990s, the policy approaches utilized to deal with it, and its effects on the domestic economy. The first section describes the dimensions and composition of capital inflows. There follows a discussion of the policy approaches utilized to deal with capital surges and an analysis of their macroeconomic impacts. The chapter concludes with a discussion of policy lessons that can be drawn from Chile's experience.

TABLE 10.1.   Net Capital Inflows and Deficit on the Current Account, 1960–2000 (as a percentage of GDP)

	Net Capital Inflows		Deficit on Current Account
	Current Prices	Constant Prices 1986[a]	Current Prices
1960–70	2.6	4.3	2.5
1971–73	1.2	2.1	2.9
1974–77	2.7	3.4	1.9
1978–81	12.2	19.7	8.0
1982–89	5.5	6.4	6.2
1990–95	6.9	6.9	2.5
1996–97	8.0	9.2	5.7
1998–2000	1.2	1.3	2.4

Source: Based on *Balanza de Pagos* and national accounts data from the Central Bank of Chile.
[a]The constant price series was derived by deflating the dollar series by an index of foreign prices faced by the Chilean economy. As for the denominator, GDP at constant prices was transformed into 1986 dollars using the 1986 peso-dollar exchange rate.

Recent Capital Inflows: Magnitude and Composition

The period since 1990 corresponds to the return to democratic rule and is roughly coincident with the two latest episodes of foreign capital abundance and the implementation of a set of active macroeconomic policies, especially the policies oriented toward managing capital inflows in the first half of the 1990s. During the decade, the economy expanded briskly and was close to its output capacity up to 1998. This was determinant of a record investment ratio, in a virtuous circle.

The data in table 10.1 show that capital inflows, as a proportion of GDP, were substantially larger in the 1990–98 period than in the 1960s and, surprisingly, only slightly higher than during the debt crisis of 1982–89. However, it should be taken into account that Chilean GDP is much larger now (in dollar terms) than in previous periods. Consequently, in absolute terms capital inflows are of a much larger order of magnitude. Moreover, in 1997 total inflows soared, reaching levels that were much higher than earlier in the decade and accounting for 10 percent of GDP.

In the mid-1980s, and in spite of the debt crisis, capital inflows were relatively large, both in nominal terms and as a share of GDP.[2] The disappearance of voluntary bank lending was partly compensated for by substantial support from multilateral financial institutions (see chap. 6).

2. This partly reflects the effects of the debt crisis itself, which led to the dramatic real devaluations of 1982–85, with the consequent fall in the dollar value of Chilean GDP from U.S.$32.6 billion in 1981 to U.S.$16.0 billion in 1985.

Thus, public flows became the main form of international financial resources available to the Chilean economy during the 1980s.

Private capital began to return to Chile in 1986, but the initial spurt was associated almost exclusively with the debt-equity swap program started by the authorities in the second half of 1985. It was not until 1989 that other private flows became significant (see fig. 10.1). In part owing to the large exchange rate subsidy implicit in the swap scheme, the program was successful in attracting significant amounts of foreign investment in the form of swaps (see chap. 7). The swap program was abandoned by foreign investors in 1991, mainly because the rise in the international price of Chilean debt made it no longer profitable to invest via debt swaps. However, FDI not associated with the swaps continued to grow apace. During the 1990s, FDI represented an overwhelming part of the capital inflows into Chile.

The supply of short-term private inflows also figured prominently in the capital surge, though at a much lower scale than FDI. For interest-arbitraging capital inflows to take place, the domestic interest rate must exceed the international rate by a margin that is more than sufficient to compensate for the expected exchange rate depreciation and the country risk premium. These conditions have prevailed in Chile since the late 1980s. On the one hand, in 1992 and 1993 international dollar interest rates reached a thirty-year low, and, while they have risen since then, they have remained moderate and are still much lower than they were in the 1980s. On the other hand, notwithstanding the record high investment ratio of Chile in the 1990s, it still has a low stock of productive capital, associated with its U.S.$5,000 income per capita. Obviously, that shortage of productive capital results in a higher level in its trend market rate of return or price. Therefore, the interest rate must tend to be higher than in a developed economy. Thus, monetary policy, in order to be consistent with sustainable macroeconomic balances, must hold real interest rates over the foreign ones. In the Chilean case, additionally, an adjustment process accompanied this "structural gap" in 1990, which relied on a significant rise in domestic interest rates (see Ffrench-Davis 2000, chap. 7).

The other two requirements for interest arbitrage were also favorable to capital inflows. Chile experienced 130 percent appreciation in 1982–88, and, as it emerged from the debt crisis, expectations regarding the real exchange rate turned from depreciation to appreciation. Improving terms of trade in the late 1980s also contributed to the change in expectations. Moreover, in the early 1990s expectations of exchange rate appreciation, owing to the capital inflow itself and an improved current account position, made short-term round-tripping appear very profitable. Also, the "emerging markets" mania of recent

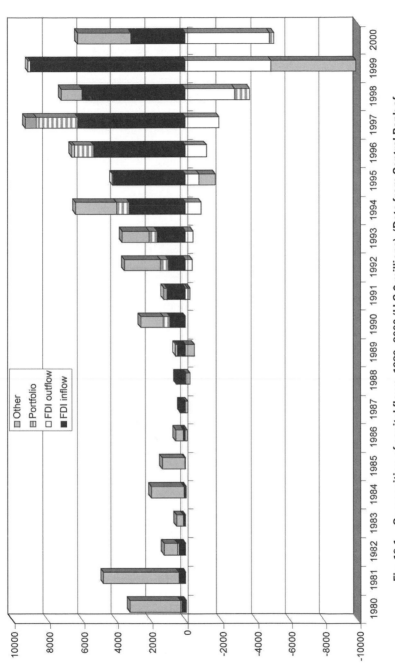

Fig. 10.1. Composition of capital flows, 1980–2000 (U.S.$ millions). (Data from Central Bank of Chile.)

years in international stock markets can be interpreted as a dramatic reduction in perceived country risk. Short-term private flows were very important until 1992, when they began to fall as a consequence of the policy measures adopted to stem them.

Portfolio inflows have taken two forms: investments through mutual funds set up in the major international capital markets and the issue of American Depositary Receipts (ADRs) by large Chilean corporations. The ADR is a mechanism by means of which foreign corporations can issue new shares on the U.S. stock markets. The "primary" issue of ADRs represents an opportunity to expand the capital of firms at a relatively low cost, since capital costs in international markets naturally tend to be lower than in Chile. The relatively developed domestic stock market, the low country risk, and the burgeoning use of ADRs for placing shares in the U.S. stock markets made Chilean stocks a prime candidate for investors seeking new and more exotic financial vehicles.

There is also a "secondary" issue of ADRs through the purchase of the underlying stock in the Chilean market by foreigners and its subsequent conversion into ADRs (for a thorough discussion, see Ffrench-Davis, Agosin, and Uthoff 1995). This operation does not constitute an enlargement of the capital of the issuing company but only a change in ownership from nationals to foreigners. At a moment when foreign exchange is overabundant and there are significant downward pressures on the exchange rate, it may be necessary to discourage them. These shifts in ownership involve exposing the economy to an additional degree of uncertainty and volatility, since when foreign investors' mood changes they can easily reverse the operation and convert their ADRs into the underlying stock in national currency for sale on the domestic stock market. These flows have played a destabilizing role.[3] They inflated the stock exchanges in 1994 and 1997 and depressed them in 1995 and 1998, in a clear case of procyclical behavior.

The Mexican and East Asian crises are illustrative of these dangers of financial destabilization. In the case of Mexico, as emphasized by Sachs, Tornell, and Velasco (1996), domestic policy failures, particularly the large increase in domestic credit that resulted from a poorly regulated domestic financial system, were important factors. Domestic credit booms in both of these crises, however, were triggered by large capital

---

3. It has been argued that foreigners who become pessimistic about a country will sell their ADRs on the U.S. stock market, therefore having no impact on the domestic stock and foreign exchange markets. However, this argument ignores the fact that the issuance of ADRs implies that stock prices in the domestic and U.S. markets must tend toward equality through arbitrage. This is in fact what happened: movements in stock prices of Chilean companies that issued ADRs in U.S. stock exchanges are highly correlated with those in the Santiago exchange.

inflows. The herding behavior displayed by foreign portfolio investors has been increasingly recognized as a critical element in the crisis (Calvo and Mendoza 1996; Griffith-Jones 1998). Since assets of firms from a particular developing country are normally a very small proportion of international investors' portfolios, it may not pay to go to the trouble of obtaining costly information. Therefore, they tend to follow "signals." The positive signal at the end of the 1980s was that Mexico was undertaking market-oriented reforms (and entering NAFTA) that would, in the eyes of the international banks, raise returns on Mexican corporate assets. In the case of Mexico, the signal for a reversal of the financial capital inflow was the notion that current account deficits had become "unsustainable" and the exchange rate had appreciated "excessively." Of course, the large current account deficits and outlier macroeconomic prices, particularly an appreciating exchange rate, had principally been a consequence of the exogenous (and collective) behavior of foreign investors in the first place.

What this boils down to is that a large component of capital inflows, particularly portfolio capital, is not only volatile but largely exogenous from the point of view of the recipient country. Even short-term credit has an exogenous component, since the so-called country risk premium has a large subjective element. Hence, paradoxically, a successful country can see its fundamentals — such as the deficit on the current account, exchange rate, domestic savings, and bank portfolio — worsened by a large capital surge (see Ffrench-Davis 2000, chap. 10).

From a theoretical point of view, what we have here is the possibility of multiple equilibria: an appreciated exchange rate with large capital inflows and a depreciated exchange rate with capital outflows. Moreover, there are dynamics involved: capital inflows appreciate the real exchange rate, and the latter, if it is gradual, encourages additional inflows. This can proceed for several years, as happened in 1976–81 and 1990–94 in several LACs. After a while, when the deficits on the current account accumulate and the stock of external liabilities has risen, the appreciation trend is replaced with expectations of depreciation, which in turn tends to lead to a reversal in the direction of flows. This indicates that there is a need for policies that reduce the more volatile components of capital inflows and demonstrates that the "fundamentals" are not independent of policies toward inflows. Moreover, some equilibria are more "desirable" than others, in terms of their effects on economic growth and sustainability.

While private flows have increased, public debt has been reduced with public outflows. During 1989–91, these net outflows were caused mainly by the public debt operations involved in debt-equity swaps. More recently, the reduction of public debt corresponds mostly to debt prepayments. These were particularly large in 1995–96. These prepayments were undertaken to alleviate the large accumulation of international reserves by the Central Bank; to reduce net financial costs; and, in doing so, to relieve appreciating pressures on foreign exchange markets and improve the balance of the bank.

Since 1991, several large Chilean corporations have been making direct investments abroad. The destinations are mainly neighboring countries. The largest investments have been in electricity generation and distribution (mostly in recently privatized companies, first in Argentina and then in other Latin American countries), but other sectors such as light manufacturing and retailing are also represented (Calderón and Griffith-Jones 1995). In 1996, after a persistent expansion since 1991, investment abroad represented 1.7 percent of GDP.[4] A major rise in 1997–99 is commented upon later.

The Policy Response and Its Effects

In the 1990s, Chilean monetary authorities have deployed a wide range of policies to regulate the surge in capital inflows. On the one hand, the Central Bank has attempted to discourage short-term and speculative capital inflows while maintaining open access to the economy for FDI. On the other, it has sought to moderate the impact of capital inflows on the domestic economy, by intervening in foreign exchange markets so as to prevent an excess supply as a result of unduly appreciating the real exchange rate and sterilizing almost completely the monetary effects of the rapid accumulation of international reserves (see Ffrench-Davis, Agosin, and Uthoff 1995).

Two other policy factors have contributed to the success achieved in managing capital inflows. First, fiscal policy has been very cautious. Higher levels of social expenditure have been financed through new taxes. Chile ran a significant public sector surplus during the 1990s, amounting to 1 to 2 percent of GDP.[5] The prudent stance of fiscal policy, including compliance with the rules of a copper stabilization fund,[6]

---

4. Balance of payments data underestimate the size of these investments because a large share of them is financed with funds raised on international capital markets that never enter the country. A similar situation emerged regarding Korean investments in its neighbors.

5. In 1999, a deficit was recorded, determined by the significant drop in fiscal income. This was associated with the severe adjustment process that depressed aggregate demand.

6. Given copper's weight in the balance of payments and fiscal accounts, and the instability of its price, a Buffer Fund was created in the 1980s under an SAL from the World Bank. The fund accumulates a share of price increases in order to compensate for future

eased the task for the monetary authorities in managing capital inflows and preventing undue exchange rate appreciation during most of the decade. Second, as a result of the 1982–83 banking crisis, prudential banking regulations were introduced and have been perfected over the years. This, again, prevented capital inflow from unleashing a lending spree by the commercial banks, which, in turn, eased the task of keeping the current account and the exchange rate within sustainable bounds up to 1996.

Policies Aimed at Managing Capital Inflows

In a context of massive capital inflows, the two main goals of exchange rate and inflow management policies were, first, that in an economy prone to huge cycles (recall that in 1975 and 1982 Chile experienced the sharpest recessions in all Latin America) achieving sustained macrostability should be a priority. The second goal is to protect the growth model adopted by the authorities, which grants a leading role to the expansion and diversification of exports.

For exports to continue to act as an engine of growth for the Chilean economy, the level and stability of the real exchange rate are crucial. This objective could have been placed in jeopardy if capital inflows had caused excessive exchange rate appreciation and greater future volatility when the direction of net flows went into reverse. A summary of policy actions to tackle the excess supply can be found in table 10.2.

The Chilean authorities opted to regulate the foreign exchange market in order to prevent large misalignments in the real exchange rate relative to its long-term trend. The option chosen to make long-term fundamentals prevail over short-term factors influencing the exchange rate assumes (correctly, in my view) that there exists an asymmetry of information between the market and the monetary authorities, because the latter have better knowledge of the factors driving the balance of payments and principally because they have a longer planning horizon than agents who operate intensely at the short-term end of the market. However, in the face of market uncertainty, rather than a unique price, the authorities have used an exchange rate band centered on a reference price linked to a basket of three currencies, in which the dollar, the deutsche mark, and the yen are represented with weights associated with their share of Chilean trade.

Here I give an analytical account relating policy changes to the events that elicited them. The changes taking place in global markets,

low-price periods. The fund was active throughout the 1990s and plays a stabilizing role for fiscal income (see table 1.2).

the increasing international approval of Chilean economic policies, high interest rates in Chile, and a smooth transition to democracy stimulated a growing capital inflow in mid-1990.

These events were quickly reflected in a real appreciation of the market exchange rate. Beginning in July 1990, the exchange rate was at the floor of the band (in Latin American terms, i.e., the appreciated extreme). Even during the Iraq crisis in September 1990, the market rate stayed at the floor, despite the fact that Chile was then importing 85 percent of its oil needs; Chile reacted to this crisis by drastically raising

TABLE 10.2.   Regulations on Capital Flows in Chile, Second Quarter of 1998

Foreign direct investment

The only restriction on FDI inflows is the requirement that investments remain in Chile for a one-year period. There are no restrictions on profit remittances. FDI must be financed with a maximum debt component of 30 percent (70 percent equity). This limit was reduced from 50 percent in October 1997.

Portfolio investment inflows through ADRs

Minimum amount of ADR issue is U.S.$25 million, reduced from U.S.$50 million in September 1994. Minimum risk rating of BBB required for nonfinancial firms and BBB+ for banking companies. 30 percent reserve requirement on secondary ADRs since July 1995.

Other financial and portfolio inflows

Subject to the 30 percent reserve requirement up to June 1998, then reduced to 10 percent. These include trade credits, foreign currency deposits, loans associated with FDI, and bond issues. Bond issuers face the same quality-enhancing restrictions as ADR issuers. In September 1998, the reserve requirement was set at zero. Subject to a minimum stay in Chile of one year, except in the case of ADRs, which can be retired at any moment.

Foreign investment by the Chilean nonfinancial private sector

Investors not wishing to have access to the official foreign exchange market need only inform the Central Bank of their investments abroad. Those wishing to have access to the official market need permission from the Central Bank. This is not difficult to obtain. At the present time, the formal and free market exchange rates are similar.

Foreign investment by Chilean institutional investors

Foreign investments by pension funds, mutual funds, and life insurance companies are subject to certain limits as to the amounts and type of foreign assets that they can hold. Pension funds are allowed to hold up to 12 percent of their total assets in foreign assets (raised to 16 percent in 1999), and stocks are limited to one-half of total foreign holdings.

Foreign investment by banks

Foreign financial investments by commercial banks are limited to 25 percent of bank capital and reserves and are restricted to fixed income securities issued or guaranteed by foreign governments or Central Banks. Banks are authorized to use foreign currency deposits to finance trade among countries belonging to the Latin American Integration Association (LAIA). Commercial banks may hold equity in foreign banks provided that they have a capital adequacy index of at least 10 percent.

Source: Adapted and updated from Budnevich and Le Fort 1997.

the domestic price of fuel (together with reducing nonsocial fiscal expenditure), which caused an inflationary shock in September and October. The CPI, whose inertial component implied a rise of about 2 percent monthly at the time, jumped to 4.9 and 3.8 percent, respectively, in those months. The speed and close coordination with which the Central Bank and the government reacted to external events may explain why pressures in the foreign exchange market continued to encourage appreciation and inflation was quickly reduced.

In early 1991, the strict crawling peg system that had been followed by the monetary authorities was modified and, in order to introduce "exchange rate noise," which would discourage short-term flows, the rate was moderately revalued on three occasions and then, in compensation, devalued in the following months. Thus, at the end of each of these moves the "official" rate returned to its initial real level; the real devaluations within each move made it more costly for short-term funds to enter the country and thus served as an effective tool for temporarily stemming the excess supply of foreign exchange. However, the measure could not be repeated too often, since the market would then anticipate the revaluation and the policy would lose its effectiveness, which actually happened in the third move. Nevertheless, during almost six months the authorities gained time to design a policy that would act efficiently in a more prolonged transition period. This policy reform had to advance against the opinion of multilateral institutions and financial agents, which stressed the need for an across the board opening of the capital account. The reform, against the fashion, was based on the perception that the large supply of financing was not stable, and short-term factors affecting the current account, such as the high price of copper, the incentive of high domestic interest rates, and the temporary depressed level of imports, would tend to change in the near to medium term.

It was recognized, however, that part of the observed improvement in the current account — a considerably improved nonfinancial services account, a more vigorous nontraditional exports sector, and a reduction in the external debt burden — was more structural or permanent. In June 1991, in response to this combination of factors, and pari passu with a 2 percent revaluation and a tariff reduction from 15 to 11 percent, a non-interest-bearing reserve requirement of 20 percent was established on foreign loans (covering the whole range of foreign credits, from those associated with FDI to trade credits). The reserves had to be maintained with the Central Bank for a minimum of ninety days and a maximum of one year, according to the maturity of the operation. At the same time, a stamp tax on domestic credit, a rate of up to 1.2 percent, was extended to external loans. In July, an alternative to the reserve requirement was allowed for medium-term credits, which consisted of making a payment to the Central Bank of an amount equivalent to the financial cost of the reserve requirement. The financial cost was calculated by applying the London Inter-Bank Interest-Offer Rate (LIBOR) plus 2.5 percent (at an annual rate) to the amount of the reserve requirement. The reserve requirement, the option of paying its financial cost, and the tax on foreign credits all have a zero marginal cost for lending that exceeds one year, and, as will be discussed, the first two are particularly onerous for flows with short maturities.

With continuing capital inflows, over time, the system of reserve requirements was tightened and extended to most international financial transactions. Beginning in May 1992, the reserve requirement on external credits stood at 30 percent. It was extended to time deposits in foreign currency and in 1995 to purchases of Chilean stocks ("secondary ADRs") by foreigners.[7] The period during which the deposit had to be maintained was extended to one year, regardless of the maturity of the loan. The spread charged over LIBOR in the option of paying the financial cost of the reserve requirement was increased from the original 2.5 to 4 percent. In order to close a loophole through which the reserve requirements were being evaded (since equity investment is exempt), the authorities decided to screen FDI applications; permission to enter the country as FDI exempted from the reserve requirement was denied when it was determined that the inflow was disguised financial capital. In such a case, foreign investors had to register their funds at the Central Bank as financial investments subject to the reserve requirement.

With the Asian crisis, and the sudden sharp scarcity of financial inflows, the reserve requirement rate was reduced to 10 percent and then to zero in 1998. The authorities announced, however, that the policy tool would remain available in case of new capital surges (Massad 2000).

Since 1991, an attempt has been made to facilitate capital outflows as a way of alleviating downward pressure on the exchange rate. In particular, Chilean pension funds (AFPs) have been allowed to invest up to 16 percent of their total assets abroad. With similar intentions but also the objective of enhancing the productive development of Chilean firms, residents who wished to invest abroad were granted access to the formal foreign exchange market. The policy was effective in encouraging significant flows of FDI and purchases of foreign firms by Chilean companies in neighboring countries (so-called Chapter XII; see Calderón and

---

7. It is not difficult to impose reserve requirements on foreign portfolio investments. If funds that will be used for the investment are deposited with a Chilean bank, the foreign deposit is liable to reserve requirements. For funds that do not use a Chilean bank as an intermediary, the reserve requirement can be imposed when the asset is registered in the name of an agent with a foreign address. In order to be converted into ADRs, such assets must also be registered with the Central Bank.

Griffith-Jones 1995). However, higher rates of return on financial assets in Chile than abroad and expectations of peso appreciation discouraged foreign financial investments by Chilean pension funds and recently authorized closed-end mutual funds. These investments had been rising slowly as domestic firms and pension funds obtained more and better information about foreign financial assets. In mid-1997, the AFPs had only U.S.$200 million invested abroad, which represented 0.5 percent of their funds.[8] An immediate effect of liberalizing outflows has probably been to encourage additional inflows as a result of a fall in the country risk perceived by international investors (Williamson 1993; Labán and Larraín 1997). Consequently, the resulting effect tends to be the opposite of the desired one.

When does the market take advantage of opportunities to place foreign currency abroad? Obviously, this occurs when expectations of appreciation are replaced with expectations of depreciation. As is evident, in face of expectations of exchange rate devaluation there were massive outflows in the channels opened; for instance, outflows from pension funds rose sharply only when expectations changed from appreciation to depreciation after late 1997. In fact, these outflows from AFPs, between January 1998 and June 1999, climbed to the equivalent of 4.8 percent of 1998 GDP and 12 percent of their whole fund.[9] Something similar occurred with chapter XII, mainly in the form of financial investment in places such as the Cayman Islands, in an evident distortion of the chapter's initial purpose.

Exchange Rate Policy

Exchange rate policy has also experienced substantial change over time. The use of a fixed nominal exchange rate in 1979–82, in the context of an increasing and eventually complete liberalization of capital account transactions, was abandoned after the crisis of 1982–83, during which GDP declined by 17 percent (measured in 1986 pesos). In 1983–89 the

---

8. One obstacle to the liberalization of outflows by institutional investors is the lack of knowledge that regulators have of foreign financial assets. Thus, the fear that liberalization will lead to a worsening of the asset quality of institutional investors has been a key factor explaining the gradual approach to the liberalization of outflows.

9. A hasty financial liberalization risks leaving too many doors open for outflows, which tend to be massive in cases of market nervousness and shifts to expectations of currency depreciation, as was advised in due time (see Ffrench-Davis, Agosin, and Uthoff 1995). This could make more difficult the achievement of exchange rate and macroeconomic stability and more costly the international financial crises, as illustrated by the Chilean experience of 1998–99: pension funds and residents investing abroad, through Chapter XII, were the main agents behind the losses in reserves by the Central Bank and the 10 percent drop in domestic demand.

authorities utilized a crawling peg, with a floating band of ± 2 percent (widened to 3 percent in 1988 and ± 5 percent in mid-1989). The "official" rate was devalued daily, in line with the differential between domestic inflation and an estimate of external inflation. On a number of occasions, discrete nominal devaluations were added, which helped stimulate a remarkable degree of real depreciation following the 1982 crisis: 130 percent between 1982 and 1988 (see fig. 10.2).

The large capital inflows of the early 1990s put persistent pressure on the real exchange rate. In order to moderate this trend, the authorities operated through exchange rate policy, as noted earlier. However, pressures on the foreign exchange market continued in the ensuing months, although short-term capital inflows remained at low levels in response to the regulatory policies that had been adopted and a reduction in domestic interest rates. It should be noted that the stages of the business cycle in Chile and in its "financial center" (the United States) coincided during most of 1991, although this was no longer true by the end of the year and in 1992.

The pressure on the market in 1991 stemmed from long-term inflows, but mainly from a very favorable current account, with a small surplus.

Many observers began to hold the view that a modification of exchange rate policy with a significant revaluation was unavoidable. Consequently, the official rate began to lose its allocative capacity. In January 1992, the official exchange rate was revalued by 5 percent and the floating band in the formal market was expanded to ± 10 percent.[10] The observed rate abruptly appreciated by 9 percent in the market, that is, a little less than the sum of the appreciation of the official rate and the lowering of the floor of the band. There followed an overwhelming wave of expectations of more revaluations, which was fed by capital inflows in the formal and informal markets. These flows were encouraged by the certainty that the Central Bank, under its own rules, could not intervene within the band. In fact, in a market persistently situated near the floor, it intervened only by buying at the bottom price. The market's expectation was that, if something changed, the floor exchange rate would be revalued, as in fact it had been in January 1992.

---

10. It must be noted that Chile was emerging from a profound debt crisis, which was accompanied by a sharp exchange rate depreciation. Consequently, there was space for some appreciation. However, as Chile was moving from a restricted to an overabundant supply of external savings, the authorities wanted to avoid an overadjustment of the exchange rate. One specifically troublesome feature is that, as the expectations of foreign agents change from pessimism to optimism, they seek a higher desired stock of investment in the "emerging market" over a short period of time. This implies excessively large inflows for a while. Obviously, these are transitory rather than permanently higher levels of periodic inflows.

For a long time, the proposal had been circulating in the Central Bank that a "dirty" or regulated float should be initiated within the band; proponents of this view argued that the prevailing rules, with a pure band, an increasingly active informal market, and a more porous formal market, would lead to an observed exchange rate leaning toward either extreme of the band (on the ceiling in 1989–90, on the floor later). The sudden revaluation of the observed rate by nearly 10 percent between January and February 1992 contributed to the bank taking the decision to initiate the dirty float in March of that year. The observed rate fluctuated then for several years within a range of one to eight points above the floor (i.e., normally not on the floor itself), with the bank continuing to make active purchases but also frequent sales (though with a significant accumulation of reserves).

The widening of the band apparently had signaled that the Central Bank had renounced the attempt to deter revaluating pressures in defense of the export strategy, allowing the market, dominated by the short-termish segment, to determine the observed rate within a very wide range. On the contrary, the establishment of the dirty float gave back to the Central Bank a greater management capacity, enabling it to strengthen long-term variables in determining the exchange rate for producers of exportable and importable goods and services.

In the ensuing months, U.S. interest rates continued to decline, exerting pressure on the Central Bank. However, the Chilean economy was booming, and its GDP growth rate had risen well into two digits (about 15 percent over twelve months). Consequently, for reasons of macroeconomic equilibrium, the Central Bank wanted to raise rather than lower domestic interest rates. To avoid encouraging arbitrage, it decided to raise the reserve requirement rate on capital inflows. In May 1992, reserve requirements on external credits were raised to 30 percent and the period of deposit was fixed at one year.

Finally, in July of the same year, the dollar peg of the official rate was replaced with a peg to a basket of currencies (of which the dollar represented 50 percent, the deutsche mark 30 percent, and the yen 20 percent) as the new benchmark exchange rate. The purpose of these measures was to make arbitrage of interest rates between the dollar and the peso less profitable and to introduce greater exchange rate uncertainty in the short term, given the daily instability of international prices among these three currencies. The replacement of a peg to the dollar for a basket of currencies also tended to give greater average stability to the peso values of proceeds from exports. Indeed, unlike financial operations, which are largely dollar-denominated, trade is fairly diversified in geographic terms, with the United States representing only one-fifth of the total, and also operates with a more diversified basket of currencies.

As a result of the policy mix implemented in 1990–94 (plus some "good luck," the improvement in the terms of trade in 1995), Chile was enjoying a solid external sector (a small deficit on the current account, a sustainable exchange rate, and a limited amount of external short-term liabilities) when the Tequila crisis exploded in late 1994 and its contagion effect reached Argentina in 1995. Therefore, the across the board cutoff in liquid resources for Latin America did not dampen the Chilean economy. Toward mid-1995, speculative capital flows began to return to the region and with special intensity to Chile.

Given the existence of expectations overwhelmingly in favor of currency appreciation, after the Tequila shock appeared to have been left behind, the large interest rate differential between the peso and the dollar (together with good prospects for large Chilean companies) gave foreign portfolio and short-term investors what amounted to a very profitable one-way bet, in spite of the toll they had to pay for entering domestic financial markets in the form of the reserve requirement (see table 10.3). This trend toward appreciation could have been softened by intensifying price restrictions on inflows (i.e., by increasing the reserve requirement). The generalized overoptimism that financial crises had been left behind and the risky temptation to speed the reduction of domestic inflation with exchange rate appreciation weakened a highly successful policy of sustainable macroeconomic equilibria. In fact, the external deficit increased jointly with exchange rate appreciation and rapid aggregate demand growth, which were stimulated by the capital inflows of 1996–97.

Exchange rate management did not help deter speculative inflows after 1995. In spite of its formal adherence to a crawling band in 1996–97, the Central Bank was in fact maintaining a nominal, almost fixed, exchange rate. Moreover, in order to lower the floor of the band, in 1997 the authorities tinkered with the weights assigned to each currency in the basket, making less credible the peg to a currency basket rather than the dollar.[11] In addition, they factored a 2 percent rate of annual appreciation into the calculation of the central rate, ostensibly to account for higher productivity growth in Chile than in its main trading partners.

The effects of the Asian crisis, including notably worsened terms of trade in 1998 (now combined with some "bad luck"), found Chile with an appreciated exchange rate (which had not happened prior to mid-

---

11. In November 1994, the weight of the U.S. dollar was reduced from 50 to 45 percent, reflecting the falling incidence of that currency in Chilean trade. In January 1997, it was arbitrarily raised to 80 percent. For a comparative analysis of bands in Chile, Israel, and Mexico, see Helpman, Leiderman, and Bufman 1994. For an analysis of Chile, Colombia, and Israel, see Williamson 1996.

1995; see fig. 10.2) and a deficit on the current account twice as large as the average for 1990–95.[12]

The Strengthening of Banking Supervision

As noted, a tough bank supervision and regulatory environment prevented the excess liquidity of banks from fueling a consumption boom and deterioration in the quality of bank assets (as clearly took place in Mexico). This was a legacy of the banking crisis of 1981–86 in the aftermath of the preceding foreign capital surge, which led to a virtual collapse of the entire banking system (see Díaz-Alejandro 1985 and Held and Jiménez 2000). Some elements of prudential supervision adopted since then include the continuous monitoring of the quality of bank assets; strict limits on lending by banks to related firms; the existence of automatic mechanisms of bank equity adjustment when its market value falls below the limits required by the regulators; and faculties to freeze banking operations, impede fund transfers outside of troubled banks, and restrict the payment of dividends by institutions that fail to comply with capital adequacy requirements. Chilean financial markets have also acquired a depth that allows for the orderly infusion of new funds, and for their withdrawal, without significantly affecting the quality of bank portfolios (Aninat and Larraín 1996).

Capital adequacy ratios along the lines of the 1988 Basle Accord have been incorporated into the new banking law approved by Congress in 1997. But banks' capital, in practice, is well above the Basle norm of 8 percent. In addition, the Central Bank imposes limits on banks' open positions in foreign exchange, although these are still fairly crude in that they do not differentiate between loans made in foreign currency to firms that earn foreign currency and to firms whose earnings are in domestic currency. Neither do these limits differentiate between different foreign currencies. Currency risk is only one aspect of credit risk evaluation systems, which as a whole are quite good in Chile. Therefore, this compensates for the weaknesses in the norms on open positions in foreign exchange.

Nevertheless, despite the quality of prudential supervision, there are other macroeconomic variables — imbalances that cause abrupt devaluations, overly high interest rates, and bubbles in stock markets, among others — that can dampen the banking portfolio. Sustainable

---

12. An enlarged deficit on the current account, duly adjusted by the trend terms of trade, is a revealed proof of an overly appreciated exchange rate, which moved faster than net productivity improvements. I contend that in 1990–95 there was equilibrating appreciation, while in 1995–97 there was an outlier overvaluation.

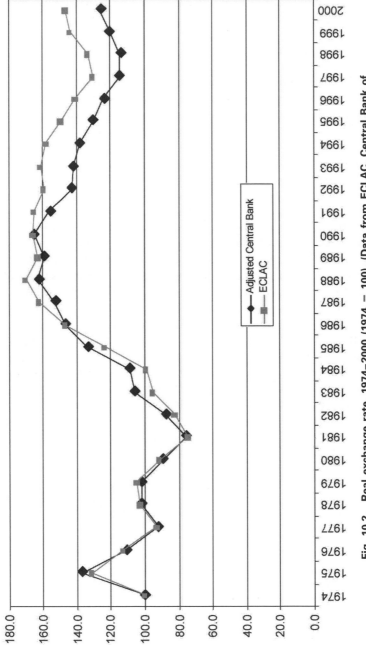

Fig. 10.2. Real exchange rate, 1974–2000 (1974 = 100). (Data from ECLAC, Central Bank of Chile, and Ffrench-Davis 1984. The main difference between ECLAC and Adjusted Central Bank methodologies is that the former uses CPI to measure external inflation, while the latter uses wholesale prices. The first is more consistent with available estimates of real exchange rates for Latin America.)

macroeconomic balances are unavoidable partners of sustainable prudential supervision.

Effectiveness of Measures

What have been the financial costs imposed by the system of reserve requirements and taxes on foreign lending? The total tax consists of the extra interest costs imposed by the reserve requirements and the tax on foreign credits. The calculations can be seen in table 10.3. As a result of the lengthening (in 1992) of the reserve requirement holding period to a full year, and regardless of the maturity of the financial transaction, the implicit tax rate on foreign borrowing increased dramatically as maturities shortened. This characteristic of the system, which is similar in its effects to a unilateral Tobin tax (Tobin 1978), is the rationale behind the requirement that reserves be held for an entire year. Before its imposition, the implicit tax rate (on an annualized basis) was identical on transactions as short as a quarter (the minimum holding period up to May 1992) or as long as a year. These very large estimates of the implicit tax rate on short-term operations suggest that, if the regulations were not evaded, they must have implied strong discouragement of short-term and portfolio flows.

How effective has the reserve requirement (together with exchange rate management) been in deterring short-term flows and preventing excessive exchange rate appreciation? There are two kinds of evidence that one can use. The first is qualitative. There is broad consensus that Chile faced a larger supply of external finance (relative to its GDP) than other countries in the region, because of its better economic performance and greater political stability. However, during the first half of the 1990s exchange rate appreciation and the current account deficit (as a share of GDP) were smaller than in other countries in the region that

TABLE 10.3. Implicit Cost of Reserve Requirement on Foreign Borrowing, 1991–99 (annualized rates)

	1991 (II)	1992 (I)	1992 (II)	1996	1997	1998 (I)	1998 (Q3)	1999 (Q4)
Reserve requirement (%)	20	20	30	30	30	30	10	0
Minimum holding period (months)	3	3	12	12	12	12	12	0
LIBOR	5.5	4.3	3.6	5.6	5.8	5.7	5.6	5.3
Implicit cost								
1 year	1.4	1.2	1.5	2.4	2.5	2.4	0.6	0.0
3 months	1.4	1.2	6.4	10.2	10.6	10.4	2.6	0.0

Source: Calculations based on data from the Central Bank of Chile. 1.2 percent tax is not included.

were major recipients of foreign capital (see Ffrench-Davis 2000, chap. 10). In addition, FDI represented a much larger share of inflows in Chile than in other countries.[13] Second, there is econometric evidence that policies directed toward the capital account have worked rather well. Recent studies indicate that the combination of disincentives to short-term inflows with the reforms in the exchange rate regime, at least up to 1994, had been able to reduce the inflow of short-term, interest-arbitrage funds significantly (Agosin 1998; Schmidt-Hebbel, Hernández, and Gallego 1999). As will be discussed, the situation changed markedly in more recent years in the face of both a new capital surge toward the emerging economies and restrictions that paradoxically were left unchanged by the autonomous Central Bank rather than increasing them in response to the huge capital surge of 1996–97 (see Le Fort and Lehmann 2000).

Some observers have claimed that the efficacy of measures intended to discourage capital inflows is only temporary, as private sector operators usually find ways to evade them (for an example of this literature, see Valdés-Prieto and Soto 1998). In principle, this can be done through several mechanisms. One is the underinvoicing of imports or the over-invoicing of exports. The second is to delay payment for imports or accelerate export receipts. Third, it is possible to bring in funds through the informal foreign exchange market. Fourth, there is also the possibility of registering short-term funds as FDI. However, this could be a costly option, since Chilean law requires that FDI remain in the country for at least one year before repatriation. Nonetheless, it was becoming a significant loophole, which, as already noted, the authorities have moved to close. Fifth, it is possible for agents to arrange back-to-back operations in which, for example, an agent pays for imports with a bank deposit in Chile rather than with foreign exchange; at the same time, the exporter is paid in foreign exchange by a bank in his or her country. All of these (and other forms of evasion as well) are possible, but they are not costless, and some of them may have undesirable effects on tax liabilities. While some evasion is inevitable, there is no hard evidence that the measures meant to discourage short-term capital inflows have been massively evaded.

However, it is clear that maintaining the reserve requirement at an unchanged rate and/or failing to supplement it with other measures came to be insufficient in the face of the new capital surge of 1996–97. Additionally, depressed stock market prices in late 1995 and a real exchange rate that was widely expected to appreciate further over time attracted portfo-

---

13. It should be noted that the loans associated with FDI were subject to the reserve requirement. Since the average maturity of these loans was about seven years, the incidence of the restriction was low. However, this avoided the danger that short-term credit would be disguised as long-term credit.

lio inflows, as witnessed by the very heavy inflows into the Chilean stock market in 1996–97. But large financial inflows are inevitably bound to turn into outflows at some point. Contagion from the Asian crisis had such an effect in 1998–2000, although it was moderate.

In addition, actual exchange rate management (in contrast to what the authorities claimed they were doing) did not contribute to discouraging speculative inflows. In spite of its formal adherence to a crawling band in 1996–97, the Central Bank was in effect managing a quasi fixed nominal price for the dollar.

In the period after 1993, the secondary issue of ADRs became an important source of short-term capital inflow with particularly volatile characteristics. Thus, the extension of reserve requirements to these inflows in 1995 can be considered to have been an attempt to deal with an incipient problem that was already causing difficulties in policy management and could become even more important in the future. It is likely that, in the absence of reserve requirements, portfolio inflows would have been much larger. However, after a temporary lull in 1995, they again surged beginning in early 1996, paying the corresponding cost of the reserve requirement. The evidence suggests that the entry fee came to be perceived as cheap in the face of positive fundamentals and a strong likelihood of further real exchange rate appreciation.

In opposition to the several studies that show a significant effect over short-term inflows, another line of attack against the use of disincentives has been to claim that, with regard to their behavior, it is impossible to distinguish between capital inflows such as FDI or long-term lending, on the one hand, and short-term or liquid flows on the other. Claessens, Dooley, and Warner (1995) claim that balance of payments categories have nothing to do with the stability of flows themselves, long-term flows being just as likely to be unstable as short-term flows.[14]

In order to check their hypothesis for Chile, a series of tests were run to determine the degree of persistence of different types of private flows (see Agosin 1998). In the first place, an autoregressive analysis of quarterly data on the components of flows for the period 1983–95 reveals that, indeed, FDI and long-term borrowing have the most persistence. On the other hand, for portfolio flows and for short-term private borrowing there is no persistence at all.

---

14. Part of the explanation of the finding that FDI is just as likely to be volatile as short-term flows may stem from the fact that, for the countries that they selected, FDI flows were a very small percentage of total foreign financing, as reported by IMF statistics. Fluctuations in small numbers tend to be greater than fluctuations in large ones. On the other hand, the period covered excludes the Tequila crisis, when portfolio flows played a significant destabilizing role. It is evident that instability must be tested in critical situations rather than during bonanzas.

Second, the coefficient of variation and the R^2 of the time trends of the same four categories of flows indicate that FDI is more stable than short-term borrowing and portfolio flows. Finally, unit root tests for FDI and other net capital inflows in real annual terms for the long period 1960–95 demonstrate that FDI does have a unit root, while other flows are stationary (without a constant or trend). Therefore, in Chile FDI has behaved as a "permanent" variable and other flows as "transitory" disturbances.

A controversial issue is assigning fiscal responsibility for the aggregate demand excess in 1996–97. In this period, an expansionary fiscal policy was recorded, with government expenditure growing faster than GDP (7.9 compared to 7.4 percent per year). However, it must be considered that the fiscal expenditure with macroeconomic effects represents only 20 percent of the economy; therefore, the large majority of the pulls behind the 8.5 percent growth in domestic aggregate demand in the period were in the private sector, accounting for 90 percent of the expenditure increase. Thus, a fiscal contribution to moderate global expenditure would have been insufficient and socially costly,[15] especially considering that the fiscal budget showed a surplus and consequently was not the source of disequilibrium. Here, once again, imbalances were of external origin and overwhelmingly private. The government's responsibility in this case lay in the lack of more effective efforts to enforce coordination between the Central Bank and the Ministry of Finance.[16] This shortcoming, which is related to the Central Bank's autonomy, was a "taboo" issue. It ignores the fact that there is no single form of autonomy in the world but several alternative ones.

Thus, we can conclude that FDI is considerably less volatile than other kinds of capital inflows and that it is advisable to target policies of prudential macroeconomic management (such as the reserve requirement on short-term or liquid inflows). This is what the Chilean authorities attempted to do, with more success in the early years of application than more recently. *Undoubtedly, short-term and portfolio inflows would have been much larger in the absence of the reserve requirement.* Additionally, sterilized intervention in foreign exchange markets prevented undue exchange rate appreciation and a consumption boom, thus keep-

---

15. The main growing components in fiscal expenditure were education, justice, and infrastructure, all fields in which there were major and widely demanded transformations, with a political consensus around increasing spending on them.

16. The lack of coordination between the Central Bank and the government was evident. As mentioned, the Central Bank authorities expressed no concern about imbalances in the external sector, while, for instance, the minister of economics said that "it is necessary to intensify and strengthen policies such as the reserve requirement to reduce exchange rate appreciation" (*Estrategia,* September 26, 1997).

ing the current account deficit within reasonable bounds, except in 1996–97.

The policy mix also had financial costs for the authorities. The accumulation of large volumes of foreign exchange reserves imposes a financial cost, which is also a social cost on the economy, since the returns on these assets have been inferior to the interest payments on the Central Bank liabilities that were issued to sterilize the monetary effects of reserve accumulation, generating large losses for the Central Bank (estimated at about 0.5 percent of GDP per annum). That is the cost of "insurance" for economic stability, but it was probably unnecessarily high given an excessive reserve accumulation. Undoubtedly, more flexible and restrictive management of the reserve requirement and other prudential macroeconomic policy tools by the authorities would have moderated that cost.

Saving, Investment, and Growth

The period since 1989 marks a clear-cut improvement in growth performance, in comparison with not only 1974–89 but the more favorable 1960s (see table 10.4). The ratio of gross fixed investment to GDP rose steadily since its trough in the mid-1980s, from about 15 percent in 1983–84 to more than 30 percent in 1995–98. Even taking longer averages, the investment ratio rose sharply, from 18 percent in 1974–89 to 28 percent in 1990–98. This increased ratio allowed Chile to sustain growth of GDP averaging 7 percent per annum in the 1990s. The increase in the national

TABLE 10.4. Investment, Foreign Savings, and Growth Indicators, 1960–2000 (as a percentage of GDP)

	GDP Growth	Gap GDP/GDP*	Gross Fixed Investment	Foreign Savings	National Savings
1960–70	4.2	2.0	21.2	2.5	—
1971–73	0.5	3.6	16.8	2.9	—
1974–81	3.3	8.8	17.8	5.0	12.6
1982–89	2.6	11.6	18.2	6.2	11.5
1990–95	7.8	1.8	26.1	2.5	22.1
1996–97	7.4	−0.9	31.6	5.7	21.2
1998	3.9	2.0	32.2	6.2	21.2
1999	−1.1	8.5	26.9	0.2	21.8
2000	5.4	7.5	26.6	1.6	21.9

Source: Calculations based on national accounts data from the Central Bank of Chile.

Note: Columns 1 and 3 are in 1986 constant prices for 1974–2000 and rates of change in 1977 prices for previous years. Column 2 is the ratio between actual GDP (GDP) and potential GDP (GDP*). Columns 4 and 5 are in current prices.

saving rate was also strong, rising from 11 percent in the 1980s to 22 percent in the 1990s (in current prices). This reveals that domestic and foreign savings worked as complements, as opposed to the substitution that took place in Mexico before 1995 and in Chile before 1982 (see Uthoff and Titelman 1998). At the same time, the use of foreign savings declined sharply, from 6 to 3.6 percent of GDP.

The Chilean policies directed toward restraining capital surges and moderating exchange rate appreciation can be credited with a significant share of the success achieved with regard to investment, saving, and growth rates. On the one hand, the management of inflows has had a positive impact on macroeconomic stability and has contributed to keeping effective demand close to productive capacity, which is essential for investment expenditures to rise. On the other hand, there is evidence that foreign and domestic savings have tended to exhibit a high degree of substitutability in emerging economies when capital arrives in surges rather than trends and when it takes the form of volatile financial flows rather than FDI or financing of imports of capital goods.[17] Foreign savings stimulate consumption through their effects on domestic liquidity, the exchange rate, and asset prices. Thus, success in keeping the current account deficit and aggregate demand within sustainable bounds contributed to the sharp increase in saving rates (Agosin 1998, 2001; Uthoff and Titelman 1998).

Some Policy Lessons of the Chilean Experience

The Chilean experience with the prudential macroeconomic management of capital inflows provides us with several important lessons. For developing countries, the swings in capital flows can be of extraordinary magnitude relative to the size of their economies. Over the last two decades, Latin American countries have gone from a severe shortage of financing during the debt crisis (and the shorter lived Tequila and Asian crises) to an overabundance of foreign capital during most of the 1990s. Totally passive policy stances will inevitably result in enormous volatility in key domestic macroprices (exchange and interest rates) and economic aggregates. By depressing investment, these fluctuations have adverse effects on long-term growth and productive employment.

By and large, policies aimed at regulating capital inflows and exchange rate management appear to have discouraged the more volatile

17. The data suggest that some crowding out occurred in 1996–98, associated with excessive inflows, exchange rate appreciation in the three-year period, and worsening of terms of trade. Nonetheless, the savings rate was significantly higher than in 1985–89. See table 1.3.

forms of inflows and prevented excessive exchange rate appreciation in 1990–95. However, in 1996–97 financial capital inflows overwhelmed the capacity of the authorities to control them with the unchanged intensity of policy tools they were using. Then, the Central Bank was unable to prevent a significant real appreciation of the peso in spite of heavy purchases of foreign exchange. The ensuing real exchange rate appreciation contributed to a widening of the current account deficit, which climbed to 5.7 percent of GDP. It must be stressed that the Central Bank did not dismantle its policies, as several other countries in the region and Asia opened their capital accounts. Nonetheless, there was clear evidence that a strengthening of the instruments used to deal with financial surges had become necessary in Chile by 1996–97.

Then the economy experienced the downside of large financial inflows: outflows of financial capital were concentrated in 1998–99 (see table 10.1), with exchange rate depreciation, in a price correction process after the significant imbalance created in macroprices. However, in response to the active management of inflows in the first half of the 1990s, and at least its subsistence in subsequent years, the accumulated deficit on current account was moderate, with a rather low stock of external liabilities, and the share of volatile funds was minor. Together with large international reserves, Chile was able to face the sharp terms of trade shock brought on by the Asian crisis. Despite the soft recession recorded in 1999, the social and economic costs, with an output loss of U.S.$ 7 billion in 1999, were significant. This roughly reflects the gap between the 1999 productive frontier and actual GDP. The gap persisted in 1999–2001, with a negative impact on employment and productive investment.

Contrary to conventional wisdom, it is possible to discriminate between flows that are stable, are of a long-term nature, and do contribute to the country's growth (such as FDI when it creates new capacity) and those that are basically speculative and lead to excessive domestic volatility. In the Chilean case, the market-based discouragement applied to speculative flows had no adverse effects on FDI, which reached unprecedented levels during the decade. The large share of FDI in capital inflows, in fact, has mitigated the effects of Asian contagion on the Chilean balance of payments.

Some evasion is inevitable: any system of discouragement makes it attractive for some operators to attempt to circumvent it. In the Chilean case, it was necessary to close loopholes when it became obvious that agents were using them. However, circumvention can be kept to a minimum with a well-designed and transparent system such as the reserve requirement on capital inflows (*encaje*) implemented by Chile and the continued monitoring by authorities in the first half of the 1990s.

The objective of sustaining economic growth in the face of volatile capital flows (or volatile export prices, as in Chile) requires the use of a battery of policy instruments. In the Chilean case, the combination of taxlike instruments meant to deter speculative inflows, a crawling band with intramarginal intervention (in my view, this was too sparsely utilized), increasing short-term exchange rate uncertainty, and sterilizing the monetary effects of capital inflows worked well for several years. It should be remembered that reserve requirements alone (or any other policy that increases the cost of external borrowing), while clearly useful, do not deter speculative attacks when large exchange rate changes are anticipated.

There is a series of possible complements to the present set of policies in the face of a new surge. Two recommendations — based on the experiences of emerging economies, especially the Chilean one — emerge. On the one hand, significant exchange rate appreciation, as in 1996–97, must be avoided. On the other, a flexible policy package, rather than a single rigid policy tool, is desirable when a new capital surge emerges.

With respect to portfolio inflows, the period of application of the reserve requirement could be increased beyond one year during capital surges in order to raise the cost of financial investments in Chile during those conjunctures. On the other hand, recently Chilean star enterprises have been massively acquired by foreign capital. These operations generate major inconsistencies in light of the recommendation that the country achieve sustainable macroeconomic balances and capital flows that reinforce productive investment. Massive operations, which take advantage of the necessary gap between domestic and international interest rates (with their strong impact on the present value of enterprises), and the depressed prices caused by macroeconomic adjustment greatly impact the exchange rate market: it is foreign investment that buys existing assets instead of creating them, the strategic command emigrates, and Chile loses its bridgehead for globalization. All this for what? We are in the forefront of a new "populism"; the benefits for a minority are seen, while the social costs are ignored. The oversupply allows choosing, and choosing allows us to better face the subsequent shortage period.

With regard to the exchange rate regime, the Central Bank should return to active intermediate policy and prevent the exchange rate from sticking to extreme appreciation or depreciation. It must be stressed that the crawling band — the intermediate regime in force in Chile until 1999 — lost prestige because of evident mismanagement that included the lack of vigorous dirty floating (active intramarginal intervention); the fact that the weights assigned to each currency in the basket used to determine the central rate were arbitrarily changed to achieve short-term exchange rate objectives; and the overly long time that authority took to recognize the need to devalue an excessively appreciated rate.

In fact, the Central Bank behaved asymmetrically, allowing the exchange rate to appreciate in 1996–97 and then moved to slow depreciation by the end of 1997 for the sake of a lower inflation rate. This provided a convergence between advocates of a free floating exchange rate and exporters (who should not support a permanently free floating exchange rate because of the enormous instability this implies). This way, in September 1999 the Central Bank announced the suspension of the exchange rate band. This would be advisable as a temporary measure intended to speed the devaluation of the exchange rate in the direction of a level more consistent with a sustainable external balance and then, before the next capital surge, return to an implicit or explicit band. In contrast, if the suspension is thought of as permanent this would mark the peak of a series of measures that amount to a renunciation of sustainable macroeconomic policies as they are defined here and in Ffrench-Davis 2000, chap. 6 (with a level of demand kept close to the productive frontier and "right" macroprices). A free exchange rate, in the context of massive volatile flows worldwide, would fluctuate considerably, with great damage to nontraditional exporters and productive investment.

Actually, there has been significant volatility of the exchange rate, notwithstanding that capital flows have not been fluctuating widely recently. In fact, the financial markets for emerging economies have been rather dry.

The liberalization of the exchange rate in September 1999 led to a rapid devaluation (to $550 per dollar) that lasted until November 1999. This allowed the real exchange rate to return to the average level of 1995. Nevertheless, the recovery of optimism regarding the Chilean economy, plus an improved price of copper and a still depressed level of imports during the first quarter of 2000, was reflected in a significant revaluation (to $500). However, when adjustments of the U.S. stock exchange came during the last quarter of 2000 the RER recovered part of its lost value (to $580); then occurred some recovery of confidence in international markets (in early 2001) and a revaluation (down to $557) and finally a spread of pessimism and a devaluatory process that by August had depreciated the rate to $690. This, according to my estimates, is a rather "right" price, probably the closest to "equilibrium" that the Chilean economy has had since the mid-1990s. Nonetheless, nothing assures that, with the present foreign exchange regime, this "equilibrium" plateau would be sustained by a totally free market. This confirms our expectations about the extreme instability of a free-floating exchange rate. Any good or bad, international or domestic, short-term news will tend to affect the spot and "futures" exchange rates significantly. Evidently, instability would be more damaging with a long process of appreciation, in a pronounced cycle resulting from a new capital surge.

CHAPTER 11

Conclusions and Challenges

Classifications and categories tend to be arbitrary, but if they are coherent they provide a guiding framework for analysis and policy actions. Following are four groups of economic lessons or conclusions drawn from the recent decades of Chilean economic history. They are followed by a ten-point grouping of future challenges.

Four Conclusions

First of all, the challenge of making growth consistent with distributive equity is ever more important, especially in light of the sharp drop in the standard of living of a wide segment of the population in the 1970s and 1980s and the fact that two democratic governments have only partially met the expectations they aroused in the 1990s. It is clear that substantial political consensus among the main social and political groups will be required to meet the challenge. Only in this way can the country implement action over time that will distribute the costs and benefits of economic growth in a more equitable fashion, with progressive improvement in the distribution of opportunities, productivity, and income. Democracy requires that growth and equity progress together.

Second, there is overwhelming evidence that macroeconomic balances are crucial to the success of any development strategy. One component that tends to be omitted from the catalog of macroeconomic factors, and should always be in the foreground, is the relationship between new productive capacity creation and actual increases in production (or utilization of capacity). As has been pointed out, there were deep imbalances in the relationship between the two variables during the Pinochet regime (fig. 11.1).

Underutilization was notably high, both in 1975–79 and in 1982–87. In both periods capital formation plunged, reducing sharply the creation of new capacity, productive employment, and equity. In fact, the consequences of that macroeconomic disequilibrium were long lasting. The same sort of disequilibrium emerged in 1998–2001, even though much milder. Consequently, the effects are also negative —

240

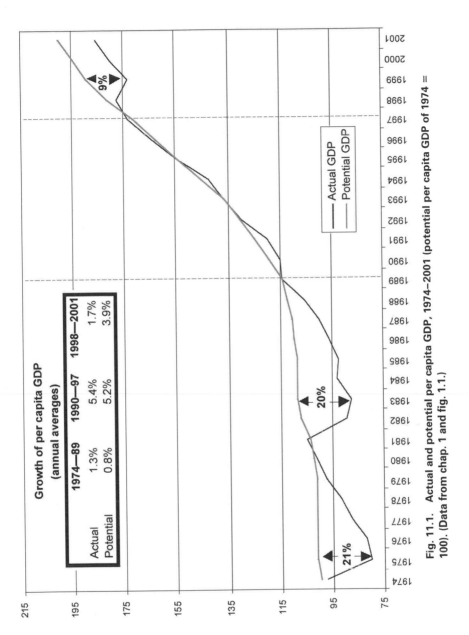

Fig. 11.1.   Actual and potential per capita GDP, 1974–2001 (potential per capita GDP of 1974 = 100). (Data from chap. 1 and fig. 1.1.)

lower capital formation, higher unemployment, less equity — but notably milder than in the two older conjunctures. It must be stressed that the most significant macroeconomic balance is the sustainable use of economically productive capacity. An economy working on the production frontier, with right macroprices, achieves higher productivity, encourages larger capital formation, and fosters the demand for labor.

The cost of such macroeconomic imbalance is high, indeed. Besides the fact that such a situation leads to a reversal of the initial success that may have been achieved in growth and redistribution, experience shows that it entails costly political losses for governments that succumb to populist temptations, whether from the Left (as with unfunded social spending) or the Right (e.g., with tax cuts that make it impossible to finance the investment in the human capital that is essential for growth with equity or with the excessive financial deregulation that paves the way for macroeconomic imbalances).

The ways of achieving macroeconomic balances can be very diverse. They may have progressive or regressive effects and may be procyclical or anticyclical depending, among other things, on the relative weight given to variables such as inflation and economic activity, the composition of public spending and revenue, the nature and condition of financial institutions, and public actions that contribute to building the capacity and organization of low-income segments of population. Sustainable comprehensive macroeconomic balances are essential, and they must be consistent with macrosocial balances.

Third, in the 1970s and 1980s there were several reforms directed at modernizing the country's economic organization. Undoubtedly, many constitute permanent and valuable bases for democratic development strategies. The changes included significant growth and diversification of exports, the achievement of a more efficient fiscal budgeting process, and the development of a new generation of entrepreneurs more dynamic and modern than the traditional business class. This progress achieved in the 1980s contributed considerably to the outstanding performance of the 1990s.

Finally, structural reforms suffered from various failures that had severe repercussions for potential economic growth and the population's welfare. The 1990s saw significant *reforms to the reforms* of previous decades, with the specific objective of introducing more pragmatism. These *reforms to the reforms* did reflect a great concern to reduce the vulnerability of the Chilean economy to the international environment, with its increased volatility, while stressing policies that contribute to greater equity in distributing opportunities, productivity, and income. The results of this change of focus, despite a number of contradictions, were notable. During almost the entire decade, Chile saw an expansion of its productive capacity unprecedented in its previous history, along with very important achievements in the fight against poverty. The recessive gap of 1999–2001, nevertheless, pointed out failures and insufficiencies and the lack of greater *reforms of the reforms* (see Ffrench-Davis 2000). From an optimistic perspective, this recession can help us to recognize these problems and find ways to solve them. With this book, I hope to contribute to the thinking and dialogue needed if we are to achieve growth with equity.

Ten Challenges

How can vigorous growth be achieved while advancing toward equity? First, there must be an understanding of how this can be achieved and what the country's real record is so far. Development occurs when growth is sustainable over long periods of time. If we measure progress in Chile by the decade, counting both good and bad years, only in the 1990s do we observe a figure of 6 to 7 percent. In the 1960s, GDP grew by 4.3 percent and in the 1970s and 1980s at less than 3 percent. It is not easy to live up to standards of exceptional performance. Some outstanding priorities that need to be kept in mind if the country is to replicate the exceptional record of the 1990s and grow with more equity are grouped here under the ten points that follow:

1. Chile must regain a macroeconomic environment of sustainable development with three features. The first is to achieve, as between 1991 and 1997, a level of effective demand close to the productive capacity of the Chilean economy—always a key objective for efficient macroeconomic balances and vigorous productive investment. This implies avoiding unsustainable booms and applying vigorous and consistent actions during recessions. Otherwise, if we are in the middle of a recession and there are expectations of other crises, how can one expect businesspeople to invest? Second, it will be necessary to maintain a competitive and stable real exchange rate, which is not feasible with corner solutions (a fully free rate or dollarization). Third, interest rates must be kept within a moderate range. These three objectives require a more flexible fiscal policy, with effective anticyclical measures (in the fiscal budget, monetary policy, and banking supervision) and an increased ability to discourage excesses in speculative capital inflows. The great danger is a "populist" attitude that fails to weigh the broad negative effects on the economy of excessive capital flows that are speculative, short term, merely financial, or aimed at purchasing what already exists without creating new productive capacity. In fact, the main cause of the recession of 1999 was the huge capital inflow in 1996–97, as shown in chapter 10.

2. Export dynamism is a determining factor for the ability to grow. Several main traditional natural resource exports will lose speed in this decade. We cannot afford to continue simply doing more of what we have always done. Markets become saturated and resources are exhausted or become less profitable. We must develop new types of exports, without losing what we have gained. This means (i) moving forward strongly to add value and technology to the traditional natural resources and develop the production of intermediate goods and services as well as capital goods linked to the productive process in those traditional areas, (ii) developing nontraditional natural resources, and (iii) finding niches for the ability and experience of national entrepreneurs and technicians in order to acquire competitive advantages. This will require an intense national effort to *complete* markets for technology, labor training, and long-term capital.

3. As far as exports are concerned, negotiating access to Latin American markets, taking advantage of geographical proximity, will be crucial. (Geography still counts for a lot, as the North Americans, who sell half their exports to their two nearest neighbors, can testify, or as the Europeans, for whom the corresponding figure is 60 percent can confirm.) MERCOSUR and its eventual future connection with the Andean Community should be key ingredients in export diversification because they would provide more accessible markets for nontraditional exports. New problems will probably emerge—among them, the macroeconomic instability of country members—but they must be confronted constructively, and mature thinking must be brought to the task. A well-designed regional integration is one way to *make,* rather than *take,* globalization.

4. Development always leaves some productive sectors behind. It is better to anticipate malaise than ignore it and have to deal with a moribund patient later. Comprehensive macroeconomic stability can make a great contribution to development and can help minimize the number of associated losers, but pragmatic, forward-looking sectoral and regional policy is also indispensable. Significant sectors of agriculture and mining are urgently in need of further thought and timely action for reconversion.

5. Growth is not possible without physical investment. The years 1999 and 2000 were recessive because of faulty macroeconomic management and the Asian crisis. The Chilean economy needs more, not less, productive investment. First, a dangerous rent-seeking bias, intensified in recent years, must be avoided: there are too many efforts and capabilities devoted to mergers and transfers of existing assets. It is necessary to strengthen creative skills; upgrading the quality of macroeconomic policies and enhancing actions to *complete* markets of factors and exports

are essential. Second, domestic capital formation is an overwhelming proportion of investment everywhere in the world. Only one of every ten dollars invested in the world comes from abroad. Domestic saving and investment are determinant. We must design the way to assure that Chile's long-term savings — such as those of the pension funds — go to domestic firms, especially SMEs. Funding for productive innovation also must be improved.

The prevailing tendency in Chile to transfer the funds of the private pension system abroad presents an unfortunate contradiction to the objective of raising the domestic savings rate so as to increase capital formation in Chile. The purpose of increasing the savings rate should be to provide financing for higher productive investment in Chile. Priority should be given to improving the transmission channels between those long-term funds and productive investment — naturally, always with guarantees and prudential principles to protect the savings of workers. This is consistent with the fact that average profitability is higher in Chile than in most developed countries.

6. Investment in human capital is a key input for stability and growth with equity. The educational reform of the mid-1990s has been a great step forward, but it is only the beginning. We must give it the priority it deserves, always keeping in mind that education is dependent on teachers. Social trust and recognition of their importance must be rebuilt. Education, however, operates over the long term. Most of the labor force of the first decade of this new century will consist of Chileans who have already finished their formal education. Chile faces the great challenge of enhancing the flexibility of the supply of labor with a farsighted and well-focused national labor-training program (looking to the year 2010, when Chile will be completing its second century of independence).

7. The environment has become a leading issue in modernization. Chile must make up for its lag in addressing environmental issues and in integrating them into the design of public policies. A highly pragmatic and participatory approach is needed to reconcile the development of today's productive capacity with preventive action, sustainability over time, and the present welfare of citizens.

8. Income distribution is highly inequitable. Chile must intensify its efforts to improve the quality and coverage of social spending, make an effective impact on hard core poverty, and eliminate the possibility that a young, intelligent person will not receive a good education because of a poor social origin. Strengthening the fight against tax evasion and the regressive loopholes that still exist in the system would provide financing and contribute to social equity. Once again, global consistency of policies and their interrelations are crucial. The quality of macroeconomic

policies strongly affects poverty and income distribution. In 2001, the regressive bias of 1999–2000 was still present with the impact of the recessive adjustment on productive investment and employment.

9. The state must be reformed. The main issues here are professionalizing public administration, raising productivity, improving the quality of public service, making space for participation of people in identifying priorities and failures (in education, health, public works, labor training, etc.) and heightening transparency in government. Simultaneously, salaries must be gradually raised to levels consistent with those prevailing in the private sector.

10. Paradoxically, since the return to democracy the quality and intensity of thinking about Chile have eroded. They have become too focused on the short term and concentrated on what "the market finances." Too much confidence has been placed in what other countries think and do (some specialists even believe that other countries should drive our macroeconomic policy, e.g., through the dollarization), and too little attention has been paid to the importance of each country's or region's specific characteristics and targets. The figure of globalization has taken the shape of mythic immutability. However, globalization is a highly heterogeneous process, incomplete, and rather unbalanced with respect to social and economic factors. It is urgent that Chile rethink the role of globalization in its economic life in order to understand how to move more effectively toward sustained growth with equity and to position itself to act cogently as it moves into this new decade.

References

Agosin, M. R. 1998. "Capital inflows and investment performance: Chile in the 1990s." In Ffrench-Davis and Reisen 1998.

———. 1999. "Trade and growth in Chile." *CEPAL Review* 68 (August).

———. 2001. "What accounts for the Chilean saving 'miracle'?" *Cambridge Journal of Economics*. Forthcoming.

Altimir, O. 1982. *Extent of Poverty in Latin America.* World Bank Staff Working Papers, no. 522. Washington, D.C.: World Bank.

Álvarez, R., and G. Crespi. 2000. "Impacto de las políticas de fomento sobre el dinamismo exportador chileno." Working Paper no. 3, Economics Department, University of Chile, April.

Aninat, A. 1978. "El programa de liberación y el Arancel Externo Común en el Acuerdo de Cartagena." In *El Pacto Andino: Carácter y perspectivas,* E. Tironi, ed. Lima: Instituto de Estudios Peruanos.

Aninat, E., and C. Larraín. 1996. "Capital flows: Lessons from the Chilean experience." *CEPAL Review* 60 (December).

Arellano, J. P. 1983. "De la liberalización a la intervención: El mercado de capitales en Chile, 1974–83." *Colección Estudios CIEPLAN* 11 (December).

———. 1985. *Políticas sociales y desarrollo, 1924–84.* Santiago: Ediciones CIEPLAN.

———. 1989. "La seguridad social en Chile en los años 90." *Colección Estudios CIEPLAN* 27 (December).

———, and R. Cortázar. 1982. "Del milagro a la crisis: Algunas reflexiones sobre el momento económico." *Colección Estudios CIEPLAN* 8 (July).

———, and M. Marfán. 1986. "Ahorro-inversión y relaciones financieras en la actual crisis económica chilena." *Colección Estudios CIEPLAN* 20 (December).

———, and J. Ramos. 1987. "Capital flight in Chile." In *Capital Flight and Third World Debt,* D. Lessard and J. Williamson, eds. Washington, D.C.: Institute for International Economics.

Bacha, E. 1983. "Apertura financiera y sus efectos en el desarrollo nacional." In *Las relaciones financieras externas: Su efecto en la economía latinoamericana,* R. Ffrench-Davis, ed. Lecturas de El Trimestre Económico, no. 47. Mexico City: Fondo de Cultura Económica.

———, and C. Díaz-Alejandro. 1983. "Mercados financieros: Una visión desde la semiperiferia." In Ffrench-Davis 1983a.

Balassa, B. 1977. *Policy Reforms in Developing Countries.* New York: Pergamon.

Baldwin, R. 1981. "Restricciones no arancelarias del comercio internacional." In *Lecturas sobre intercambio y desarrollo,* R. Ffrench-Davis, ed. Mexico City: Fondo de Cultura Económica.

Bande, J., and R. Ffrench-Davis. 1989. "Copper policies and the Chilean economy, 1973–88." *Notas Técnicas CIEPLAN* 131 (June) and Institute for Developing Economies, Tokyo.

Behrman, J. 1976. *Foreign Trade Regimes and Economic Development: Chile.* New York: NBER.

Benavente, J. M., and G. Crespi. 1998. "Sesgos y debilidades del SNI en Chile." In *Sistemas nacionales de innovación: ¿Qué puede América Latina aprender de Japón?* M. Agosin and N. Saavedra, eds. Santiago: Dolmen Ediciones.

Bergsman, J., and W. Edisis. 1988. "Debt-equity swaps and foreign direct investment in Latin America." International Finance Corporation, Washington, D.C., August.

Beyer, H. 1997. "Distribución del ingreso: Antecedentes para la discusión." *Estudios Públicos* 65 (summer).

Bhagwati, J. 1978. *Foreign Trade Regimes and Economic Development: Anatomy and Consequences of Exchange Control Regimes.* New York: NBER.

Bitar, S. 1979. *Transición, socialismo, y democracia: La experiencia chilena.* Mexico City: Siglo XXI.

Bosworth, B., R. Dornbusch, and R. Labán, eds. 1994. *The Chilean Economy: Policy Lessons and Challenges.* Washington, D.C.: Brookings Institution.

Bouzas, R., and R. Ffrench-Davis, eds. 1990. *Conversión de deuda y financiación del desarrollo en América Latina.* Buenos Aires: Grupo Editor Latinoamericano.

Bravo, D., and D. Contreras. 1999. "La distribución del ingreso en Chile, 1990–96: Análisis del mercado del trabajo y las políticas sociales." Department of Economics, Universidad de Chile.

———, and A. Marinović. 1998. "Wage inequality in Chile: Forty years of evidence." Department of Economics, Universidad de Chile.

Brunner, J. J. 1981. *La cultura autoritaria en Chile.* Santiago: FLACSO.

Budnevich, C., and G. Le Fort. 1997. "Capital account regulations and macroeconomic policy: Two Latin American experiences." In *International Monetary and Financial Issues for the 1990s,* vol. 8. New York and Geneva: UNCTAD.

Caballero, R., and V. Corbo. 1989. "The effect of real exchange rate uncertainty on exports: Empirical evidence." *World Bank Economic Review* 3 (May).

Cabezas, M. 1988. "Revisión metodológica y estadística del gasto social en Chile, 1970–86." *Notas Técnicas CIEPLAN* 114 (May).

Calderón, A., and S. Griffith-Jones. 1995. *Los nuevos flujos de capital extranjero en la economía chilena: Acceso renovado y nuevos usos.* Serie Desarrollo Productivo, no. 24. Santiago: ECLAC.

Calvo, G., L. Leiderman, and C. Reinhart. 1993. "Capital inflows and real exchange appreciation in Latin America: The role of external factors." *IMF Staff Papers* 40 (March).

————, and E. Mendoza. 1996. "Petty crime and cruel punishment: Lessons from the Mexican debacle." *American Economic Review* 86 (March).

Campero, G., and J. Valenzuela. 1981. "El movimiento sindical chileno en el capitalismo autoritario." Working paper, ILT-Academia de Humanismo Cristiano/IPET, Santiago, December.

Central Bank of Chile. 1988. "Conferencia de inversiones en Chile." *Estudios Monetarios* 10. Conference organized by Euromoney and Central Bank, Santiago.

————. Various issues. *Balanza de Pagos, Boletín Mensual, Deuda Externa de Chile, Estudios Monetarios,* and *Memoria Anual.*

CIEPLAN. 1982. *Modelo económico chileno: Trayectoria de una crítica.* Santiago: Editorial Aconcagua. Confiscated by the police.

————. 1983. *Reconstrucción económica para la democracia.* Santiago: Editorial Aconcagua.

Círculo de Economía. 1980. *Seminario sobre políticas económicas para el desarrollo y la igualdad.* Santiago: Academia de Humanismo Cristiano.

Claessens, S., M. P. Dooley, and A. Warner. 1995. "Portfolio capital flows: hot or cold?" *World Bank Economic Review* 9 (January).

Coeymans, J. 1999. "Determinantes de la productividad en Chile, 1961–97." *Cuadernos de Economía* 107 (April).

Contreras, D., and J. Ruiz-Tagle, Jr. 1997. "¿Cómo medir la distribución de ingresos en Chile?" *Estudios Públicos* 65 (summer).

Corbo, V. 1985. "Reforms and macroeconomic adjustments in Chile during 1974–84." *World Development* 13 (August), special issue, *Liberalization with Stabilization in the Southern Cone of Latin America,* V. Corbo and J. de Melo, eds.

Cortázar, R. 1983. "Chile: resultados distributivos, 1973–82." *Notas Técnicas CIEPLAN* 57 (June).

————. 1996. "A labor policy for a new reality." In Pizarro, Raczynski, and Vial 1996.

————, and J. Marshall. 1980. "Indice de precios al consumidor en Chile, 1970–78." *Colección Estudios CIEPLAN* 4 (November).

————, and J. Vial, eds. 1998. *Construyendo opciones: Propuestas económicas y sociales para el cambio de siglo.* Santiago: Dolmen Ediciones.

Cowan, K., and J. De Gregorio. 1996. "Distribución y pobreza en Chile: ¿Estamos mal? ¿Ha habido progresos? ¿Hemos retrocedido?" *Estudios Públicos* 64 (spring).

Dahse, F. 1979. *Mapa de la extrema riqueza: Los grupos económicos y el proceso de concentración de capitales.* Santiago: Editorial Aconcagua.

————. 1982. "El poder de los grupos económicos nacionales." Mimeo.

De Gregorio, J., and O. Landerretche. 1998. "Equidad, distribución, y desarrollo integrador." In Cortázar and Vial 1998.

De la Cuadra, S. 1974. "La protección efectiva en Chile." Documento de trabajo, no. 22. Instituto de Economía, Universidad Católica de Chile. Santiago.

————. 1981. "Política cambiaria y deuda externa." *Boletín Mensual,* no. 639. Santiago: Central Bank.

————, and D. Hachette. 1992. *Apertura comercial: Experiencia chilena.* Santiago: Universidad Católica, Facultad de Ciencias Económicas y Administrativas.

Departamento de Economía. Various issues. *Comentarios sobre la situación económica.*

Devlin, R. 1989. *Debt and Crisis in Latin America: The Supply Side of the Story.* Princeton: Princeton University Press.

————, and R. Cominetti. 1994. *La crisis de la empresa pública, las privatizaciones, y la equidad social.* Serie Reformas de Políticas Públicas, no. 26. Santiago: ECLAC.

————, and R. Ffrench-Davis. 1995. "The great Latin American debt crisis: A decade of asymmetric adjustment." In *Poverty, Prosperity, and the World Economy,* G. Helleiner, ed. London: Macmillan. Reprinted in Ffrench-Davis 2000, chap. 4.

Díaz, A., and J. Ramos. 1998. "Apertura y competitividad." In Cortázar and Vial 1998.

Díaz-Alejandro, C. F. 1985. "Goodbye financial repression, hello financial crash." *Journal of Development Economics* 19 (September–October).

DIPRES. 1978. *Somos realmente independientes gracias al esfuerzo de todos los chilenos.* Santiago: Ministerio de Hacienda.

————. Various issues. *Estadísticas de las Finanzas Públicas.*

Dornbusch, R. 1988. "Our LDC debts." In *The United States and the World Economy,* M. Feldstein, ed. Chicago: University of Chicago Press and NBER.

————, and S. Edwards, eds. 1991. *The Macroeconomics of Populism in Latin America.* Chicago: University of Chicago Press.

ECLAC. 1965. *External Financing in Latin America.* Santiago: United Nations. E/CN.12/0649/Rev.1.

————. 1988. "La evolución del problema de la deuda externa en América Latina y el Caribe." *Estudios e Informes de la CEPAL* 72.

————. 1991. "Una estimación de la magnitud de la pobreza en Chile, 1987." *Colección Estudios CIEPLAN* 31 (March).

————. 1997. "Evolución reciente de la pobreza en Chile." LC/R. 1773. ECLAC, Santiago, December.

————. 1998. *Policies to Improve Linkages with the Global Economy, 1995.* 2d ed. rev. Santiago: Fondo de Cultura Económica. In Spanish.

————. 2000. *Growth, Equity, and Citizenship.* Santiago: United Nations.

Edwards, S., and A. Cox-Edwards. 1987. *Monetarism and Liberalization: The Chilean Experiment.* Cambridge, Mass.: Ballinger.

Elórtegui, C. 1988. *Endeudamiento externo y conversión de deuda en la economía chilena.* Valparaiso: Ediciones Universitarias de Valparaíso, Universidad Católica de Valparaíso.

Encina, F. 1911. *Nuestra inferioridad económica.* Rpt. 1955. Santiago: Editorial Universitaria.

Eyzaguirre, N. 1988. "La deuda interna chilena, 1975–85." In Massad and Zahler 1988.

Felix, D., and J. Caskey. 1990. "The road to default: An assessment of debt crisis management in Latin America." In *Debt and Transfiguration? Prospects for Latin America's Revival,* D. Felix, ed. New York: M. E. Sharpe.

Feres, J. C. 2001. "Evidencia empírica en torno a la medición de la desigualdad: Algunas advertencias metodológicas." Mimeo.

Ffrench-Davis, R. 1964. "Elementos para una política de comercio exterior." In *Diálogos sobre el Desarrollo Económico de Chile.* Santiago: Instituto de Economía, Universidad de Chile. Reprinted in 1965 in *Cuadernos de Economía* 5 (April).

———. 1973. *Políticas económicas en Chile, 1952–70.* Santiago: Ediciones Nueva Universidad.

———. 1979a. *Economía internacional: Teorías y políticas para el desarrollo.* Mexico City: Fondo de Cultura Económica.

———. 1979b. "Exports and industrialization in an orthodox model: Chile, 1973–78." *CEPAL Review* 9 (December).

———. 1981. "Exchange rate policies in Chile: The experience with the crawling peg." In *The Crawling Peg: Past Performance and Future Prospects,* J. Williamson, ed. London: Macmillan.

———. 1982. "External debt and balance of payments of Latin America: Recent trends and outlook." In IDB, *Social and Economic Progress in Latin America, 1982: The External Sector.* Washington, D.C.: Interamerican Development Bank.

———, comp. 1983a. *Relaciones financieras externas y desarrollo nacional en América Latina.* Mexico City: Fondo de Cultura Económica.

———. 1983b. "Una estrategia de apertura externa selectiva." In *CIEPLAN* 1983.

———. 1984. "Indice de precios externos: Un indicador para Chile de la inflación internacional, 1952–83." *Colección Estudios CIEPLAN* 13 (June).

———. 1992. "Adjustment and conditionality in Chile, 1982–88." In *Cross-Conditionality: Banking Regulation and Third-World Debt,* E. Rodríguez and S. Griffith-Jones, eds. London: Macmillan.

———. 2000. *Reforming the Reforms in Latin America: Macroeconomics, Trade, Finance.* London: Macmillan and St. Martin's Press New York.

———, M. R. Agosin, and A. Uthoff. 1995. "Capital movements, export strategy, and macroeconomic stability in Chile." In Ffrench-Davis and Griffith-Jones 1995.

———, and J. P. Arellano. 1981. "Apertura financiera externa: La experiencia chilena en 1973–80." *Colección Estudios CIEPLAN* 5 (July). Reprinted in Ffrench-Davis 1983a.

———, and J. De Gregorio. 1987. "Orígenes y efectos del endeudamiento externo en Chile: Antes y después de la crisis." *El Trimestre Económico* (Mexico City) 213–14 (January–March).

———, and S. Griffith-Jones, eds. 1995. *Coping with Capital Surges: The Return of Finance to Latin America.* Boulder: Lynne Rienner.

———, P. Leiva, and R. Madrid. 1992. *Trade Liberalization in Chile: Experiences and Prospects.* Trade Policy Series, no. 1. Geneva: UNCTAD.

———, and M. Marfán. 1989. "Selective policies under a structural foreign exchange shortage." *Journal of Development Economics* 29.

―――, and D. Raczynski. 1990. "The impact of global recession and national policies on living standards: Chile, 1973–89." 3d ed. Notas Técnicas CIEPLAN, no. 97. Santiago: CIEPLAN (November).

―――, and H. Reisen, eds. 1998. *Capital Flows and Investment Performance: Lessons from Latin America.* Paris: OECD Development Centre and ECLAC.

―――, and B. Stallings, eds. 2001. *Reformas, crecimiento y politícas sociales en Chile desde 1973.* Santiago: ECLAC/LOM Ediciones.

―――, and E. Tironi, eds. 1974. *El cobre en el desarrollo nacional.* Santiago: Ediciones Nueva Universidad.

Fischer, R. 1999. "Income distribution and trade liberalization." Documento de Trabajo, no. 67. Departamento de Ingeniería Industrial, Universidad de Chile, Santiago.

Fontaine, J. A. 1988. "Los mecanismos de conversión de deuda en Chile." *Estudios Públicos* 30 (autumn).

―――. 1989. "The Chilean economy in the 1980s: Adjustment and recovery." In *Debt, Adjustment, and Recovery: Latin America's Prospects for Growth and Development,* S. Edwards and F. Larraín, eds. Oxford: Basil Blackwell.

Foxley, A. 1980. "Hacia una economía de libre mercado: Chile, 1974–78." *Colección Estudios CIEPLAN* 4.

―――. 1983. *Latin American Experiments in Neoconservative Economics.* Berkeley: University of California Press.

―――, E. Aninat, and J. P. Arellano. 1980. *Las desigualdades económicas y la acción del Estado.* Mexico City: Fondo de Cultura Económica.

Frank, C., K. Kim, and L. Westphal. 1975. *Foreign Trade Regimes and Economic Development: South Korea..* New York: NBER.

Frenkel, R. 1983. "La apertura financiera externa: el caso argentino." In Ffrench-Davis 1983a.

Garcés, F. 1990. *Normativa vigente para la inversión extranjera (Capítulo XIX).* Boletíns Mensual, no. 747. Santiago: Banco Central de Chile.

Gémines. 1987. "Operaciones con pagarés (Capítulo XIX)." Informe Gémines, no. 84. Santiago: Gémines.

Griffith-Jones, S. 1998. *Global Capital Flows.* London: Macmillan.

―――, and E. Rodríguez, comps. 1992. *Cross Conditionality, Banking Regulation, and Third World Debt.* London: Macmillan.

Hachette, D. 2000. "La reforma comercial." In Larraín and Vergara 2000.

―――, and R. Lüders. 1992. *La privatización en Chile,* CINDE, Santiago.

Harberger, A. 1985. "Observations on the Chilean economy, 1973–83." *Economic Development and Cultural Change* 33 (April).

Held, G., and F. Jiménez. 2001. "Liberalización, crisis, y reforma del sistema bancario: 1974–99." In Ffrench-Davis and Stallings 2000.

Helpman, E., L. Leiderman, and G. Bufman. 1994. "A new breed of exchange rate bands: Chile, Israel, and Mexico." *Economic Policy* 19 (October).

Hofman, A. 1999. *The Economic Development of Latin America in the Twentieth Century.* Aldershot, U.K.: ECLAC and Edward Elgar.

INE. 1999. "V Encuesta de Presupuestos Familiares, 1996–97." *Serie de Estadísticas Sociales* 1 (June).

Jadresić, E. 1986. "Evolución del empleo y desempleo en Chile, 1970–85: Series anuales y trimestrales." *Colección Estudios CIEPLAN* 20 (December).

———. 1990. "Salarios reales en Chile, 1960–88." *Notas Técnicas CIEPLAN* 134 (September).

Jorgensen, E., and J. Sachs. 1988. "Default and renegotiation of Latin American foreign funds in the interwar period." Working Papers, no. 2636. Cambridge, Mass.: NBER.

Krugman, P. 1990. *The Age of Diminished Expectations.* Cambridge: MIT Press.

Labán, R., and F. Larraín. 1997. "Can a liberalization of capital outflows increase net capital inflows?" *Journal of International Money and Finance* 16, no. 3.

Lahera, E. 1981. "The transnational corporation in the Chilean economy." *CEPAL Review* 14 (August).

Larraín, F. 1988. *Debt-Reduction Schemes and the Management of Chilean Debt.* Washington, D.C.: World Bank.

———. 1991. "Public sector behavior in a highly indebted country: The contrasting Chilean experience, 1970–85." In *The Public Sector and the Latin American Crisis,* F. Larraín and M. Selowsky, eds. San Francisco: ICS Press.

———, and A. Velasco. 1990. "Can swaps solve the debt crisis? Lessons from the Chilean experience." *Princeton Studies in International Finance.*

———, and R. Vergara. 2000. *La transformación económica de Chile.* Santiago: Centro de Estudios Públicos.

Larrañaga, O. 2001. "Distribución de ingresos: 1958–2001." In Ffrench-Davis and Stallings 2001.

Le Fort, G., and S. Lehmann. 2000. "El encaje, los flujos de capitales y el gasto: Una evaluación empírica." Documento de Trabajo, no. 64. Banco Central de Chile, Santiago.

Little, I., T. Scitovsky, and M. Scott. 1970. *Industry and Trade in Some Developing Countries.* London: Oxford University Press.

Lüders, R. 1980. "Estrategias de desarrollo industrial y sus resultados: El caso de Chile." Paper presented at the international symposium Política Industrial en los 80s, Ministerio de Industria y Energía, Madrid, May.

Marcel, M. 1989. "Privatización y finanzas públicas: El caso de Chile, 1985–88." *Colección Estudios CIEPLAN* 26 (June).

———, and P. Meller. 1983. "Indicadores líderes de recesión y expansión económica." *Colección Estudios CIEPLAN* 11 (December).

———, and P. Meller. 1986. "Empalme de las cuentas nacionales de Chile, 1960–85: Métodos alternativos y resultados." *Colección Estudios CIEPLAN* 20 (December).

———, and A. Solimano. 1994. "The distribution of income and economic adjustment." In Bosworth, Dornbusch, and Labán 1994.

Marfán, M. 1984. "Políticas reactivadoras y recesión externa: Chile, 1929–38." *Colección Estudios CIEPLAN* 12 (December).

———. 1992. "Re-estimación del PGB potencial en Chile: Implicancias para el crecimiento." *Cuadernos de Economía* 87 (August).

———, and B. Bosworth. 1994. "Saving, investment, and economic growth." In Bosworth, Dornbusch, and Labán 1994.

Marshall, J. 1981. "El gasto público en Chile, 1969–1979." *Colección Estudios CIEPLAN* 5 (July).

Massad, C. 2000. "Capital flows in Chile: Changes and policies in the nineties." In *The Globalization of Financial Markets and the Emerging Economies.* Santiago: ECLAC and the Jacques Maritain Institute.

———, and R. Zahler, eds. 1988. *Deuda interna y estabilidad financiera.* Vol. 2. Buenos Aires: Grupo Editor Latinoamericano.

McKinnon, R. 1977. "La intermediación financiera y el control monetario en Chile." *Cuadernos de Economía* 43 (December).

———. 1981. "Foreign exchange policy and economic liberalization in LDCs." In *Alternativas de políticas financieras en economías pequeñas y abiertas al exterior.* Estudios Monetarios, no. 7. Santiago: Banco Central de Chile.

Meller, P., ed. 1996. *El modelo exportador chileno: Crecimiento y equidad..* Santiago: CIEPLAN.

———. 1997. *Un siglo de economía política chilena, 1980–1990.* Santiago: Andrés Bello.

———, and A. Solimano. 1984. "Inestabilidad financiera, burbujas especulativas y tasa de interés real: Chile, 1975–83." Mimeo, CIEPLAN.

Mendive, P. 1978. "Protectionism and development." *CEPAL Review* 6, no. 2.

MIDEPLAN. 1999. *Resultados de la VII encuesta de caracterización macroeconómica nacional (CASEN 1998).* Documento, no. 1. Santiago: MIDEPLAN.

Ministry of Finance. Various issues. *Exposición sobre el estado de la Hacienda Pública.*

———. 1985. *Financial Package.* Santiago: República de Chile.

Mizala, A. 1992. "Las reformas económicas de los años setenta y la industria manufacturera." *Colección Estudios CIEPLAN* 35 (September).

Moguillansky, G. 1999. *La inversión en Chile: ¿El fin de un ciclo en expansión?* Santiago: Fondo de Cultura Económica and ECLAC.

———, and D. Titelman. 1993. "Análisis empírico del comportamiento de las exportaciones no cobre en Chile: 1963–90." Documento de Trabajo, no. 17. ECLAC, Santiago.

Molina, S. 1972. *El proceso de cambio en Chile.* Santiago: Editorial Universitaria.

Monckeberg, F. 1998. *Jaque al Subdesarrollo Ahora.* Santiago: Dolmen Ediciones.

Morandé, F., and R. Vergara, eds. 1997. *Análisis empírico del crecimiento en Chile.* Santiago: Centro de Estudios Públicos and ILADES.

Morgan Guarantee Trust. 1987. "Debt-equity swaps." *World Financial Markets* (June–July).

Moulián, T. 1982. "Desarrollo político y estado de compromiso, desajuste, y crisis estatal en Chile." *Colección Estudios CIEPLAN* 8 (July).

———, and P. Vergara. 1979. "Coyuntura económica y reacciones sociales: Las fases de la política económica en Chile, 1973–78." *Apuntes CIEPLAN* 22 (November).

———, and P. Vergara. 1980. "Estado, ideología, y políticas económicas en Chile, 1973–78." *Colección Estudios CIEPLAN* 3 (June).

Muñoz, O. 1986. *Chile y su industrialización: Pasado, crisis, y opciones.* Santiago: Ediciones CIEPLAN.

———, and A. M. Arriagada. 1977. "Orígenes políticos y económicos del estado empresarial en Chile." *Colección Estudios CIEPLAN* 16 (September).

Ortega, E. 1987. *Transformaciones agrarias y campesinado: de la participación a la exclusión.* Santiago: CIEPLAN.

Perry, G., and R. Junguito. 1983. "Política económica y endeudamiento externo en Colombia en la década de los setenta." In Ffrench-Davis 1983a.

Pinto, A. 1973. *Chile, un caso de desarrollo frustrado.* Santiago: Editorial Universitaria.

Pizarro, C., D. Raczynski, and J. Vial, eds. 1996. *Social and Economic Policies in Chile's Transition to Democracy.* Santiago: CIEPLAN and UNICEF.

Política y Espíritu. 1975. "Informe económico." *Política y Espíritu* 357, Santiago.

Raczynski, D. 1996. "Targeting social programs: Lessons from the Chilean experience." In Pizarro, Raczynski, and Vial 1996.

———, and C. Oyarzo. 1981. "¿Por qué cae la tasa de mortalidad infantil en Chile?" *Colección Estudios CIEPLAN* 6 (December).

Ramos, J. 1975. "El costo social: Hechos e interpretaciones." *Estudios de Economía* (second semester).

———. 1986. *Neoconservative Economics in the Southern Cone of Latin America, 1973–83.* Baltimore: Johns Hopkins University Press.

———. 1993. "Macroeconomic equilibria and development." In Sunkel 1993.

Reinstein, A., and F. Rosende. 2000. "Reforma financiera en Chile." In Larraín and Vergara 2000.

Robbins, D. 1994. "Relative wage structure in Chile, 1957–1992: Changes in the structure of demand for schooling." *Estudios de Economía* (October).

Robichek, W. 1981. "Some reflections about external public debt management." In *Alternativas de políticas financieras en economías pequeñas y abiertas al exterior.* Estudios Monetarios, no. 7. Santiago: Banco Central de Chile.

Rodrik, D. 2001. "Why is there so much economic insecurity in Latin America?" *CEPAL Review* 73 (April).

Roldós, J. 1997. "El crecimiento del producto potencial en mercados emergentes: El caso de Chile." In Morandé and Vergara 1997.

Roningen, V., and A. Yeats. 1976. "Non-tariff distortions of international trade: Some preliminary empirical evidence." *Weltwirtschaftliches Archiv* 112.

Ruiz-Tagle, J. 1979. "Scis años de política social: Una revolución en marcha." *Revista Mensaje* 282.

———. 1980. "Desarticulación de la educación." *Revista Mensaje* 291.

———. 1981. "Reformas en la educación superior." *Revista Mensaje* 297.

Ruiz-Tagle, J., Jr. 1999. "Chile: 40 años de desigualdad de ingresos." *Documento de trabajo,* no. 165. Department of Economics, Universidad de Chile, Santiago.

Sachs, J. 1987. "Trade and exchange rate policies in growth-oriented adjustment programs." In *Growth-oriented Adjustment Programs,* V. Corbo, M. Goldstein, and M. Khan, eds. Washington, D.C.: International Monetary Fund and World Bank.

———, F. Larraín, and A. Warner. 1999. "A structural analysis of Chile's long-term growth: History, prospects, and policy implications." Report prepared for the Ministry of Finance.

———, A. Tornell, and A. Velasco. 1996. "Financial crises in emerging markets: The lessons from 1995." *Brookings Papers on Economic Activity,* no. 1.

Sáez, S. 1991. "Indicadores para las exportaciones chilenas: 1950–89." *Notas Técnicas CIEPLAN,* no. 138 (January).

Sanfuentes, A. 1987. "La deuda pública externa de Chile entre 1818 y 1935." *Notas Técnicas CIEPLAN* 96 (March).

Sanhueza, G. 1999. "La crisis financiera en los años ochenta en Chile: Análisis de sus soluciones y su costo." *Economía Chilena* 2 (April).

Scherman, J. 1981. " Estadísticas básicas del sector industrial externo chileno." *Notas Técnicas CIEPLAN* 35 (August).

Schmidt-Hebbel, K. 1988. "Consumo e inversión en Chile (1974–1982): Una interpretación 'real' del boom." In *Del auge a la crisis de 1982,* F. Morandé and K. Schmidt-Hebbel, eds. Santiago: ILADES.

———, and L. Servén. 1999. "Saving in the world: The stilized facts." In *The Economics of Savings and Growth: Theory, Evidence, and Implications for Policy,* K. Schmidt-Hebbel and L. Servén, eds. Cambridge: Cambridge University Press.

———, L. Hernández, and F. Gallego. 1999. "Capital Controls in Chile: Effective? Efficient?" Documento de Trabajo, no. 59. Banco Central de Chile, Santiago.

Servén L., and A. Solimano. 1993. "Economic adjustment and investment performance in developing countries: The experience of the 1980s." In *Striving for Growth after Adjustment: The Role of Capital Formation,* L. Servén and A. Solimano, eds. Washington, D.C.: World Bank.

Stiglitz, J. 1998. "The role of the financial system in development." Paper presented at the fourth annual World Bank Conference on Development in Latin America and the Caribbean, San Salvador, El Salvador, June.

Sunkel, O., ed. 1993. *Development from Within: Toward a Neostructuralist Approach for Latin America.* Boulder: Lynne Rienner.

Tironi, E., and J. Barría. 1978. "La Disputada: De la Enami a la Exxon." *Revista Mensaje* 271.

Titelman, D. 2001. "Reformas al sistema de salud en Chile." In Ffrench-Davis and Stallings 2001.

Tobin, J. 1978. "A proposal for international economic reform." *Eastern Economic Journal* 4 (July–October).

Torche, A. 1987. "Distribuir el ingreso para satisfacer las necesidades básicas." In *Desarrollo económico en democracia: Proposiciones para una sociedad libre y solidaria,* F. Larraín, ed. Santiago: Ediciones Universidad Católica de Chile.

Tybout, J., J. de Melo, and V. Corbo. 1991. "The Effects of Trade Reforms on Scale and Technical Efficiency: New Evidence from Chile." Policy Research and External Affairs Working Papers, no. 481. Washington, D.C.: World Bank.

Uthoff, A., and D. Titelman. 1998. "The relationship between foreign and national savings under financial liberalization." In Ffrench-Davis and Reisen 1998.

Valdés, R. 1992. "Cuantificación de la reestructuración sectorial generada por la liberalización comercial chilena." *Colección Estudios CIEPLAN* 35 (September).

Valdés-Prieto, S. 1989. "Orígenes de la crisis de la deuda. ¿Nos sobreendeudamos o nos prestaron en exceso?" *Estudios Públicos* 33 (summer).

———. 1992. "Financial liberalization and the capital account: Chile, 1974–84." In *Financial Reform: Theory and Experience,* G. Caprio and J. Hanson, eds. Cambridge: Cambridge University Press.

———, and M. Soto. 1998. "New selective capital controls in Chile: Are they effective?" *Empírica* 25, no. 2.

Vergara, P. 1980. "Apertura externa y desarrollo industrial en Chile, 1974–78." *Colección Estudios CIEPLAN* 4 (November).

———. 1981. "Las transformaciones de las funciones económicas del Estado de Chile bajo el régimen militar." *Colección Estudios CIEPLAN* 5 (July).

Vial, J. 1988. "An econometric study of the world copper market." *Notas Técnicas CIEPLAN* 112 (May).

Vignolo, C. 1980. "Inversión extranjera en Chile, 1974–79." *Revista Mensaje* 286.

———. 1982. "El cobre en el desarrollo nacional: Evolución reciente, perspectivas, y estrategias." Working paper, Centro de Estudios del Desarrollo, Santiago.

Williamson, J. 1981. "The crawling-peg in historical perspective." In *The Crawling-Peg: Past Performance and Future Prospects,* J. Williamson, ed. London: Macmillan.

———. 1993. "A cost-benefit analysis of capital account liberalization." In *Financial Opening: Policy Issues and Experiences in Developing Countries,* H. Reisen and B. Fischer, eds. Paris: OECD.

———. 1996. *The Crawling Band as an Exchange Rate Regime: Lessons from Israel, Chile, and Colombia.* Washington, D.C.: Institute for International Economics.

World Bank. 1997. "Chile: Poverty and income distribution in a high-growth economy: 1987–1995." Report no. 16377-CH, November.

Yáñez, J. 1979. "Una corrección del índice de precios al consumidor durante el período, 1971–73." In *Comentarios sobre la situación económica.* Santiago: Departamento de Economía, Universidad de Chile (second semester).

Zahler, R. 1980. "Monetary and real repercussions of financial opening-up to the exterior: The case of Chile, 1975–78." *CEPAL Review* 10 (April).

———. 1988. "Estrategias financieras latinoamericanas: La experiencia del Cono Sur." *Colección Estudios CIEPLAN* 23 (March).

———. 1998. "The Central Bank and Chilean macroeconomic policy on the 1990s." *CEPAL Review* 64 (April).

Zañartu, M. 1980. "Gasto social en los pobres." *Revista Mensaje* 290.

Index

References to figures are in italics; references to tables are in bold.